SERVING
IN SILENCE

Vietnam Nurse, Mother of Four, Highest-Ranking
Officer to Challenge the Military's Antigay Policy

. . . .

by

MARGARETHE CAMMERMEYER
with Chris Fisher

Jeannine'
thank you for taking
on bias & changing the
world -

authorHOUSE™

1663 LIBERTY DRIVE, SUITE 200
BLOOMINGTON, INDIANA 47403
(800) 839-8640
WWW.AUTHORHOUSE.COM

colonel
Margarethe
Cammermeyer
16 June 06
Portland

First published by AuthorHouse 07/23/05

ISBN: 1-4208-4400-8 (sc)

Printed in the United States of America
Bloomington, Indiana

This book is printed on acid-free paper.

·················

Acknowledgments

This book came about because of the extraordinary work of a lot of wonderful people. It started when, as a naive colonel, I wanted to change a military regulation. It didn't take long to realize that I could not do that alone. The Military Law Task Force, Lambda Legal Defense and Education Fund, and the Northwest Women's Law Center all joined my legal team. Mary Newcombe, an attorney with Lambda, has been my guiding light through the legal maze. She also gently nudged me to come out to my family and children, and celebrated with me when I was not rejected. Jeffrey Tilden and Michael Himes, collaborating attorneys with the NW Women's Law Center, provided expertise to deal with the local legal system. Their continuous support, wisdom, and savvy gave invaluable assistance in our battle. Captain Margaret Bond, Judge Advocate General Corps, was appointed later and provided the military demeanor to the case, which she handled with extreme grace. Without them there would have been no story, just another soldier who had served and lost.

When the news of my challenge to the military broke, I faced another, very different onslaught, this timed it was the media. There were an amazing number of phone calls, interviews, letters, and a *Primetime Live* segment produced by Lisa Cohen that generated even more interest and support.

George Greenfield became my agent and encouraged me to speak out. He convinced me there was a story, which needed to be written. Mindy Werner, at Viking, agreed, and has been as caring as she has been rigorous in helping put this book together. For the last eighteen months, Chris Fisher and I have talked, worked, written, and rewritten, explicating the story, which is my life. Her unique ability to write in my voice, to use my words to tell my story is her extraordinary gift. Our friendship has evolved, been fed, and prospered during these months of work, and I treasure it.

For my children, the time has been difficult. Their support for me as their mother has been unwavering. But the experience has taken its toll also. The coming-out process involves the whole family, and can be difficult when one is young and dealing with one's own struggle for identity. My sons are learning the price of freedom, of civil rights, of being labeled through association, and they daily face the fear of being rejected not because of who they are but because of who their mother is. These are my children, of whom I am most proud.

And through it all-the failures, the highs and lows, the long evenings and early mornings, the midnight flights across the country-my companion and partner, Diane, has been there. Together we have taken this journey, lost our privacy, and gained our freedom. She has made the trip worth traveling. I cherish her, for she has helped make me whole. I cannot serve in silence any longer.

CONTENTS

CHAPTER 1

. . . .

Prologue

On April 28, 1989, I started to work at half-past six, as I did every morning, expecting the day to be like any other. Friday was clinic, when I met with patients one after another, reviewed the progress of their treatment strategies, monitored their medications, and listened to their concerns. Immediately after the last appointment, I was expected at my realtor's office to sign an offer on a new home, just south of Seattle, with a view of Puget Sound. And wedged in between almost unnoticeable in the crush of other demands-I had a meeting with Agent Brent Troutman of the Defense Investigative Service, as part of my military work. I remember clearly the agent's requesting a face-to-face interview with me and how difficult it had been to find time in my schedule.

As I parked my car and entered the hospital, I decided it would be best to meet with Agent Troutman in my office, away from the distractions of the clinic. I didn't feel apprehension. After all, this was my turf. He had courteously promised it would take no more than forty-five minutes of my time and would be a routine interview.

And that's what I expected it to be. From my protected position as colonel and Chief Nurse of the Washington State National Guard from naiveté, and perhaps from denial, I wasn't apprehensive about answering questions concerning my application for a top-secret clearance.

But something made me schedule it on the busiest day of my week. Something kept me from thinking about the kinds of questions the agent might ask and what my answers would be.

With classes, weekend duty in the National Guard, and research on my doctorate, this was the earliest time I had been able to squeeze him into my schedule. Fortunately, a graduate student training with me was available to cover my brief absence. The student could handle my patients during that time-and I'd be close at hand should anything come up she needed me for-so I'd agreed to meet with him at eleven o'clock.

While demanding and busy, my life now was filled with average sized joys and disappointments. It had a rhythm I liked. The trajectory of change through which I had been propelled so rapidly after my divorce in 1980 had slowed. I called my own shots and counted my own blessings, which were many. And most important, my life was filled with the needs and accomplishments of my four sons.

I believed the turmoil in my life was over.

At forty-seven, I had just a few more goals to achieve before a graceful military retirement. I had wanted to be national Chief Nurse and a general since I first joined the Army in 1961. Now I had the background, the military experience, and the professional education (particularly since my doctorate was almost completed) to compete for that position. I had already taken the Basic and Advanced Officers' courses, the Command and General Staff course, and the Chemical Casualty Care Course, but

I had not been to the War College. To position myself for my next promotion, I needed to take courses there, which required I upgrade my military clearance to top secret. And to do that I had to meet with Agent Troutman.

After a morning of examining and evaluating patients, I greeted Brent Troutman. We chatted pleasantly as we walked to my office. Ironically, it was in the basement in a remote part of an adjacent building. Built below ground level, it had only one little window up near the ceiling. As the interview dragged on, the forty-five minutes stretching to hours, the room began to feel like a prison cell. Before it was over, I felt that I had spent the day in a dungeon undergoing an interrogation as part of a spy drama.

Agent Troutman spread out papers on the desk and began asking the questions on his list, which I answered without hesitation. Midway through these routine inquiries, he read from his form a question that concerned homosexuality. Curiously, I don't remember the exact wording, though my answer would change the tenor of the interview and my life.

I took a breath; a little moment passed. Up to a few years before, I wouldn't have been hesitant. I would have affirmed my heterosexuality and the interview would have proceeded without a hitch. But I had changed, had painfully and slowly come to terms with my identity.

I really had no idea that day in 1989 what the consequences of my honesty could possibly be. This was before the media focus on gays in the military. I wasn't familiar with the few lawsuits challenging the policy. Personally, I'd never known anyone who had been investigated or discharged because of his or her sexual orientation. In fact, I didn't know what the regulations actually said. I assumed commanders had discretion in handling these matters. I believed the Constitution I had sworn to defend as a soldier permitted those, like myself, with unblemished records to serve regardless of the color of their skin, their ethnic background, their religion, or their sexual orientation.

As the question hung in the air, I had no choice about what my answer would be. This was a top-secret clearance, I was asking to be deemed worthy of trust and to prove I couldn't be blackmailed by anyone. Of course, I'd tell the truth. Even though it was a truth I'd given a name to less than a year before. Even though the small clutch in my throat told me this might change everything.

I said, "I am a lesbian."

The routine interview turned into an interrogation. Agent Troutman stayed until 4:00 p.m. He then came back an hour later with a statement he had written for me to sign. They weren't my words, but he wanted me to sign my name to them as though they were. He'd condensed a five-hour interview into a short paragraph. There were phrases I'd never used, comments I'd never made. I crossed them out and signed only what was left.

As I was investigated and discharged, this statement served as the basis of my prosecution. My four words had begun an ordeal. At the time, hurrying out of my dungeon-like office to get to my last patients of the day, I tried to shake off the feeling that the military I loved would now become my adversary.

I finished at the clinic, and I got to the real-estate office in time. I wasn't late. But that's all I remember. The world was spinning. I felt numb.

The next years would be a journey both lonely and exposing. I have been interviewed, quoted, avoided, and sought after. There were times I felt helpless times I wanted to hide. I waited with anguish for the mail, hoping for, yet dreading, the letter from the military that would tell me what was going to happen next. Would the Army accept me or discharge me? Would I be court-martialed or retired? Would the regulation banning gays be changed or would I be drummed out in shame? Waiting, walking to the mailbox, hoping this day's delivery would have news of what the military would do.

I have been luckier than many others who have suffered discrimination in the armed forces. My investigation, while filled with intimidation and unsubstantiated innuendos, was not the witch-hunt others have endured. I wasn't arrested or put in prison, as has happened too often. I wasn't beaten up or killed—the tragic fate of Allen Schindler and others who were not protected by the government they served and loved. I didn't lose my civilian job. A strong family surrounded me. My brothers and my father have never wavered in their support. My sons and daughters-in-law have lovingly, tenaciously stood by me with good-natured irritation at all the fuss. But still, my military career has been taken from me. Despite the mollifying words of the officer who headed my military hearing " You are a great American," I was discharged.

I'm not angry at the military—it gave me the honor and opportunity to serve my adopted country for twenty-six years. And though no longer in uniform, I still serve. My mission now is to dispel people's stereotypes of gays and lesbians. The chains of prejudice are made of ignorance and fear.

So I've folded my uniform and put it away. I avoid the flag (although even now, if alone, I sometimes salute it, because it's not the flag but the government that's a fraud). At ceremonies, I rise with everyone and begin the pledge of allegiance, but catch my breath in the middle, stop. I cannot say the last line because it is not true.

During my years in uniform, I served according to the motto: duty, honor, and integrity. Those ideals defined the military for me. Several times in this ordeal, soon after my first meeting with Agent Troutman and through the years of investigation that followed, other officials asked me if I wasn't just "stressed" or confused when I said I was a lesbian. They offered me opportunities to recant, to return to silence, and all would be forgotten. There is no choice. I'd rather sacrifice my uniform than my integrity

But I never really thought that would be the way it would play out. No, as naïve as it sounds, I didn't think that in America I would have to choose between being honest and serving my country. Not in the hours with Agent Troutman in April 1989, not in the two and a half years of investigations and hearing, not in the numerous meetings—explaining my position, my record, my commendations for service—did I believe it would come down to losing my military career because of prejudice and hate. Not until my last day in uniform, the day of my discharge did reality set in.

I had always dreamed that I would retire with full military honors, in a parade with a band playing and tears flowing. But the tears on the day of my discharge were not expressions of pride and honor. I put on my uniform and medals for the last time, arrived on post to turn in my field gear, keys, and identification card. I would no longer drive up to the gate, present my badge to the entry guard, receive and return a smart salute, with permission to pass onto the post. It was over. It really had come to that.

The servicemen-and-women under my command gave me their final salute. Hugs, and smiles, and tears broke our military demeanor. There were people from the media, attorneys who were carrying my case forward, well wishers from the National Guard. Everyone was warm and generous. I felt shame, but I didn't let anyone know that by the way I presented myself. I had not convinced the military to let me stay and serve, had not persevered to change a regulation: I felt the shame of failure. Honesty brought wholeness to my life and shattered it.

At the end of the goodbyes, with the press conference over and the attorneys and TV crews packing to go, a pickup truck drove up. A man in slacks and a sport shirt and a woman in a jogging suit jumped out. The woman paced in the parking lot, yelling to be heard above the quiet conversations around me. She pointed to the man, stuck out her chin, and screamed at me, "My husband spent forty years in the Air Force, forty years of his life to protect our country from people like you."

Everyone stopped talking. I said quietly, "No, that's not what he was protecting us from."

She cut me off, yelling, "I feel like vomiting."

I started to walk toward her. My attorney put her hand on my arm, saying, "Don't, Grethe."

"At least," I explained to my lawyer, "if she has someplace to throw the darts they won't be thrown at so many others."

Something drew me to her. Here I was in my uniform, my unit behind me. Soldiers don't retreat. I could confront her.

She waved her fists in the air. "You're tearing down the American family, you're tearing down the America that I love, that I would give my life for."

I was next to her. My voice was calm, an automatic response to someone out of control. "I almost gave mine for it…"

She spat the words in my face: "I wish you had." Someone behind me gasped.

I stood as tall as I could, without anger or surprise or fear.

I had learned to steel myself against hatred during my divorce.

Suddenly, as I looked into this woman's furious eyes, the memory of those times hit me. Nine years before, after my weekly visits with my sons, my ex-husband, Harvey, would line up the boys and make them join him in jeering at me. They would chant: "Dyke, queer." These little men, ages four to eleven, yelling, their faces twisted in pain and confusion. I would drive away speechless, cowed, crying. The words weren't true for me then. I believed it was only an expression of Harvey's anger, but even so, I couldn't defend myself. I went away. Rebuilt my life. Did my work, won awards, was obedient, missed my sons, avoided controversy, found my life partner, and forgot to be apprehensive about hate.

Until the day of my discharge.

What began as a simple challenge to a governmental regulation cost me my military career but gave me my freedom. My task in telling this story now is a new one for me, and I'm not sure how to go about it. Before, my job was always to listen and understand others, follow and give orders, tend to my patients' wounds and needs. Describing what happened to me personally was not something I did much. But nursing has taught me to listen to the human voice, its words and silences, fears and dreams. I will try to use that instruction on myself- and on my many past selves-to show what has brought me here.

Margarethe (Grethe) Cammermeyer
June 1994

CHAPTER 2

· · · · · · · · · · · · · · · · · ·

Origins and Inspirations

My very first military operation was a stunning success by all accounts (and since I don't remember a thing about it, the accounts will have to do). My mother smuggled guns past Nazi headquarters in Oslo to a rendezvous with Norwegian resistance fighters. The method of transportation was my baby carriage with, of course, me in it. Apparently I performed my role well.

· · · · · · · · · · · · · · · · · ·

History, even that distant abstraction called "world events," has a curious way of affecting our lives. It can do it whether we want it to, or not, whether we're even there to participate in it. On another April day, forty-nine years before my meeting with fate and Agent Troutman, and two years, in fact, before I was born, Germany invaded Norway. After a busy year swallowing countries in Eastern and Southern Europe, Hitler waited until spring to send his armies to my homeland. The warmer weather allowed King Haakon and his overwhelmed Norwegian troops to retreat to the northern interior and wait for the promised help from the British and French. But the now common "too little, too late" Allied response to more Nazi aggression failed to prevent disaster. The northern resistance did hold for a brave while. Soon, however, as the German advance in France threatened that country's independence, the British decided that Norway would have to be abandoned to the invaders. In a quick retreat, all Allied forces left Norway and headed south to protect Paris. Still the king refused to abdicate and legitimize the Nazis. On June 10, 1940, he and what was left of the government sailed off, along with the Norwegian Navy, to five years of exile in Britain.

Now, as in other parts of Europe, Norway's moral and spiritual survival was up to the underground resistance fighters and the individual citizens throughout the country who daily risked their lives to fund, feed, and hide them. Norwegian citizens like my parents.

My father was raised in the Belgian Congo, where his father, a physician, had a clinic. After his childhood in Africa, my father returned to Norway to attend the university, following in the family tradition to become a doctor. If he'd dreamed of travel then, I don't know. The war in Europe altered many plans.

My mother's background was more traditional-at least geographically. Her father, a psychiatrist, was the director of the first psychiatric hospital in Norway. In the early part of the century, he was considered a pioneer in this emerging field of medicine. Set outside Oslo, on a stunning sweep of countryside in Drammen, the institute was a haven for the treatment of this new category of human ailments: mental diseases. Then shock treatments and more arcane methods were employed, but the attitude of curing not condemning people who are mentally ill was a new and liberal approach. Consequently, my mother was never judgmental or frightened of those who were different. She had, and imparted to her children, the humanist's fascination and compassion for all types of people. Her upbringing also qualified her, in our eyes, as an authority on psychology.

Her true passion was painting. After high school, she went to London to art school. But with the unexpected death of her father, and the economic hardships on the family that followed, she abandoned her dreams of being an artist, returned to Norway, and began preparing for one of the few professions open to women: nursing. She was a Red Cross nurse when she met my father, the young doctor, and they married in 1940.

I was born in March 1942. Directly across from the apartment building in which I spent the first years of my life, the Nazis established their Norwegian headquarters. The adults in my world shielded me as much as possible from the intrigue, suspense, and fear of those years. I can't separate my memories from my mother's stories or the creations of my vivid imagination. It probably doesn't matter, because each had the same effect. I always wondered if I would have the resistance fighters' courage to withstand adversity.

While the Norwegian Army was still intact, my father was with them in the northern interior. After the Nazis captured the country, he returned to our apartment and continued in his outward life as a researcher at the University of Oslo. But both my parents worked in sheltering the resistance forces. That underground war was fought with all the means available-and it was a war women shared equally with men. A war planned in the kitchens and bedrooms, carried out by feeding and hiding people whose very presence in your home could bring arrest and execution, not only to them, but also to your family.

Hitler's henchmen and their Norwegian supporters, led by Vidkun Quisling-the man who gave us a new word for traitor-had spent the two years since 1940 instituting hatred and intolerance in every area of Norwegian daily life. Schools and churches received decrees instructing them on the ways and means of imparting this "new order." When teachers refused to cooperate and the state church courageously broke with the puppet government, large numbers of arrests and deportations followed. The members of the forty-three-organization-strong medical association, my father among them, publicly protested against the Nazification of the profession. The Germans responded to this affront by rounding up the leaders of the group. Those who escaped arrest went underground.

Women had a particular advantage in the resistance. That first military operation of mine occurred when I was just months old. A friend of my mother's arrived at our apartment with a package. She explained that the parcel contained weapons that had to be delivered to an address on the other side of town. Soon the two women emerged from our apartment, out for a stroll with me in the baby carriage. They pushed me up and down the streets of Oslo for hours, casually chatting and window-shopping, a young mother and her friend on an afternoon outing. Suddenly they popped into an alley, stopped at a doorway; two men jumped out. Mother lifted me up; the men pulled all the weapons out from underneath my blanket and vanished. Seconds later, we were back out in the street continuing our leisurely wandering.

My mother's sister, Aagot, was with the exiled Norwegian forces in Canada. They were centered in a place they called, appropriately enough, Little Norway. Aagot was involved in training with the resistance to be ready to come back with the Allied forces when Norway was liberated.

During those first years of my life we had members of the resistance forces sheltered with us. If there were ever an unusual sound anywhere in the apartment building, our guests would hide. If the doorbell or phone rang during meals, they would immediately get up, take their plates and silverware, and hide to give the appearance that just our family was at the table. It was an automatic behavior that I mimicked as well, jumping up with my plate and hurrying to hide with them. My parents would not correct me. They felt that bringing attention to this game by disciplining me would more likely make me mention it to my friends when I was playing outside. That could alert the Nazis. Rumors and innuendos were often the ways resistance sympathizers and helpers were uncovered.

Now this was no problem except that after the war I kept doing it. Born into the situation, I didn't know that leaping up and hiding was not the expected behavior when you felt a little tense during meals. This came to a head when I was five, and we lived for a time in the home of a prominent American neurologist during my father's sabbatical on a Rockefeller fellowship. Our two families shared evening meals together in their stately Boston home. Our hosts were surprised, and my parents chagrined, to see me, at unexpected sounds, jump up, take my plate and utensils, and leave the table. Finally my parents had to explain to me that it was no longer appropriate or necessary behavior. Though it must have been funny, no one ever laughed at me, but instead offered their reassurance that there was no longer any need to leave the table with my food. Yet even now, I automatically jump up and respond to the sound of the phone or doorbell-a reminder of how powerfully the past keeps its hands on us.

Throughout my childhood, I was enthralled by the stories of courage displayed by the Norwegian resistance, especially the women, during the war. Movies and books about their struggle against the Nazis made a powerful impression. I was shown the prison in Oslo where the Norwegian freedom fighters had been tortured and killed. I envisioned myself there-in fact, these fantasies were so compelling they became as real as my own experiences.

I learned women could be partners in the daily struggle for freedom. I saw them risk their lives and save others by feeding those in need, sheltering those who were hunted, strolling with the baby and the guns past the Nazis. Those images shaped me throughout my life. And they inspired my attraction to the military.

For me, being a soldier meant more than merely firing a gun or flying on a bombing raid. Would I be woman enough, as the models I revered from childhood were, to do the hard job of fighting for country and freedom? Would I be able to choose the greater good over personal safety? Would I stand up regardless of the cost-for what was right?

The Norwegian resistance and the support they received from their fellow citizens forced the Germans to keep far more troops occupying the country than they'd planned. By the war's end, the constant disruption by only 40,000 resistance fighters had diverted more than 350,000 German soldiers to Norway, weakening the Nazi forces elsewhere. The Allies, primarily American soldiers, liberated Oslo on May 8, 1945, and were cheered in parades and celebrations. For five long years, through despair and terror, my family and country had sacrificed, struggled, waited for this day. Though I was very young, it set in my heart and mind a love for the United States and an unquestioning belief in its military that even fourteen months in Vietnam would not shake.

My parents were strong individuals and very different from each other. The values and roles they displayed at home were conservative and traditional, yet they participated in the resistance and, after the war, picked up their family and immigrated to a distant country. My father lived and breathed for his research in neuropathology. Whether in his lab at the hospital or the university, or at home in the evenings and on weekends, he was immersed in his papers, books, and journals. My mother's great gift was with people. Once in our home, you noticed only her presence (fortunately, because her hypertension didn't allow her to do much housework). But for all their differences, my parents presented a united front. There were no disagreements or negotiations.

Father never talked much about himself or his childhood in Africa. But that early taste of other cultures gave him an acceptance and ease with new places that lasted his entire life. In the Congo he had, as was the colonial custom, an African companion whom he referred to in terms I find deeply offensive. His "boy" was assigned to him for the twelve years he was there. He still refers to him, as a "boy" -that is, a black person to cater to his whims, to be his playmate and valet. Prejudice is terrible, insidious and destructive. While Father didn't denigrate people of different ethnic backgrounds or race, he wrongly assumed, like others of his class, his superiority as a white. He assumed his superiority as a man over any woman-including his wife and his daughter.

As a scientist, he is much honored in his field. While friends of mine have told me they enjoy his wit, I have seen only his reserved authoritarianism. It's not that he's insensitive, rather that he does not express feelings. It may be a Scandinavian way of acting-but it isolates him a great deal and makes it hard to get close.

In addition to his physical reticence, he has a superstition that prevents him from hugging his own sons. He was always afraid that embracing them would make them become homosexual. This ridiculous myth had apparently circulated in his childhood. Though a brilliant scientist, he has held on to it all his life. It shows again how powerfully that hand from the past rules our thinking in the present–silencing new information, preventing new experiences. Because his prejudice was unconscious, my father's fine intellect never focused on it and so he unthinkingly accepted an isolating and destructive myth. Even to this day he shakes the hands of his children and grandchildren to say goodnight.

When I think of my father, I hear "No." It was constant, unemotional, clear, and unbending. Whenever I had a need, I'd first talk to Mother-that was always lovely and fun. But we both knew she couldn't provide what I wanted. So soon enough, she would send me in to see Father. He would inevitably be sitting working on his scientific papers at the dining room table. I would stand before him and state my request-to use something, do something-and I can't recall his ever saying yes to anything. It was just no. A final no. Not a no that had room for any future negotiation. Never a maybe. And if I tried (not to argue because his authority was never to be questioned) to see if I could get him to change his mind, it never happened.

This was both a burden and a gift. It constrained me because I always struggled to believe in myself, in my own value. But its positive side, the gift I've lately come to appreciate, is that it made me decide that I would try never to say no, but rather, to ask, Why not?

When my sons ask me for something, I think, well, why not? And if I don't have a good answer, I allow them to have it. As a military leader, I tried to make people understand the whys of an order. I have also been prompted to challenge rules and regulations throughout my career-almost always successfully because common sense usually wins. Usually.

My mother's response, on the other hand, was an implicit yes. But her yes never came as a contradiction of my father. She did not allow us to do something he had forbidden-this was a Norwegian household, where the father's voice prevailed. So her affirmation was not able to change our practical world. It was crucial to us, though, and acted as a radiant beacon showing us that we ourselves were wonderful. It didn't mean we could play after supper, or borrow the car, or get a new pair of baseball shoes. My father's no in practical matters was all-powerful. Her yes told us we were profoundly worthy and good: yes, she would always listen to our ideas and laugh at our jokes; yes, we were loved and valued. She was the light that filled the room.

I love the smell of formaldehyde. When I go to the lab at the hospital to pick up slides or data, I linger as I pass the door where the anatomists work. People in the lab will look at me and ask, "What's the matter?" I try to explain that the smell is wonderful to me, but they think I'm kidding. I'm not. It reminds me of going to visit my father at his lab. And those are all good memories-most particularly, my memories of the mice.

After the war, I was old enough and life was calm enough for me to visit my father at work. He was a neuroanatomist and neuropathologist at the University of Oslo. What a wonderful world that was to enter. As I walked up to the laboratory, a curious, new smell engulfed me. It was the pungency of formaldehyde mixed with the aroma of fresh cedar chips and, of course, the animals. The mice were the best part, and he would take me to their cages, grab them by the tail, give them to me to hold and play with. More than the fun of having these little white creatures running up and down my arm was the sense that *this is the place where something is happening.*

When I was five, my father became the first
Norwegian to receive a Rockefeller fellowship, allowing
him to do research for nine months in the United States.
It was a dream come true for him. So in 1947 our family
traveled to America for the first time.

We stayed with Dr. Ray Adams, a neuropathologist
who was working with my father on his research. Dr.
Adams and his family graciously entertained us in their
Boston home. Father and Dr. Adams conducted their
experiments and performed bench work dissecting brains
at labs of the Boston City Hospital. It was a productive
collaboration and they published several papers together
explaining the results of their work on brain diseases.

In Norway, Father had worked alone as a
microanatomist of the brain. At that time, there were few
other specialists outside the United States in this new
field. Going to Boston and working with colleagues was
professionally exhilarating for him. When the Rockefeller
fellowship ended and we moved home, Father had come
to the conclusion that to fully contribute in his specialty
he needed to work in America on permanent basis.

After we returned to Norway in 1947, our family
began a series of moves that was to last the rest of the
time I lived with my parents. Initially, we went back to
the apartment in Oslo where we'd lived during the war-
apartments in Oslo are owned and normally stay in the
family. Then my grandfather died and we moved to the
family home outside town. But soon it was put up for
sale because of my father's decision to immigrate to the
United States.

In 1950, the American government offered him a
position at the Armed Forces Institute of Pathology and,
expecting to move to Washington, D.C., immediately, our
family sold the country home. But the Korean War had
started and immigration quotas for Scandinavians were

cut back. So we lived in a haphazard succession of hotels and other people's homes as we waited for our American visas to be granted.

Finally, in February 1951 our permission to emigrate came through. My parents were clearly thrilled with the opportunities offered us. Only nine years old, I, however, didn't want to leave my home. But as the big sister to my brothers Jan Wilhelm, seven, and Tom, eighteen months, I tried to put up a good front as we packed and prepared to leave. Yet I remember saying to my best friends, Randi and Ellen Piro, on the way to the airport, "I will return in five years." (That ambitious promise didn't get fulfilled.) It was my way of coping.

It didn't work, of course. There was still the trauma of leaving everything familiar behind. All I knew was that we were going someplace very far away. Off into the skies. I had no recollection of the earlier trip; it was really like going into vacantness. An open-ended nothing. I didn't have any idea of what was on the other side. I didn't even know how getting there was going to take place. I sat on the plane, looking out at my two friends who were waving goodbye, and felt very sad and empty

We had moved many times. Since the sequence of places and people had been caused by my father's successful career, each move was a sign of something positive happening, and so it felt improper to be sad now. I don't think my parents realized the price of this disruption on my brothers and me, or, if they did, had any way to minimize it.

We were not alone in this-throughout Europe and Scandinavia families were relocating and rebuilding after the war and the realignment of national boundaries. Even so, there are lasting effects of this almost nomadic time in my life. In many ways the past does not exist for me. There's no thread that ties together the events of my childhood. It was broken too many times by a move, a new home, a new community. Perhaps I coped with the changes and the losses by feeling that nothing was real. I didn't attach importance to any person or place, didn't allow myself to care about it, because all too soon, I knew, I would leave it behind. That's hard on a child. Knowing its effect has made me ensure that my own sons remain stable and grounded in their lives at almost any cost.

So I have few memories of arriving in my new country. I recall the odd experience of getting on the airplane, being lifted up out of my world, and on the same day being put down on a new continent, with a new culture and language.

We first settled into a hotel in Washington, D.C. It was near Union Station-the hub of trains, buses, and cars in and out of the busy city, just a few blocks from the Capitol building itself. My parents took us out to see the sights. My experience in Oslo hadn't prepared me for the speed and intensity of life in this new place. People bustled by in every direction. They spoke English, a language I didn't understand. I was struck with the foreignness of everything. I became even more protective of my younger brothers, and as the oldest, saw my job as paving the way for them in this new and unfamiliar world.

Along with our homesickness and unease came wonderful discoveries, too. Father went to the nearest grocery store and came back to our hotel room with bunches of bananas. He'd loved them as a child -in Africa, and they weren't available in Norway those days, so this was a big treat. To us children this proved that America really did have almost anything you'd ever want.

Father began working at the Armed Forces Institute of Pathology. But after a few years, he was disappointed to still be limited to reviewing cases and unable to do original research. Then he was invited to the National Institutes of Health for a position he was pleased to accept. Staying there until his retirement, he performed independent and experimental work in brain anatomy and found it very fulfilling. The titles of his scientific papers were complex; I remember just a few of the projects he said he'd worked on–such as the study of Albert Einstein's brain. His main contributions to neuropathology were in describing the anatomical aspects of both normal and abnormal brains so that others would be able to make distinctions between them.

As my father's career evolved, we kept moving to homes that were either more comfortable or closer to his job. From 1951 to 1959, we lived in four houses and I went to five different schools. It was hard to develop a sense of place and community, and I spent much of my youth alone.

We first settled in a rather splendid house in Washington, D.C. Since I couldn't speak English, the talk of people on the street and in school and the stores made no sense to me. Wanting to maintain our Norwegian culture and heritage, we spoke Norwegian as our primary language at home whereas my brothers and I struggled to learn English at school as quickly as possible. After a frustrating day trying to converse at school, we'd switch back to Norwegian the minute we walked in the house. The first few years in America, all of us managed the bilingual discipline well. But as we became more assimilated into our American schools and lives, our determination flagged. By junior high, Norwegian was a chore, not a relief, and I nearly forgot how to speak it. Feeling different and wanting only to fit in, I failed to see any advantage to being bilingual. Fortunately, by college I'd reclaimed my passion for all things Norwegian and regained my ability to speak my native language.

Our first house in America was close enough to my elementary school so I could walk there. Late spring in Washington was nothing like that season in Oslo. The heat and humidity were unbelievable. But on my trek to classes, I found a way to beat the tormenting weather. Alongside the road, the leaves on the bushes were nice and cool and within easy picking distance for a third-grader. I pulled them off their branches and put them all over my face and eyes. So comforting and moist, they gave me a wonderful respite from the heat. They also gave me welts-they were poison ivy. By the time I came home from school, my eyes were swollen shut and my face a mass of blisters. My parents had no idea what this malady could be and sought medical help.

Looking back, the only thing more amusing than putting the leaves on my face in the first place was that I did it more than once. I'm sure my parents and our doctor told me to stay away from poison ivy. But I didn't. I'd walk to school in that unbearable heat and humidity, pull off the cool, moist leaves, put the leaves back on may face and soon the welts were back. All I can say in my own defense is that unless you've suddenly been set down in a new physical world, it's hard to imagine the hundreds of occurrences that your own ignorance makes into crisis. Many times in America, my parents' pride and reticence prevented us children from finding easy solution to these ordinary problems. Unlike my younger brothers, who could learn from my stumbling example, as the firstborn I had to forge environment on my own-welts and all.

The school system didn't help much. Because I towered over my fellow classmates, it was decided that I should skip fourth grade and go directly into fifth. I could barely speak English, but I advanced anyway. I suspect the teachers moved me ahead because I could "speak" math well, and they assumed the rest of my skills were similarly advanced.

Entering fifth grade, I was a crucial year younger and still struggling with English. I was immature next to my classmates, ignorant of how things worked in America, and talked with an accent-all of which made me feel out of place, awkward, and stupid. That's my one overriding memory of those years: feeling so very different from everyone else, and hating it.

When I moved from elementary school to junior high, I made a fool of myself the first day of class. Knowing nothing about this new regime, I raised my hand and asked the teacher, "When is recess?" The room burst into laughter. They made it clear that recess was something for little kids in wimpy elementary school, not for sophisticated junior-high-schoolers. Of course, I felt dumb and humiliated. My worst fear was of being laughed at. After that, I didn't ask questions about American customs: I didn't participate spontaneously but held back until I knew exactly what was expected.

But with my younger brothers I could show off and follow the usual rites of passage. I was quite a tomboy, playing Kit Carson in my baby-blue cowboy hat, and I showed Tom and Jan how to "ride" our pretend, stick horses. In later years, I practiced throwing knives with them in our backyard, and taught Jan, just two years younger, to smoke my mother's Lucky Strikes, and gave him his first taste of beer.

While quiet and shy in school, I loved sports. In high school, I became president of the girls' athletic association. That broadened my circle of friends and gave me a sense that I could do something that didn't just revolve around schoolwork.

One of my best friends was Diane, a classmate of mine, who was a year behind me in school. When she was younger, a tumor had been removed from her spinal cord, and she was now a paraplegic. She was in a wheelchair and our school had no elevators, so I would help her when she had classes on the second floor. She wore braces on her legs in the morning, and we'd slowly work our way up the stairs together. Then I'd bring up the wheelchair, unlock her braces, help her back into the chair, and she'd be off to classes.

Her sister played on the Arcade Pontiac semiprofessional, fast pitch softball team. One day, knowing how much I loved sports, Diane invited me to come with her and watch them practice. The team took one look at me-fifteen and almost six feet tall-and asked me to play some catch with them. I threw a mean softball. After a more rigorous tryout, they formally asked me to become a member of the team, and I was delighted.

But first I had to get past my father's no. I went to my mother with the great news of being chosen to play. Underneath her happiness for me I could sense concern as well that my father would disapprove of my devoting more time to sports. Though I did well in school without needing to study very much, the work ethic ruled at our house. In fact, it was so revered by Father that we rarely took vacations.

Then my mother showed me a marvelous way around Father. Although it was new to me, I got a sense she'd developed the tactic over the years to circumvent his no. This time I wasn't sent in to ask his permission. Instead, my mother simply started driving me to every practice and game. It was that easy. He either didn't notice or didn't care. In fact, I don't recall his ever coming to watch me play during the three great years I was on the team.

I played bench most of the time, but you'd be surprised how much work there is in sitting on the bench. I came home hoarse from every game. The team companionship was wonderful. For out-of-town games, some of my teammates brought their guitars and ukuleles.

They taught me the words to their songs, and soon I was learning to play the baritone uke. Around them, life began to feel right and comfortable. Even though I was taller than most of the other women, they sensed my inexperience and took me under their collective wing. I became, in a way, the team mascot.

In return for this new camaraderie, I put together a special lucky charm for the team and carried it to every game. A cat's eye. A real cat's eye, that is.

That year in science class, I'd had a project on the comparative anatomy of the eye. I enjoyed the work so much, I set up a lab in my bedroom—a lab like my father's. I enlisted him in bringing home the basic equipment and supplies. On a long board across the length of my wall, bottles of formaldehyde held different animals and snakes. My father would sometimes offer to teach me the more delicate aspects of dissecting. But he never did the work for me. Always he gave me the freedom to do it on my own.

I specialized in eyeballs—fishes', frogs', and snakes' eyeballs. My mother, trained as a nurse and the wife and daughter of doctors, was very liberated. She believed that if I wanted to fill my bedroom with anatomical specimens, it would be more interesting than collecting stamps.

During one summer in high school, I volunteered at the National Institutes of Health cleaning lab equipment, and my collection of specimens grew. Then one day my father brought me the cat's head. With great deliberation, I dissected it, describing each procedure in my notebook. When I finished, I had a cat's eye. It was remarkable and I wanted to do something different with it—not just throw it away. What better thing to do than keep it as a good-luck piece? So I found a lovely little glass bottle to hold the eyeball, covered it with formaldehyde, and carried it around in my purse. Sometimes I'd show it to people, particularly at our softball games. It would unnerve the other team a bit, and that was always helpful-we said our cat's eye might even bring the national title into sight. The local press loved the story and, though I said that my prized possession was just the result of a science project, I enjoyed being a little outrageous. My plan was eventually to preserve it in paraffin. But one day I dropped my purse and the bottle broke, spilling formaldehyde, eyeball, and bits of glass over everything. Luckily I liked the smell.

During my years on the team, Mother continued to drive me to practice several times a week. This gave us more time to talk and I enjoyed that very much.

One day, on the way to the field, she said, out of the blue, "You know, there are several women on your team who are homosexual. It's nothing to worry about. It is a mental illness."

In hindsight, I realize it was a remarkable comment from my mother. But back then; I heard it—coming, as it did, so unexpectedly—as a statement of fact about the world. It was as if she'd remarked that the planets revolve around the sun. She didn't personalize the observation, didn't mention names or point out any behavior. There was no emotion in her voice-no judgment or disapproval. She made the comment and then changed the subject.

We never discussed the issue again. Perhaps because sex was not mentioned in our home (this was the mid-1950s and we were Norwegian), either I didn't feel any desire to question her about it or I suppressed any curiosity I felt. I don't remember being upset or fearful. I certainly didn't think the subject had anything to do with me.

Since I respected my mother, particularly on issues of psychology, I tried to observe my teammates with a little more awareness during the next few days. But I saw no signs of mental illness. So I stopped this secret scrutiny and once again became immersed in the challenges and joys of our team's progress. I remember feeling a bit relieved at having been spared the supposed mental affliction of homosexuality. But basically all I really cared about was playing a great game.

My upbringing was conservative, and expressions of warmth or affection were very rare in our family. So sexuality was somewhat of a mystery. At school, those were the days when boys wore their blue jeans hanging down so low you could see the crease between their buttock cheeks. Except for occasionally worrying that their pants would fall off, I didn't think about feelings of attraction or non-attraction to boys in high school

I liked boys as teammates and friends and competitors. Several guys in my neighborhood taught me to box with thin gloves, something I thoroughly enjoyed. But I dated less than others in my school, and that made me feel unattractive and unworthy. I didn't want to be different; I wanted to be like everybody else, and everybody else wanted to date. I wasn't pursued, and it was inappropriate for a girl to express interest first. A girl's role back then was to be pretty, available, and passive.

Even my mother would tease me about my awkwardness, strength, and height. Once when I opened the refrigerator door in a hurry, I ripped the handle off. Mother was in the kitchen and laughed, saying "And to think, I wanted a dainty little girl." It was affectionate, not critical, but a common refrain for her. Some months later, my strength got the better of me again. I came home after a bowling game with friends. My parents had gone to bed early forgetting I was still out, my father put the chain on the front door. When I came home and unlocked the door I felt a little resistance and just pushed a little harder. The entire doorframe came off. My father rushed out in his pajamas and apologized and my mother stood in the hall, looked at the mess, and laughed at her not-so-dainty daughter again.

As I got older and more self-conscious, I decided I was too tall to be asked on dates and my internal voice said that I was too ugly or too fat. My self-identified faults brought me the same types of uncertainty and torment every other teenager experiences also. My saving grace was my interest in sports and science.

However, and here is the belated ah, ha, I did have a crush on my junior-high gym teacher. She was the most wonderful teacher in the school-athletic, fighting for our needs, pushing us to excel, yet also able to be caring and understanding. Many of us were just beginning our menstrual periods, we were so embarrassed and too shy to say anything but desperate for our privacy. Ms. D. knew without a word what our concerns were and exempted us from the workouts or showers. My crush consisted only in thinking, " Gee, wouldn't she be fun to know outside of school?"

When I got to high school, I developed a similar crush on my new gym teacher. She, too, was absolutely wonderful-sensitive, strong, and compassionate.

But then I had no context in which to put my feelings. I felt an admiration and emotional bonding with them, but there was no favoritism on their part because I got into my fair share of trouble when I didn't perform up to their standards. Gym teachers were always admired by their students, and I assumed others shared my feelings as we strove to gain their attention and respect. But with the perspective of time, I realize there was something else involved, too. Something I didn't understand at all then.

There was one other time I experienced this undercurrent of emotion toward one of my professors. This time it was in college and she was my medical surgical professor. She was brilliant, very strict, yet there was something about her that was compelling and unnerving to me. Back then; all I could understand about feeling drawn to these women was this sense of "difference." These three women were different from others in my life. It was as if they had something in common. What that something was would remain a mystery to me until I reached my mid-forties.

In my senior year of high school I finally ended up with a "boy friend". We met when I was babysitting his sister's daughter. He was very sweet and we were both very young and inexperienced in life. He had a stick shift car, which he drove with such expertise and taught me how to drive it. The high school senior prom approached for both of us and I was pleased when he asked me. I enjoyed dressing up, having our pictures taken, and hearing our parents tell us how grown-up we looked. I finished high school feeling a little more part of the social scene and perhaps I was not such an ugly duckling.

Yet for all my desire to fit in with my classmates, never in my growing-up years did I envision myself getting married. Neither of my parents discussed the issue at all. And my Aunt Aagot was a wonderful example of someone who had a full and adventurous life without ever marrying. As I looked forward to college, my dreams of the future all concerned my career as a doctor.

Being successful in sports had been fun and taught me to delight in teamwork and discipline. But that success hadn't given me one thing I really needed. Only by going to medical school could I get what I wanted most. By becoming a doctor I would finally achieve something very important that had, so far, been out of my grasp: my father's approval.

CHAPTER 3

. . . .

Choosing Your Battle

Several years ago, my father wrote our family history. In it he described his offspring this way: "I have three children." Though I am the firstborn, his three children are my three brothers Jan, Tom, and Paal. It caused uproar. My brothers and their wives were outraged; I was deeply hurt. And yet it was good to get out in the open the message I had struggled with all my life: that as a woman, no matter what I did, I would never count.

. . . .

There have been a few times in my life when I haven't done what I said I was going to do. Those failures have shaped me as much as any successes, and the memory of them stays sharp and constant. I don't think that's a bad thing, although a part of me would prefer my pride to be untarnished.

The first promise I broke was that of becoming a doctor.

I come from a family of doctors. Both of grandfathers, my father, and four cousins were physicians. As early as I can remember, I knew I would join their ranks. The doctor's daughter would be a doctor. My summer, as a teenager, at the National Institutes of Health confirmed my interest in medicine and research. There was the little matter of college before the real challenge of medical school, but I believed I'd handle that with the same ease as I'd managed high school. The future was obvious and clear. My confidence that I would soon be a doctor counter-balanced the uncertainty that came from looking and feeling different-too tall, too shy, and too Norwegian next to the American teenagers.

So becoming a doctor was going to be my vindication in many ways. But there were more challenges to this goal than I saw at the time. Just seventeen when I entered college, I was very young and naive. Towering over my peers by inches, I mistakenly assumed I'd surpass them in achievement just as easily and as well.

I entered the University of Maryland in the fall of 1959. College was an exciting new world. As the first in my family to attend an American university, I was not only a pioneer but also a standard-bearer. My performance would set the pace for the Cammermeyers in their adopted country and pave the way for my brothers. To prove my genius status, I enrolled in a grueling schedule of premed courses: microbiology, chemistry, zoology, calculus, history, and English in my first semester.

For the first time I was on my own. Even though I lived in the dorm and had a dorm mother, I said to myself, "Great, no rules, no regulations, I can do my own thing." I made friends with a few of the people I worked with in the dining room, and together we discovered the local pub. I went overboard. Since I'd done well in high school without studying, I took advantage of all the evenings at the local hangouts, playing pool and socializing. At the time, my behavior seemed perfectly justified. I wasn't home, where I had to be a proper role model for my younger brothers and feel the quiet constraints of my parents' propriety. Also, this was a way to fit in. You didn't do that sitting over books in the library, but by drinking with friends in the local tavern. Even a genius needs to be well rounded. Social life took precedence over studying, and as a result, I didn't do very well in school.

By the end of my first semester of premed courses and playing at the pub, the results were in: my grades were so bad I was put on academic probation. Disaster. I needed top grades to compete for medical school; and I worried that I'd never manage the cost of medical training without a scholarship.

I had already asked my father for financial help in covering college tuition. He said he couldn't afford it with his other family obligations. He seemed to meet any request for money with "I can't afford it"–another form of his no. My mother ran our household on a strict allowance that never seemed to be quite enough, and so she would have to ask him for additional amounts if my brothers or I needed, for example, a new pair of shoes. I hated her lack of autonomy and freedom. Father was a scientist at a major government agency, so we were not poor. Rather, he was selectively frugal. And my mother's subservient position prevented her from telling him she needed more money to cover our basic needs. Instead, she compensated by going without, by doing our laundry by hand long after other families had washing machines, by making all our clothes, by knitting Norwegian sweaters and selling them to acquaintances. When Father rejected my request for tuition assistance, I was not surprised-but I was humiliated. I determined to make it completely on my own.

But with no money and insufficiently good grades for scholarships, I didn't know what to do. Becoming a doctor had been my only plan.

My mother, seeing my devastation, tried to dissuade me from abandoning school. She gently inquired how I would make a living without a degree. We analyzed my past employment: one summer as a secretary and another assignment as a lab assistant at NIH. I could drop out of school and be a secretary or wash laboratory beakers. But to continue in science, I would definitely need a degree. We sat there in silence. It was January 1960. We were women raised in the 1930s and '50s when the array of choices was not particularly. And we were women in my father's house.

My father has three children: they're my three brothers. My father accepts this belief in the subordinate place of women, as his father accepted it before him. To him women are subservient: loved, valued-but less than men. They do not carry the family name. When they marry, they take another man's name, and when they bear children, they are contributing to another man's heritage. So not carrying the family name, I do not exist to my father. It is, I see now, the message that defined my childhood and that I've sought to overcome all my life, a message that is no less powerful for being subliminal-it's been like fighting a shadow.

I fought it from the beginning. As a child, I had a lab, like his. I planned to become a doctor, like him. He didn't discourage me from any of these things. He hardly noticed. I rarely could get his attention.

Inevitably, my mother did not help my dilemma. She, too, lived the unspoken rule of our house that women could not expect to compete with men, and tried to pass it on to me in daily homespun doses. I don't blame her for that. Her job was to prepare me for the world-the world she knew. That meant keeping me in check, as she had been, dutifully abandoning art school in England to return to Norway to study nursing and marry. As her mother had done for her, she sought to shape me so that my role in life as girl and woman would fit without binding. Whenever I was high on myself, thrilled by a dream or a success, Mother would say, "Come down to earth, prima donna." And I would. Down to earth, eyes closed, down among the shadows. I was cocky on the outside quick witted, ready with a pun or a joke-but inwardly so doubtful of my own abilities that one semester of bad grades sent me tumbling into despair. I had no reserves, no separate, internal sense of entitlement or self that I could find strength or solace in. Now I can see I had set myself up to fail. In away, by taking a double schedule of classes and then spending evenings in the pub, I had proven my father's message: I was nothing.

When I dropped out of premed, my father didn't say anything about my abandoning my goal. Just as he didn't approve, he didn't disapprove.

But no longing of my life then or for years to come is more indelible than the wish that he would say, once, "I'm proud of you, you've done a good job." My medals did not do it, my marriage and four sons did not do it, my awards for service and clinical achievements did not do it. It wasn't until I got my doctorate-and I insisted he come to that graduation, the only graduation ceremony of mine he ever attended—that we made a sort of peace. Only then, as I grasped my doctoral diploma, he finally, off-handedly, remarked, "You know, I should have gotten my Ph.D. also," and I felt, Oh, I have been *released!*

But that took another thirty years.

Being put on academic probation made medical school seem unattainable. However, I did see another way if I lowered my expectations. This course would allow me to pay for my education and remain in the field I loved, but meant choosing a career I'd always said was the lowest in the world: nursing. Because it was a woman's job and to get my father's approval I had to excel in something that counted to him, nursing felt like a defeat. I faced an important lesson in choosing my battles: Do I set myself up to succeed or to fail? Even though I was lowering my aspirations, nursing was a way to turn this adversity of bad grades and no money into something positive: something that would at least give me a career.

Nursing was to give me something even more important than an income. With this throwing up of my hands and giving up my dream of becoming a doctor, I was acting out the "poor me" scenario. I had to bear so many burdens: I was the firstborn; I was cut off from my childhood by our immigration; I had to pave the way for my brothers because my parents didn't know anything about American society; I had to be the spokesperson for our family; I had to set a good example; I had to toe the line. Nursing gave me the opportunity to see beyond myself. It made me deal with other people's suffering. Nursing forced me to find what I most lacked at that time: compassion for others—which eventually led me, much later, to have it for myself.

In many ways, nursing is the crummiest job in the world. You're dealing with urine and blood and vomit. You see people at their worst, in agony, and they're totally dependent on you, it can seem like a thankless job. You are subservient to doctors; you are considered dumb. Day after day, year after year, you perform the most elemental tasks-intimate, dirty, repetitive tasks. You are the arm for someone who doesn't have one, the legs for someone who can't walk, the hands that give food and medicine.

Yet doing these tasks, patient after patient, hour by hour, something happens. It occurs for some in a flash. For others, like myself, it's a slower transformation. As you bathe, monitor, and inject each patient, you begin to realize you are also a healer, the hope that may not have surfaced yet, the touch that gives comfort, the voice that says, "You matter," and, when healing is no longer possible, you're the eyes that say goodbye. And then you understand that nursing is the most important job in the world.

But when I was seventeen, that knowledge was years away. All I knew then was that I was a young woman and a nothing, and the only job that suited both was the crummiest job in the world. So I stayed in college and transferred my major to nursing. Even though becoming a nurse meant lowering my expectations, I knew I could succeed. On the surface, it made my life easier. I played the part: did better in my new courses, never cut classes, saved my money, and spent evenings with my fellow students at the local hangouts.

Those first two years of college, I had two good friends. Working with me in the mess hall dishing up food and bussing was a wonderful bear of a guy named Doug. He became the big brother I'd never had. When it was party time we'd go down to the pub together and I'd make a fool of myself. One night I saw a fellow open a bottle of beer with his teeth. I said to Doug, "Well, shoot, if he can do it, I can do it." I used my canine teeth. For each bottle I opened with my teeth, I got one free. It was a way to economize, and, of course, it got to be sort of a show. Doug would see that I made it home okay at night regardless of how much beer I'd had. And when I used my cross-country skis to get to classes in an unusually snowy winter, he patiently explained he would prefer it if I didn't ski down to the pub. He did not want to have to deal with getting both me and my skis back to the dorm. On weekends he would come over to my parents' house. We were there for each other. It was a buddy relationship

I treasure and still so enjoy the visits with him and his wife when I travel east.

My friendship with Alice was cemented in an unusual way, One Saturday, as we all, did our chores in the dorm, a young daredevil in a little plane began swooping down over campus. Either to impress or frighten us we didn't ever find out which-he zoomed his plane over the roofs of the dorms, just barely avoiding impact. As he buzzed our building, everybody rushed to the windows to look with both excitement and concern. Everybody but me. I crawled under my bed, terrified, I had a phobic response to the sound. It must have touched off subliminal memories of living in Norway during the bombings of WWII.

My roommate could not calm me. Alice, who lived down the hall, was brought in to handle the situation. She was ruthlessly compassionate, with a no-nonsense manner and a big heart. She analyzed the minor crisis, then knelt down and negotiated with me as I trembled under the bed. I finally shared with her my experiences of the war; She understood and didn't discount them. Soon I was up and out, carrying on with the weekend activities. Where other people saw me as distant and unusual in my manners and style, Alice and I connected. She was fearless, shrewd, and still had a powerful sensitivity and integrity. We became loyal friends.

Looking back, I see these two separate selves. I held my own with the guys at the pub, and then during the day I took classes to become a nurse —a role I felt was subservient. Unlike with all the other roles I'd been assigned and performed, practice and time didn't make nursing fit. When the dream of being a doctor ended, I struggled to find direction. The weight of being and feeling different from my classmates pulled me down. I dated, but my dates were buddies more than suitors. I had no mentors, saw no future I wanted. I began to write poems, melancholy poems, obsessed with duty and death, and yearning for the chance to be worthy of both.

I also began to have physical symptoms. I'd always been vigorous and healthy, but now I couldn't shake a series of illnesses. After a bout with mononucleosis ended, I continued to have abdominal pains. Still, I kept on trying to do all the things in my schedule taking classes, working, being the smiling student nurse.

The abdominal pains continued, but I didn't go to the doctor. I was doing some drinking. But no matter what I did, I didn't feel okay. Sometimes at night, alone in my dorm room, I would smash my fist into the wall, making a hole and crushing my knuckles. Then, a bit later, I started cutting myself. I carefully drew the razor across the skin, deep enough to draw blood and feel the pain. I told Alice, who was very concerned, that I was doing an experiment to see how fast wounds healed on the human body. Actually, I was trying to get rid of some of the inside pain by putting it on the outside.

Even though I tried to fulfill all my obligations without any sign of this inner confusion, there were occasions when I walked around campus with a black-and-blue hand, crushed knuckles, and bandaged wrists. I suppose it was just a matter of time before someone turned me in to the assistant dean. Again my college career was in jeopardy, despite my good grades and excellent hospital work.

The dean summoned me to her office. I appeared early and anxious, and managed to get through the brutally short interview without revealing any emotion. I also endured it without remembering much that was said, except that she required I see a psychiatrist before I could continue in school. My only thought was, I can't tell my parents. The firstborn cannot falter again. So I arranged to pay for the session with the psychiatrist on my own.

Nevertheless, I was outraged that I was expected not only to subject myself to this session but also to pay for it. In what I thought would be one fifty-minute interview, this stranger would determine my fate but one session was not sufficient and I had to return for a second visit. I decided that if I got through this I would never let anyone catch me in such a humiliating position again.

The psychiatrist asked about my behavior. I told him about my feelings of failure, and of not being accepted, the cutting, and the fists through the wall. By that time his diagnosis was quite clear as he told me that my behavior was just "acting out," wanting attention and schoolgirl stuff. And he did not think I was suicidal. I was incensed that his though I was seeking attention but I kept my mouth shut. He signed the papers allowing me to return to school. My friends called me the smiling melancholic, and I wanted to move beyond that but the psychiatrist didn't seem to hear my words, he only judged my actions and then discounted my emotional turmoil.

So I took the feelings and locked them away. They didn't fully emerge again until my separation and divorce.

After the visit to the psychiatrist my symptoms stopped. The dean and I never spoke about it again. I missed only a few days of classes, so my parents and classmates knew nothing of what occurred. And I promised myself I would be a model student. There were no books on getting in touch with your feelings. We all lived with the expectation that we fit into stereotypic roles and as a result my inner turmoil continued to be repressed.

The only doubts I couldn't silence concerned the path I was on in nursing. I was near the end of my sophomore year and my courses were going well. But I worried that, as a career nursing would give me nothing that mattered and I would feel trapped in a dainty, traditional role. Perhaps to my adolescent conscience becoming a nurse was penance for my earlier pride. Penance had quickly become a prison. But then, the prison gates suddenly flew open and I was once again liberated by the American military.

Unlike my childhood liberation, this one didn't start with a parade. Instead it started with a memory. I remembered a woman I'd met during a high school bowling party. We were bowling some games and she proudly walked in wearing her new Army uniform. She had graduated from the Army Student Nurse Program. She talked about the excitement of travel, the challenge of service to her country, the possibility of taking care of soldiers in combat. At the time I had not thought much about it. I assumed I was just steps away from becoming a doctor. But now, trying to find a way to make my nurse's role fit, I again saw her stride in with all that tangible future and honor. Here was a way to contribute to the greater good. Being a nurse healing soldiers would be much less demeaning than being a civilian nurse kowtowing to doctors. This is what I would do. This would be my liberation from tedious, subservient woman's work. This was the role that would not constrict, and I felt light as air and hope for the first time since my disastrous first semester of school.

My belief-born in my earliest years living across from Nazi, headquarters-that there are values worth dying for now found expression. The idea of liberty and justice for all is worth dying for and worth living twenty-six years in uniform for. It's not an esoteric concept. American soldiers, many who gave their lives, rescued me and my parents, our town and country, from Nazi conquest and tyranny, Though I was only three when our liberation came, it was and remains the event that made the rest of my life, my freedom and my family's freedom, possible. So when I came to be rescued again, I turned to the American military to liberate me as it had done before, in 1945.

It was an exciting time to join the Army. The early 1960s-this was before the debate over Vietnam-was a time of renewed patriotism in the country. John Kennedy was the passionate young leader of a never-defeated America. His contagious idealism hit my American peers like an awakening bolt of passion. But his vision didn't change my pride in being an American, it confirmed it. That America was the champion of goodness and democracy was no revelation to me. I'd known the truth of that long before I ever touched the shore of this continent, read a book in English, heard a speech by a patriotic gratitude I had taken the oath of U.S. citizenship in August 1960, put my hand over my heart and pledged allegiance to the flag. No other country in the world had ever done as much to ensure freedom and justice, and the instrument of that achievement was the American military.

I now found a role that fit without binding: I would serve as a nurse and soldier. This would also be a way for me to repay America for giving my father a place to do his work and my family a home. In addition, if I signed up for the Army Student Nurse Program, my last two years of college tuition would be covered; in return, after graduation I would serve three years on active duty. This took an enormous burden off my shoulders.

My parents met my happy announcement with uncomfortable silence. This was the spring of 1961. My father lived the life of an intellectual, and a military career for a woman didn't make sense to them. My parents worried that "women of our class don't join the military." But they did not say no, I tried to explain that

I wanted to join in order to elevate nursing to something more meaningful

They were also reluctant to make any judgment on their own, since this was a new country, so they turned to their American friends for insight. What they got was prejudice. Still lingering from the 1940s was the belief, my parents were told, that only homosexuals and whores joined the military.

Of course that ignorant stereotype resonates even today. Why is there this need to diminish a woman's desire to serve her country? Why are men who join the military manly and dedicated, while the women who do are tainted and self-serving?

Back then I was enormously perplexed by such statements. I was naïve about issues of sex and sexuality. I did not feel an attraction to men, though I certainly enjoyed their friendship. I remember a vague fear when I was in college that my feelings of alienation might be because I was homosexual. I attributed my occasional suspicion to trying to diagnose my melancholia, and the few times I considered it, I completely rejected the idea. It didn't fit me at all.

True, I wasn't interested in getting married, but that was because I wanted a career. In those days, people believed a woman had to choose one or the other. I didn't just want a career, one day I wanted to be the Chief Nurse of the entire Nurse Corps, and a general. I was sure this was the right path, and my parents accepted my explanations. So I made my appointment at the recruiter's office. Once I committed to being a nurse, I also committed to becoming a soldier.

I went alone to the Army recruitment center in the July heat of 1961, my summer dress delicate among the uniforms and medals. The atmosphere was a bit intimidating, as it was supposed to be. The military is not for wimps.

When I entered the office Major Anna Cost, a peroxide blonde with unending energy and goodwill, welcomed me. Major Cost was an Army nurse and my recruiting officer. Through the next years of my training, as I moved up in rank and graduated, she was also my role model and doting grandmother.

Joining the military as an Army student nurse, taking the oath under the flag that day, I felt a deep joy that went beyond the honor and obligation of the moment. I realized that not only would I serve and defend America, but also the military would take care of me.

I now had a credible future. I went about my work with new hope and purpose. But that vague question lingered: Why did I feel alienated from my peers? Why did I feel different? Though taller, I looked the same, dressed the same, took the same courses, enjoyed the same music. In fact, I often sang and played folk music with my classmates-music of The Weavers and The Kingston Trio that we all loved. The lyrics moved me just as they did everyone else. Still, I felt different. When people older than myself entered the room, I stood up. This, appropriate in the recruiting office, was out of place on campus, but I did it automatically. In greeting others, I always shook hands (which women never did in those days). I held the door open for people, even my classmates, but felt awkward if they did the same for me (the tallest should always hold the door). These behaviors came naturally. They felt right to me-and yet they also made me feel out of place. What was wrong?

When I was child in Norway I never felt different from others. That came when we moved to America. It occurred to me that I might find some answers in Norway, so I saved my money for a trip back. My grandmother was getting old, and I had yet to fulfill my childhood promise to visit. So in August 1962 I returned to Norway for the first time in eleven years. The trip was more wonderful and meaningful than I had ever imagined it would be. By the time the airport taxi pulled up in front of my grandmother's apartment building in Oslo, I was so excited to be home, I ran out of the cab, burst through the entrance, and raced up the five flights of stairs, so oblivious to everything but my destination that I dropped packages the entire way up the staircase. When I reached the door, grandmother embraced me happily, crying, *"Kjære Grethemor velkommen hjem."* Behind me, laughing and beaming, my aunt followed, her arms loaded with all the gifts I had dropped along the way. The sweet pleasure of belonging, just as I was, without any need to be otherwise, returned after an eleven-year absence.

I spent weeks visiting with relatives and friends, traveling to the countryside, drinking in all that was familiar and loved, savoring the words: *"Jeg er hjemme"*— I am home. I began to notice something remarkable: everywhere I went, young people stood up when their elders entered the room; women always shook hands in greeting and held the door open for others. This etiquette was expected and proper. I realized that rather than being different, with its implication that this was somehow wrong, I was doing exactly what I was supposed to be doing. I was being Norwegian. There was nothing wrong with me. I decided that all the feelings of uncertainty, loneliness, and alienation I experienced as a teenager and a college student were explained by the fact that I'd been born and raised in Norway and was Norwegian. My exoneration. I didn't have to be worried about a mysterious reason why I felt different in America. Here I was like everyone else. I fit in, I was home.

When I returned to America, I rushed into my last year of college with enthusiasm for schoolwork, though I still withdrew socially. I had a private room and, instead of joining others at the pub, I passed my spare time by playing the baritone uke and singing by myself. It was my solace and how I dealt with my melancholia. Today, when I play those songs for my teenage sons, they laugh at the despair of the lyrics and howl like animals in mourning.

After my enlistment in 1961, my advancement in the military proceeded exactly on schedule (one of the delightful aspects about such a splendidly rigid institution is that if you do what you're supposed to, the system does what it's supposed to). I was promoted from recruit to private, then to private first class, and finally commissioned as a second lieutenant.

My world was still very small. It consisted of school and the military. The social upheaval that began in the 1960s didn't really affect me. You're sheltered from the world when you're in school, just as in many ways you're protected when you're in the military. And for me, the additional benefit of having enlisted was that I didn't have to make any decisions about what I was going to do tomorrow. It was all taken care of. I liked that. It was good not to have to worry about where I was going to live, or where my job would be. I happily said, "Take me where you want, and let me learn to be an adult, without having to make other decisions." In a way, I was relinquishing responsibility; at the same time this life fit my lack of emotional maturity. I was being taken care of.

As an Army student nurse I received my first military commendation, the Good Conduct Medal, for hospital work and some recruiting I'd performed. When it was pinned on my uniform it had the full, intended effect. I was tremendously proud.

Beyond being praised and regularly promoted (hallmarks of the military regime), I was paid seventy-eight dollars a month-a handsome amount in those days. It was wonderful to be paid to go to school. With this regular income, I saved enough money to make two important purchases. First I bought my mother a washer and dryer, so she could stop doing laundry by hand. She was delighted with the gift, and I was proud to have the autonomy and the income to help make her life a little easier.

Then I bought my first car, gorgeous big black four-door 1957 Mercury. It had sleek lines with contrasting white fins protruding off the back end. The seats were leather, and the windows and gears were operated by push buttons (an innovation in those days). It was an absolute dream car. Owning it, driving it, showing off its power and style delighted me tremendously. I wasn't just at peace with myself, I was ready to go. Army, here I come!

After graduation, the only thing that stood between me and the military was passing a two-day state board nursing examination. This was the culmination of all my college and hospital training. The multiple-choice questions covered every aspect of nursing. After the test, my classmates and I dragged ourselves out of the exam center in Baltimore, so sure that we were going to fail that we made plans to get together to study for the next time the test would be given. The six weeks of waiting for the results went slowly—with fears surfacing from my earlier failure in school. Then, finally, the Army notified me I was to report for active duty. I had passed the state board examination. I was ecstatic.

The preparation was over; my career was truly beginning. I waited eagerly at my parents' home in Bethesda for my orders. Any day they would arrive and I would begin my military life. Any day I would put on my uniform, pack my bag, report for duty—and finally take my place in my new world.

"Any day " came on Sunday evening, July 24, 1963. *The* telegram arrived at the door. My orders—even the phrase was impressive. Impatiently I opened *the* telegram. I read it. I read it again. I read it a third time. My heart stopped. I didn't know what to do. These were my orders:

TC 220. BY ORDER SA FOL RSG DIR. WP TDN. FOR TVL COSTS TO AND PD AT TDY STA ONLY 2142020 32-29 P2450-21 22 25 S99-999. FOR ALL OTHER COSTS 2142010 01-1231-1233. EFF UPON EXPR PRESENT LV. TDY ENR TO STU DET, MFSS BAMC (3410-02) FT SAM HOUSTON, TEX. REPT DATE: NST 0730 HRS 23 JUL 63.

The telegram told me other things as well, an entire page of instructions. All in capital letters and commanding abbreviations and acronyms. After searching the page for clues, I decided I'd been ordered to Fort Sam Houston-but when? How? If I didn't find out, I might disobey the first orders of my career.

There had to be a solution. I couldn't get hold of my recruiter—it was Sunday night. Where were military matters best analyzed and understood? And where was I most likely to find someone on duty even on a Sunday? The Pentagon, of course. I worked up my courage, dialed the Pentagon, and asked to speak to the officer in charge. He abruptly got on the line. Flustered, hardly able to explain my reason for calling, I finally convinced him to translate the telegram. He must have considered me an absolute idiot. After all, the Pentagon had a few other obligations-like managing troops and planning for war-that were more important than deciphering a telegram for a young nurse. But at the time, it was the only thing I knew to do. And it worked. He told me what I needed to know. I was on my way.

I made travel plans so I would arrive and report for active duty no sooner than 7:30 a.m., July 23, 1963 to the Medical Field Service School, Brooke Army Medical Center, at Fort Sam Houston, Texas. Though I had no idea about military protocol or what to do once in uniform, I got out my manual that described each style of uniform and opened it on the dresser. It showed the correct positioning of all insignias and medals. Now I went to work.

I spent hours ironing my cord uniform. No longer used today, cord was the type of fabric-a lightweight, green-and-white cotton weave—that was made into a smart-looking skirt-and-blouse outfit. Once every wrinkle was out, and each crease looked sharp and perfect, I placed the brass just as it was in the manual photograph. The simple gold lieutenant's bars went parallel, one-half inch from the top shoulder seam and centered. The Nurse Corps caduceus was placed on the right lapel, perpendicular to the floor and three quarters of an inch from the edge. The U.S. insignia was centered on the left lapel and parallel to the floor. The nametag went over the right breast across from the top buttonhole and anatomically adjusted as necessary. My Good Conduct Medal was alighted over the left breast across from the top buttonhole in perfect alignment. The second lieutenant's bar graced the cap one inch from the front crease on the right side. Everything was in its proper position. I compared myself in uniform to the picture in the manual perfection. I looked beautiful.

I went out to show my mother. I don't know what pleased her more-my new look as an officer or my own excitement. By now, she and my father were allies of my decision to become a soldier. They had watched me thrive since my enlistment, and defended my new career if friends or colleagues questioned it. Mother agreed the uniform suited me very well, laughing as I paraded around, and teasing, "Come down to earth, prima donna."

But on the way to the airport, perfectly attired as an officer, I felt strange. I looked the part, but could I act it? This was just the second time I had been out in such a public place as a second lieutenant. I had dressed in my uniform to fly on standby status when I visited Aagot in Portland, Oregon, earlier in the summer (military personnel received special airline rates). Then, as now, I was plagued with questions. What was the protocol for military conduct? Where and when should I salute? And whom? My duty was to salute first anyone senior to me whether in the Army, Navy, Air Force, or Marines. That was my duty—but would I be able to tell who was senior to me? I didn't know how to read insignias—there were so many. What if I mistakenly saluted an enlisted person? That would be totally wrong. The enlisted person had to initiate the salute, but what if that didn't happen? My anxiety rising, I reached the airport.

As I entered the terminal, I didn't know whether to take off my cap or leave it on. I left it on, hoping I wasn't committing a grave error. As I waited for the plane, I decided it was the time and place to take evasive action. I scanned the airport, determined to avoid other military people. Every time people in uniform approached, I turned my eyes away. But when they had passed and were at a safe distance, I'd peek to see what they did with their hats and how they acted when they met others in uniform. I felt like an impersonator.

That was soon to change. The Army has a systematic process for reshaping the identity of each person. Not only do you get a new preface to your name (lieutenant), new clothing (uniforms), new behaviors (marching and saluting), but you also learn a new language (abbreviations and acronyms). It is accomplished in only ten weeks, and it's called basic training.

My transformation occurred at Fort Sam, as we called it. I arrived on time, with the rest of my fellow trainees, exactly as ordered, and went directly to billeting to receive my housing assignment. For the duration of basic training, we all stayed in sparse officers' quarters.

Arriving on a military post, I always feel as if I've been picked-up and set down again in a foreign culture-a culture somewhere back in time. The terrain is invariably flat. This is best for parades, of course. It also allows everybody to be, quite literally, on the same plane. Roads are more economical to build and it's easier to move equipment and vehicles quickly and safely on a flat landscape. And aesthetically it's very pleasing. The lawns are vast and green. The buildings are elegantly stoic, without ingenious designs-very straight lines, very pragmatic. Every square inch is used because Every square inch is needed. The symmetry in the landscape and architecture is mirrored by the meticulously maintained grounds, where vehicles never exceed the posted speed and people in uniforms calmly, diligently go about their work. In this place of picturesque serenity, a wonderful thing happens: impersonators are turned into officers.

At Fort Sam all high-ranking officers live in Victorian-style wooden residences. Other officers and enlisted are billeted in simple brick houses, duplexes and barracks. From there, a half-mile-long parade field, framed by rows of elegant trees, stretches up to the imposing Brooke Army Medical Center.

In the center of it all, surrounded by the vast green lawn of the parade field, stand the flagpole and the cannon. Every morning, on every military post, including Fort Sam Houston, reveille is sounded. I always made sure to be outside at 0600 hours to be a part of this awakening ritual. The cannon goes off and everything on post stops. Talk about bowing to Mecca—this is the military equivalent. If you are outside anywhere on the post—even if you are a civilian—once the cannon goes off, you stop. If you are in a car, you stop the car and get out; if you are marching or walking, you halt. The reveille or retreat sounds and everyone stands and salutes in rapt attention in the direction of the flag raising or lowering.

All these elements of military life–from the uniformity of the architecture to the defining rituals and behaviors–serve to create a sense of shared values and purposes that are vital and comforting. For example, the salute. Such a central part of military life, it is the focus of the first obligation we faced. As soon as we got on the post, we were told that military tradition requires each new officer to perpetuate a cardinal rule: to give the first enlisted person who salutes you a dollar. This happened to me the first day as I walked to my quarters. After I returned the salute, I gave the enlisted man a dollar, and blushed because he now knew I was a green "butter bar"— as the bearer of the gold-colored insignia of the second lieutenant bar is termed. The initiation was over and it had its effect. I was a member of this group, connected in gestures, rituals, and dress.

A salute is a greeting. On one level, it's the subordinate's respect for the senior rank. But it's much more than that. The salute creates a humanizing connectedness. Here are two people walking on the same street who are forced by tradition to say hello, in a society that normally is segregated by hierarchy and non-fraternization between officers and enlisted personnel. The discipline of it changes a person in good ways. I can tell who's been in the military even if they're not in uniform. Out in the civilian world, walking along the street, if I have direct, unhesitant eye contact with a stranger who says hello, we both know we have a common military history, are connected, and share a world.   '

Our immersion in military life continued in the classroom. My class of incoming members of the Army Nurse Corps studied the structure of the Army, the symbols of unit sizes and corps, the developments of battle plans. We learned the configuration of platoons, companies, battalions, batteries, and armies. As medical personnel, we learned about battle casualties, requirements for beds and supplies, medical resources, and the skills of each specialist and technician on the battlefield. In addition to the battlefield scenario, there were lectures on the care of soldiers and their families during peacetime. Most of the on-site work we did at Brooke Army Medical Center was to learn that inescapable aspect of all military service: paperwork.

The most powerful experience of my ten-week training was the course in combat nursing. Even before we boarded the buses to take us to the mock battlefield, our work began. We took the fatigues we were going to wear, wadded them up into our helmets, filled the helmets with insect repellent until the fabric was thoroughly soaked, Then we draped the impregnated fatigues out in the August sun to dry. The stench of the drying chemicals not only kept the insects away but made us dread being around one another.

The next day, dressed in our newly perfumed fatigues, we traveled by bus convoy to Camp Bullis, our field-training site. It was miserably hot and humid when we arrived, and we were soon greeted by the only residents of the desolate area. Rattlesnakes. Lots of them. And they were ready for us. Occasionally they would visit while we sat pensive and alone in the foul-smelling outhouse. Their sudden presence would eject us from our positions as though we were under incoming fire. It was a quite effective combat simulation. There was something profoundly unsettling about the slithering movement, smell, and rattle of the snake that made me feel I couldn't get out fast or far enough. But our real encounters with the snakes were not as gut wrenching as our mock encounters with war and casualties.

Prior to our own involvement in simulated combat, we were taken to an observation area to watch bombing raids and war games. It was awesome and unreal. I don't think there is a way to make pretended war feel real—and that is perhaps both a blessing and a tragedy. None of the training experience I had in the next weeks, none of my experience teaching combat medicine to medics on their way to Vietnam in following years, ever made combat anything more than a hypothetical experience of "what if." It wasn't until I served in Vietnam myself that war and what it does to people became real for me.

But then, in Texas in 1963, we were only playing war games. "Wounded soldiers" were "moulaged" with incredibly vivid, authentic-looking makeup to simulate types of battle casualties. In teams we searched for and treated these mock casualties. Each step of emergency care was practiced on the open terrain: keeping the airway open, stopping the bleeding, and assuring adequate circulation for each wounded soldier we found. At first, coming up to a badly wounded man lying on the battlefield, I was immobilized by the horror. Just the sight of the damage–even made-up damage—to the human body would cause that visceral twinge, that surge in the gut. Then we applied dressings to the wounds and prepared to transport the casualty. Two of us carried the patient—individuals often weighed more than a hundred and eighty pounds—across ravines and creeks. After three or four days, I learned to look without feeling, treat without thinking, and work without getting tired—all skills I would hone in Vietnam.

Looking back, I find it hard to imagine that we saw this as only an exercise to be mastered. But it was ten years after the Korean War, and the next war—Vietnam— was an as-yet-unrealized tragedy. So I didn't think or worry about the possibility of using these skills. And besides, I had given up making decisions.

For some, military discipline is too confining. To be told what to wear, how to wear it, what to do, where and when to do it, relieves a person of the small decisions of daily life to such a degree that some feel there is no self left. But that's not true. Trivia are eliminated so your entire attention can be directed to what matters: your mission. A nurse's mission in the Army is to conserve the fighting force and to perform that duty with honor and integrity. Those of us who stayed and embraced these values grew strong in this strenuously consistent environment.

The military's most potent weapon is the belief that we are more alike than we are different. That is the way to marshal our best impulses and actions for the greater good. Go to one parade and you'll understand-a thousand fall in and march as one. We don't get caught up in our differences. But that beautiful precision takes training. Lots of training. That's why the parade field is the centerpiece of the military post.

We started our drill training under the hot August sun. About sixty of us arrived at the parade field for our first practice. All women officers, all looking the same in our sharp uniforms, all standing in a vague group, waiting. Then our drill instructor inspected us. We stood silent, alert, and somewhat bewildered. He took a breath and called "FALL, in!" We stared. No one moved. He looked at us and quickly said: "All nurses here, line up in two rows. Now, in each row, shift so that the person standing left of you is shorter than you, and the person in front of you is shorter than you.

We did it in a flash. Suddenly we looked quite splendidly organized. He went on: "Those of you who are in the far right-hand column are the squad leaders—assume this position always. Squad leaders take your squads and practice marching.

Being the tallest, I was appointed platoon leader. This placed me in front, and in charge of, four squads. It was my job to call cadence for the platoon I had a deep, authoritative voice that projected throughout the parade grounds. I sounded more like a drill sergeant than a reserved, quiet nurse that I was. I loved putting my platoon through their paces. My voice as the key. As we worked together, I discovered the value of musical inflections. My platoon was able to tell from the way I announced the prepatory command what execution command was to follow. "FORWARD, march" —I dropped the sound down as my jaw lunged into the deep "march" and the platoon moved together as one in crisp, clean motion. "COLUMN RIGHT, march!" All heads high and direct, we'd turn sharply. We began to move with fluidity and grace. We were becoming a unit.

By the last parade at Fort Sam, we had put it all together. We joined the other new officers completing their basic training, men and women, nurses, physicians, dentists, occupational therapists —more than five hundred assembled on the parade field for a final show of marching expertise. Each platoon leader's job was to call cadence for his or her platoon as together we paraded down the field to the reviewing stand. The challenge was to make sure your platoon marched to your voice and didn't get out of sequence by listening to another's cadence. My voice really projected by then, and I loved the display of teamwork. Calling cadence, I soon noticed as we all moved down the parade field, that other platoons fell into synch with our cadence. They were following my voice. There was nothing else like it—marching, proud, five-hundred-as-one, indivisible. We were bound together by oath, duty, and values to serve the country we loved. I now was a soldier with comrades. Together we could vanquish any threat to freedom.

And for me Vietnam was only a small nation somewhere far away.

CHAPTER 4

· · · · · · · · · · · · · · · · ·

The Perfect Match: Soldier and Nurse

We were in the middle of war games on the barren, vast high desert of the Yakima Firing Range in eastern Washington State. As a colonel and Chief Nurse of the Washington National Guard, I was leading my troops in the most grueling few days of their yearly duty. Our 164th Evacuation Hospital provided medical support for all the other units. Conditions of war were meticulously created. The commanding general called a tactical briefing. He reminded us that each soldier had to give 100 percent and added forcefully: "Our job is to kill!" It was like a slap in my face. I'd been in the military for twenty-three years, but I'd never acknowledged that most basic goal of soldiering. Until this moment, still, I wanted to yell back: "No. My job is to heal!"

· · · · · · · · · · · · · · · · ·

In ten weeks of basic training at Fort Sam, I had learned the rudiments of soldiering. Next I was sent to Fort Benning, Georgia, for six months to become an Army nurse. In those days, there was a stigma to joining the military with a bachelor's degree. It came from the belief that you learned nursing by doing tasks and you could only do that by training in a school that awarded a nursing diploma. If you had gone to college, you were considered to know a lot of high falutin stuff you had learned out of a book but, when it came down to it, you really didn't know how to take care of patients. Those of us who came to active duty with four-year degrees felt we didn't have a lot of clinical experience working with people. So the Army gave us six months in a hospital to allow us to catch up with the hands-on skills of nursing.

I had quite clear ideas of what areas in the hospital I did not wanted to work in and which patients I did not wanted to care for. I definitely did not want to work on the women's ward. Women were wimps. They whined, wanted nurses to wait on them all the time, asked for the most medication. In childbirth, they would lose control and scream in pain. I was sure it couldn't be that bad (little did I know). And after my student nursing days on the pediatric ward watching two- and three year-old tyrants in high chairs throwing food and smearing feces, I was not about to become a pediatric nurse. After all, I'd joined the service to take care of soldiers.

However, the Army had other ideas and I was assigned to the women's surgical and gynecological ward. I didn't join the Army to take care of women dependents! That was not my idea of military nursing–but orders are orders. And, it turned out that it was on the women's ward that I learned to be a nurse.

After I'd reported to my new assignment and spent a few days on duty, the head nurse, who had watched me carefully, took me aside for a chat. She was wise and gave me some of the best direction and training in my career.

It made a profound difference in my work. Every patient I have ever cared for since has benefited from it.

"Lieutenant Cammermeyer," she said, "take six weeks and learn to become a clinical nurse."

She gave each new nurse officer permission to focus on the most important skills of nursing–listening and nurturing. She was saying, in effect, there's time; practice those things you've learned in school. This was a luxury because of the tremendous workload in every hospital. The general rule in those days was if you had enough time to sit and talk with a patient you were either goofing off or didn't have enough to do.

She sensed, I suspect, that despite the initials RN, USAR, ANC behind my name, and the second lieutenant's insignia on my uniform, I had very limited life experience. I knew how to perform the tasks of nursing. But my head nurse knew that was only one part of the job. I had never really been sick, had not had any deaths in my immediate family, and knew little about chronic physical pain. Also, I'd never been emotionally involved with anyone. Earlier in my training, I'd been so intent on learning tasks that I often didn't understand what my patients were feeling. My own life experiences consisted primarily of being a daughter, sister, and student, which meant that I did not have a frame of reference for understanding my patients. Either I became overly attached and sympathetic with them or I dismissed them as not being stoic enough. Either approach prevented me from functioning effectively as an empathic nurse.

And I had never been hospitalized. To me, my workplace was a model of order, discipline, and routine. However, if you're the patient that is not how you experience a hospitalization.

So, for those first six weeks, I was assigned to provide care to only a few female patients. I had the time to sit down and listen and talk with them. I learned by listening. I heard stories of pain, loss, grief, and anguish that each patient described in her own way. Women told me of the terror of waiting to have a breast removed because of cancer. I had time to sit with them and hear their fears the night before surgery. I learned the importance of listening, of a kind word, a gentle touch, and a caring back rub. I discovered that the core ethic of nursing is caring, being, and empathizing with the patient.

Whatever tendency I'd had to believe treating female patients was not worth my military-trained talents ended completely when I watched a woman die in the intensive care unit.

Gruesome. I still see her body in the stark, bare cubicle. She was lying totally exposed, comatose, like a corpse. Nothing about her was relaxed or flaccid. She was stiff—though you didn't see the stiffness, you saw the lack of movement, of humanness. Her skin was a deep yellow from jaundice. It was a profound discoloration, almost a molten color, showing that the transition from life to death had begun. Tubes and lines went from her body to machines, and a monitor registered her vital signs, though her spirit had already left her body.

She had attempted an abortion on herself. Abortions were illegal then. The year is 1963.

I left her cubicle and went to shift report. That is when you come on duty and find out the status of every patient on the ward—what his or her story is, the treatment plan, the prognosis, and anything else that's important to know. The nurse in charge gave us the report on her: "This is a twenty-two-year-old mother of two children under five who was pregnant. She decided that she couldn't deal with another pregnancy and used a knitting needle to try to abort. The knitting needle penetrated the uterus and ruptured it, causing a generalized infection. She told no one for days and suffered at home until the bacteria spread throughout her body. Her liver is no longer able to filter the poisons and toxins of the infection. Her blood has hemolyzed [a process in which the red blood cells have broken down and released hemoglobin, making the blood thick, viscous, and unable to flow easily]. There is nothing more to be done for her. Her husband, a young officer, is in shock and visits often. We're not expecting her to make it through the night."

Her story made a profound impression on me. If legal and safe abortions had been possible, my patient would not have needed to use such drastic measures.

My prejudice toward women patients–for that's what it was– began to change. It came, as most prejudice does, from ignorance. Caring for the dying young woman gave me a deep appreciation for the challenges she had faced alone. When women shared with me how it felt to be awaiting surgery, managing fears that weren't calmed by condescending doctors, I admired their strength. By the time I completed my six months at Fort Benning, I saw women as people to be respected, but still, I was more excited about caring for soldiers.

Throughout my life I'd seen evidence of the inferiority of my gender: the emphasis in my family on my father's authority, and my mother's tacit approval of her subservient status, the minimizing of women in the films, TV programs, and books of the era, and the fact that the military allowed women to serve only in the selected positions. Receiving the cultural message in many shapes and ways, I, like the men around me, negated women.

Learning to be a nurse, particularly a military nurse, is learning about the futility of extraordinary efforts to save dying patients. It's such an unacceptable lesson; you also intuitively begin to discover ways to try to cheat death.

It was my day off, but I was called in. There had been a terrible helicopter accident. Fort Benning was a training area for Special Forces. The casualties were from a parachute platoon stationed here and the helicopter crashed on a practice mission.

I hurried to the hospital.   The ward had been transformed into a makeshift burn unit. There was nothing there now except white–sterile white, patients wrapped in white gauze-quiet determination, white partitioning between casualties, and white hospital gowns and mask for the nurses– and futile hope.

The next days had a surreal quality. In the halls, cubicles, and rooms, sheets had been hung from the ceiling. Wherever we went, we moved through a maze of sheets. Their purpose was to cut down the spread of infection and isolate the patients. The entire time we cared for these men, we looked more like operating room nurses.   Dressed in sterile uniforms, we walked around with hoods, gowns, masks, and gloves, changing every time we came in contact with something that might be contaminated. The risk of infection is so great with burn patients. They have nothing left to protect them.   There was a smell you never forget. The stench of burned skin, muscle, and bone. Mixed with that was the acute, sweet smell of antibiotics. Antibiotics applied and administered in every fashion and form–in creams, in dressings, through intravenous fluid bottles. But for all our technique and equipment, our will and desire to save them, we were fighting against a formidable adversary. Nature does not design the human body to survive such pervasive burning.

Our job was to salvage these tragic victims. There were eight men. Each soldier was burned over 90 percent of his body. They were from the post–people we'd worked with.   You couldn't recognize them underneath the dressings and the swelling of their extremities. Their faces were like inflated balloons on which someone had drawn a couple of lines where the eyelashes should be and a couple of little ridges that now resembled the sides of a nose, and a parched sliver that represented a mouth. The rest of their bodies were completely charred.

That was my first experience with massive injuries and numerous casualties. You work hoping they'll make it, believing they'll make it. And when they don't, you employ another strategy—denial—as an attempt to cheat death. Otherwise you can't function.

We replaced fluids to stabilize a few of them so we could send them to the famous burn unit at Brooke Army Medical Center in Texas, where, we convinced ourselves, they would get well. But some died at Brooke, and some died with us. Although I heard or saw that they had died, each death was unreal. One way of pretending that our efforts to save these men did not fail was to say to yourself that the patients had been discharged from the hospital or had gone to another facility where they would get better. After all, they had left the hospital and that way you didn't have to deal with the tragedy and futility of their deaths. Remaining emotionally distant was a way of pretending that they didn't die.

Remaining emotionally distant was how you managed to do your job—especially in the military—to deal with the horrible things you see. When I worked at the evacuation hospital in Vietnam I believed the unit medics had it so much worse because they were on the front line treating casualties in the midst of the fighting. They denied the horror of war by pretending the nurses and doctors healed the wounded. And the nurses and doctors practiced a disassociation between bleak reality of our best hopes by total emotional detachment and not even learning the names of their patients.

I instinctively used this denial even with the first death of a patient I cared for as a nursing student. I was caring for a delightful, black woman in her fifties who looked as if she were seventy. She was suffering from congestive heart failure. She had been my patient a couple of days and I had grown very fond of her. On Friday afternoon, I said goodbye for the weekend and told her I would see her Monday. Monday morning I came to the hospital for my patient assignment walked into her room and saw her bed was empty. I couldn't believe it. Her bed was made up but she wasn't there. To stop the sinking feeling, I decided, "Well, she went home." I inquired about her status with the head nurse. I was told she had died over the weekend. But those were words I couldn't, or didn't want to hear. I decided she hadn't really died, but had been discharged from the hospital and gone home. That's how I dealt with her disappearance. It produced a very strange sense of loss because I had not had a chance said goodbye.

Unexpected death is always difficult to accept. Whether it's your patients who die unexpectantly, or your parent who dies when she's not supposed to—as I was to experience with my mother death several years later-when you haven't said goodbye, you find yourself pretending that the person is living happily ever after. When you are young and inexperienced the myth that no one dies allows you to go on to the next patient.

Fort Benning was one of the most traditional of the military posts because it was a training center for officers and enlisted personnel from airborne training, infantry and ranger training programs. There were never any surprises; soldiers were in control, and there was a sense of propriety not always present in the civilian world. Driving onto the post, through the gate guard station officers were always greeted with a salute as their blue decal was spotted. I always looked forward to this wonderful protocol. On one such marvelous occasion, I was driving my roommate Judy's stick shift Corvair. I looked and felt very much the officer, particularly as I pulled up to the guard shack and was immediately met by the gate guard, who whipped up to a sharp salute. I returned it in my most military fashion and nonchalantly put the car in gear to continue on through, but the motor died with a bang and a roar. I tried to hide my humiliation by quickly restarting the car, and drove onto the post. But my stern expression couldn't hide my beet-red face of embarrassment.

As a young Army nurse, I began each day by putting on my uniform. Because I was working in the hospital, I was issued a plain, straight white dress with belt and a ten-inch-high white cap. This thing on my head made me almost seven feet tall. The whole attire was no more functional than it was attractive. The small and too few pockets allowed us to carry only scissors and a pen. The saving grace of the otherwise plain uniform was our rank and Nurse Corps insignia pinned prominently on the lapels. But since all our patients thought nurses were wonderful, I felt wonderful, too. However, away from the hospital I much preferred to be in my regular soldier's uniform.

The nurses' and women's uniforms changed radically during the Vietnam War. It became evident that the white uniform was difficult to clean, and the skirts impractical because so many tasks could not be done without indecent exposure. We often had to climb underneath the beds to adjust them or to connect equipment. It was difficult to bend over without having the skirt ride up-though, of course, every patient was ready and eagle-eyed to get his peek at the long, sleek legs of this Army nurse. It was very disconcerting to know that guys could look up under our dresses while we were caring for a patient during an emergency.

Fortunately, combat nurses were issued fatigues in Vietnam. Also as a result of the war and the social acceptance of pantsuits for women during the 1960s, the traditional Army hospital uniform even outside the combat zone was changed to a white pantsuit. The fate of the ten-inch cap was finally sealed–how many times have I seen it knocked off by the orthopedic bed frames used for traction? It, too, was eliminated, first from the military ensemble and then from civilian nursing schools and hospitals-another example of how the military has often taken the lead in social change and custom.

The most famous example of social change created in the military was President Truman's 1948 executive order desegregating all branches of the armed forces. The military integrated all bases in the years after 1948 even though the policy went against the prevailing social norm in the segregated South. Of course, some prejudiced whites obstructed this move toward social justice, but everyone agreed that the military did a decent job in the battle for racial integration.

I realized what an achievement the integration was when I was stationed in Georgia in 1963. Inside the gates of Fort Benning, segregation was outlawed. But off-post was a very different world. Shops and restaurants displayed "Whites Only" signs. Blacks were denied equal access to schools, transportation, housing, and jobs. And with the civil rights movement growing in momentum, the sixties were a time of conflict and violence in the towns and countryside throughout the region as injustice and hatred were challenged. However, back on military soil, I saw whites and blacks working and living together successfully. Incidents of bigotry would be punished–the threat of military discipline works. If an order is given–

even when it is contrary to the civilian social norm right outside the gates of the post—that order is obeyed. From this experience, I came to believe even more in the American military's power and commitment to overcome the divisiveness that prejudice causes.

But as a young lieutenant, I had little time to think about the social turmoil in the civilian world. I had much to learn.

All nurses worked rotating shifts. We'd be given day, evening, or night duty, and the schedule was often changed, so that we learned to manage different shifts easily. We never had more than one weekend off every six weeks. Married to our hospital duties, we had to fit any social life into our rigorous work schedules.

When I first arrived at Fort Benning, I was assigned with another nurse to a two-bedroom apartment in the female officers' quarters. Judy was tall, like me, new to nursing, and new to the Army. We got along famously from the beginning. She was a very social person, always setting up dates and taking advantage of the many special opportunities of being a female on the post. There were lots of young officers and officer candidates. She would frequently arrange a blind date for me and I would dutifully go. It didn't feel possible to say no to her. I wanted to be part of my new military world, and I watched my friends and colleagues put energy into the social scene. So even though I was focused only on my career, I went on the dates Judy set up for me. I tried to avoid physical advances and felt awkward in resisting.

I saw my constant vigilance in the sexual skirmishes with the men I dated as pretty normal. Men tried to push the limits and the woman's job was to maintain them— that was the message I'd gotten at home and was part of my own life style. There was another consideration as well. Getting pregnant before marriage was not only unthinkable on a social level—but if it happened, you had to leave the military. In fact, you had to leave even if dependents under 16 years of age. Since none of us knew how to give birth to sixteen-year-olds, we simply did not engage in sex.

Looking back, I see that I wasn't interested in men on a physical level but went through the rituals of dating, anyway. I rarely allowed myself to examine those feelings of discomfort and I never discussed those feelings with friends. I came from a very private family where those things were not mentioned (and the so-called sexual revolution where people became more open about their feelings and behavior began later in the decade). The few times I thought about it at all, I decided that my hesitancy in dating was due to the fact that physical intimacy was taboo before marriage. It was only appropriate that I keep my guard up.

Being officers in the Army, we were required to attend many military-sponsored social events. At least once a month; there was a formal hail-and-farewell party. This was a ritual to welcome new officers and other personnel arriving on post and to extend a boisterous farewell to those who were leaving. The expected attire was the formal dress-blue uniform, and the main activity was consuming enormous quantities of alcohol. Although it was considered unbecoming for officers to be drunk, overindulgence was common.

I switched to bourbon and water because I had learned that if I abstained from sweet cocktails, I could drink more, remain in control, and have fewer side effects the next day. I got the reputation of being able to drink almost anyone under the table without losing control myself. Self-control was protection against sexual advances.

In addition to the hail-and-farewell parties at the hospital, the post commander held a New Year's Day reception, which everyone attended. Each unit also had its own series of parties, and then there were the officer candidate school graduations. There was always a full calendar of opportunities to drink and celebrate. There was an emphasis on partying and its accompanying indulgences of drinking and dating. After a while, the social evenings all began to blur together. Each one felt like a repetition of the same party-the same faces, the same quantities of alcohol, the same jokes and stories, the same advances.

I actually had more fun with a couple of women officers on the post. We shared similar interests-playing the guitar and singing. After we became friends, I recall, I wondered if they might be homosexual. It was probably the first time I'd used that term in my own thinking about someone I knew. But even allowing myself to think such a thing felt intrusive to them and therefore improper. They never displayed any overt affection toward one another or said anything that would confirm that their relationship was more than that of friends, so I was able to put speculation out of my mind. We spent many delightful off-duty hours together singing and talking.

My main objective at Fort Benning was to succeed in my career. The demands of nursing absorbed me mentally and spiritually. I was also determined to perform with excellence as a soldier, so I would be allowed to spend my next tour of duty in Germany.

I hated Germans. This prejudice came from my childhood. I felt the only way to confront it was to go to Germany, which I'd never done, get to know individual Germans, and then see if that hatred was justified or could be relinquished. I went to Germany to heal the wound that hatred causes. It was also where I would meet Harvey.

CHAPTER 5

. . . .

Germany and Marriage

Another blind date. This one was set up by a well-intentioned friend of a friend of a surgeon who knew a fellow he thought I ought to meet. As I got ready for the evening, I again debated about wearing high heels, as I debated every time. What does it matter if I'm two inches taller than my date, or four? I'm still taller, so the guy invariably feels that he's with a towering female and we both have a polite but awkward time and that is that. There was a knock at the door. I slipped on my heels, opened the door, and looked up. His grinning face was above mine. He looked every inch—and there were many in his six-foot, six-inch frame—the clean-cut, athletic, spit-shined soldier. Confident, polite, and an officer.

. . . .

In my mind, my two-year tour of duty in Germany is divided into two parts. The first dates from my arrival in March 1964 to August of that same year. That's when I immersed myself in both military nursing and the German culture. The second part began after Harvey and I were introduced on August 14, 1964. Our dating, engagement, and marriage added an aspect to my life I hadn't sought or anticipated.

Arriving in Germany as an officer, I wanted to be a worthy representative of America. I remembered being told of inappropriate and rude Nazi soldiers in Norway during the war. I now wore the uniform of the U.S. military officer and my behavior had to be impeccable as I was representing America. My entire demeanor encompassed the dignity and grace of America, I was so proud.

I hoped that during this time in Germany I would become a more accomplished, confident and proficient nurse by working in a large military hospital. I also wanted to learn more about Germany because I had a significant bias based on my upbringing in Oslo. I wanted to see if all Germans were as bad as the Nazis though the intellectual part of me suspected they couldn't be. My mother's half sister, Lajla, had married a German and lived in Bonn so I would have an opportunity to meet the "real people" and culture. I looked forward to visiting them and overcoming my apprehensions and ignorance.

When I first stepped off the train in Nuremberg, I found myself in another century. Seeing the old cobblestone and brick streets, churches, and buildings was enchanting. Dating back to the early days of the Crusades, Nuremberg was an old walled city that had been reconstructed after the devastation it suffered during World War II. In medieval days, the moat surrounding the town had protected it from invasion, but now it was empty and useless. But the imagination could take you back in time to imagine what it might have been like back then.

During World War II, Nuremberg had been an important hub of Nazi Germany. Remnants of Hitler's plan for a thousand-year Reich were still standing in the form of the vast parade ground and stadium. Twenty years earlier the German Army had assembled there in review and to be inspired by the Fuhrer. At each corner of the parade field there were huge prison towers built to house the chiefs of state of Britain, Russia, the United States, and other allied countries, which Hitler planned to capture. I felt the ghosts marching in goose step, saluting with outstretched arms and calling *"Hail Hitler!"* Even in town it was unnerving to feel all the hatred directed at Americans.

There was a resurgence of neo-Nazi sentiment in Nuremberg in 1964, and parts of the city were off-limits to Americans because of the threat of violence. This was the less-than-idyllic city to which I had come, hoping to get rid of my anti-German sentiment. Though I feared I would encounter German-Nazi –hatred of Americans, my own experience was to be very different.

The work at the Army hospital was challenging, making my two and a half years in Germany very busy. Yet there was always time to party, which made my off-duty time busy with other demands. As on every military base there were the hail-and-farewell parties, commander's-call socials, and other functions. However, I had decided that the way to learn about Germans and overcome my bias stereotypes was to experience the local nightlife. So days and nights both on the military base and in town my life was full of activities and adventures.

I had saved my money to buy a new car when I arrived and chose a fire-engine-red Kerman Ghia. This great little German sports car gave me the freedom to travel in style on my time off and could do 96 miles an hour on the autobahn.

I became best friends with Deanna, one of the nurses who lived in my building. We both worked rotating shifts but somehow managed to have many of the same nights free. She was great fun and shared my desire to experience German culture. But women didn't go into town in the evenings unescorted. Serendipitously that problem had been covered when I first arrived, I'd met a couple of great fellows who worked at the military radio station. Bill and Jim were young, courteous enlisted men who became our escorts when Deanna and I visited local nightclubs. We decided they were just our escorts and therefore we were not fraternizing with enlisted men in violation of military protocol.

Nuremberg was a city that never seemed to sleep. After work, even if it was midnight, we'd meet the two radio announcers and the four of us would head downtown. We toured the wine cellars and sampled the local brew for hours in the gasthauses and nightclubs. We were welcomed everywhere. In fact, when German musicians took a break from entertaining in some establishments and the four of us got up on stage, uninvited, and sang American folk songs, people applauded and we were very impressed by our talent. We had great fun wherever we went. This acceptance by our German hosts immediately eased my feelings of fear and dislike of them.

Soon I saw Germans as individuals and had to let go of my conscious prejudice. But getting rid of the subliminal prejudice is something that requires a continuous effort, education and willingness to try to overcome the prejudice. I think my training and experience as a nurse helped my efforts to get through my prejudices. Whenever I learned about a new disease or illness, I would imagine myself having it; I'd feel the symptoms and the emotional consequences that followed. Because I understood the illness and was able to imagine its effect on me step by step, it wasn't so foreign, and I lost my fear of it. And so, in turn, I was better able to understand and care for my patients. I used a similar approach to overcome my anti-

German sentiments. I still despised Nazism and those who acted out its monstrous fanaticism. But as I got to know people on a one-to-one basis, I stopped hating Germans as a whole.

My visits to Aunt Lajla and Uncle Adolf in Bonn also helped getting through that prejudice. Spending time with them eased my homesickness and educated me more about the complexities of politics and cultures. They were married before World War II began and lived together in Germany. When the war broke out, my uncle was forced to enter the military. He opposed the Nazis but followed their orders to preserve his own life. At the same time, the government took his business and his money. So, fearing repercussions because she was a foreigner and the wife of an anti-Nazi, Aunt Lajla and their daughter, Lille Mag, went into seclusion in the German countryside. Ironically, my uncle was sent to Norway in the German army of occupation. He was able to hide the fact of his marriage to a non-German; something he felt was necessary to protect both of them from the military bureaucracy. Consequently, he did not contact anyone in my family during those dangerous years in Norway. When the war ended, Lajla and Adolf were reunited; they remained in Germany, rebuilding their lives.

When I was a child after the war, I met Aunt Lajla, but not my uncle so visiting them now was new and unique. Uncle Adolf was now a successful businessman importing wood products. They and Lille Mag, my cousin, entertained me when I visited them on my weekends off from military duty. Aunt Lajla was so like my mother with her warmth and exuberance. We shared family stories, went sightseeing and they told me stories of the atrocities of war living in Germany and fighting their own Nazi occupation.

During my first months overseas, I discovered my childhood friend Randi was working in Germany. I hadn't seen her since my trip back to Norway during college. One weekend, we met in Munich for a reunion. Dachau, one of the concentration camps, was nearby. We walked through the remnant of the death camp, paid homage to all those who had been killed there, and remembered our own early lives during the war. We were overwhelmed with grief.

Being so far from my family for the first time, I communicated with them in weekly letters. Since neither my mother nor I were emotional writers, but we shared news of daily events. In fact, my letters home were usually uninformative assurances that I was fine. My mother's letters told stories of my brothers and how they were doing in school.

I enjoyed my new overseas assignment, and my life was full. I continued to work all day and play all night with Deanna, Bill, and Jim, and then come to work and somehow function the following day. Looking back, I don't know how I had the stamina. But then we had energy for everything. However, after another month of nightly trips into town, the partying became boring and too exhausting. I was now comfortable around Germans, and since both Deanna and I wanted to stay closer to our friends and colleagues on the post, we began spending our free evenings at the officers' club.

Professionally, Nuremberg was a wonderful assignment. The hospital was an old German facility that had been converted for use by the occupying U.S. forces. It was four stories high, with incredibly long wards. On each floor the corridor must have stretched for almost a quarter-mile. There were seventy-six patients on the medical ward, which included a specialty unit to care for patients who had had heart attacks and an isolation area for patients with infections.

Like most lieutenants, I worked nearly everywhere in the hospital. Fortunately, now that I was a seasoned Army nurse, I could request my assignment, and I chose not to work on pediatrics, or the women's ward, or in the delivery suite-I had spent enough time there in college and at Fort Benning. So I began working on the combination surgical ward including the recovery room, trauma unit, intensive care unit and orthopedic ward.

The orthopedic patients were great because they were healthy but grounded in bed. Most had fractured legs with pins and traction devices holding the bones in proper alignment. Patients lie in bed for weeks or months waiting for the bones to heal. They were bored, restless, and horny. Like most guys in that predicament, they teased and flirted with their nurses. I enjoyed being appreciated and complimented. They were primarily enlisted men, and I, of course, was an officer-which meant no fraternization beyond the jokes on the ward. So I felt safe. There was another important aspect to our camaraderie. I fit in, and felt part of the family of American servicemen and women in a foreign country. These patients might one day be my comrades in a war or a life-threatening emergency, and that, too, made me feel more connected to them. For all those reasons, I didn't experience the awkwardness that I had felt with men before. These patients were like my younger brothers, and I joined in the back and-forth banter and teasing.

Our facility was also the trauma center for the military training area near the East German border. The year 1964 was a time of high tension between the Communist countries and the United States. One of the most dangerous places was the border separating East and West Germany. Communist border guards regularly shot Eastern Europeans who were trying to escape, and there was a sense of danger whenever you approached the border. Graffenwoehr was the American training site for armor battalions. Tanks performing traveling to war-game maneuvers were driven through the streets of small German villages. Sometimes the tank gun turrets would not make the turn through the centuries-old street corners. This clash of new military equipment with ancient streets and a rural lifestyle frequently caused serious accidents. Soldiers who were injured during these maneuvers and war games would be evacuated to our trauma unit.

I knew very little about trauma care when I arrived but was soon educated by working with and observing the Army medics. My first and most important lesson was that the sergeants knew everything. If you were wise, you listened and learned from them. But since I was a second lieutenant there was a little charade dealing with these experienced medics. When there was a procedure I was not familiar with in this highly specialized field-for example, hooking up the traction for fractures or inserting a chest tube-I would go up to the sergeant on duty and ask if he would take care of it. Then I would stand by, watching and learning. Probably the dumbest thing to do as a new officer is to assume that you know anything, especially since no one around you will believe it anyway. So as a young second lieutenant I approached trauma nursing with the appropriate humility and decorum, trusting that any omission on my part would be forgiven because I was too young to know better. In fact, my most common confession in those days even to those below me in rank was "Well, what can you expect of a second lieutenant?" Once I said that, a sympathetic sergeant would show me the ropes.

But all that tolerance of inexperience changes as soon as you get promoted to first lieutenant, which is the main reason I needed to learn everything quickly. I was due for promotion one year after college graduation, which would be during my third month in Germany. When that automatic advancement came, I was suddenly, overnight, considered to be an old hand, and presumed to have a professional level of experience and military savvy-in short, to be a real officer. No longer the naive butter bar, I had no excuse if I did not know something about nursing or the Army. From that day forward, it was not acceptable to ask questions. I had to lead, to know the appropriate nursing and military procedures, to perform and see that my staff performed appropriately as well.

That is one of the purposes of the military hierarchy. Through constant promotions that reward achievement, it is expected that we rise to the occasion, assume more responsibility, and function at a higher level. For my staff, and me I found that the expectation of success inspired us to achieve. While that strategy doesn't always work for everyone, I've found it to be effective. Expect and demand people be good at what they do, and they will rise to the occasion.

Consequently, when I became a new first lieutenant, I did everything by the book until I disobeyed my first direct order. It was during "alert," a mock-emergency situation when all personnel are notified of a "crisis" and, whether on duty or off, has to report to their own section chief in person. This signing-in process was a rigid and important protocol during which the readiness of a unit was tested and uniforms and equipment were inspected for completeness.

I was working night duty as the only registered nurse on the ward with three enlisted medics for medical and cardiac intensive care patients when an alert was called and I was told to report to the office of the chief nurse, four floors below. There were three coronary-care patients needing close observation on the ward and I was the only registered nurse.   To satisfy this order for practice alert, I would have had to leave my patients unattended to report in and then return to the ward. It was an ethical dilemma, but my first duty was to my patients.

I called my supervisor and said I would be unable to leave my patients until a registered nurse or a physician relieved me. The supervisor reiterated that I was receiving a direct order to report and sign in. The tension in her voice matched what I felt as I told her I understood the order and I would not leave my patients. Hanging up the phone, I was sure that my military career was over.

From my first moment as an Army student nurse, I was trained that an Army order represented "God's" word. I believed that. Disobeying an order was like committing a mortal sin. However, I could not follow this order. If I left my three coronary patients for ten minutes, a crisis could occur with any one of them that the medics wouldn't have had either the training or the authority to handle. Ethically and professionally I could not leave them, but from a military standpoint I was guilty of a terrible offense of refusing a direct order and insubordination. Though very intimidated by my supervisor, I held my ground. My patients came first. Finally, the ward physician and head nurse arrived. I explained the situation to them, and then reported off and left to face what I was sure would be a court-martial for refusing a direct order.

It was a long walk to the office where my supervisor waited. As I entered, I braced myself to receive what was, in strict military rules, my due. Instead I received an apology from the very person whose order I had refused to follow. She explained she hadn't understood the severity of the medical condition of my patients and commended me for having had the integrity to refuse to leave them. Although the story ends well, and I gained new respect for how priorities can sensibly change a rigid regulation, I never forgot what it felt like to refuse a direct order. It was an almost unbearable feeling to realize that in doing the right thing, I was facing consequences that could destroy my career.

For the next years I benefited from the invaluable experience of working in a busy military hospital. Caring for soldiers was increasingly rewarding, and gave me the kind of respect and challenge I had sought by joining the Army.

After I had worked on a variety of wards, I was assigned the job of coordinating education at the hospital. I was surprised to be selected because usually a major with more experience than I possessed held this position. Though I was a first lieutenant, it was a job promotion. As a career officer, I expected to move frequently from one position to another to broaden my experience and enhance my leadership abilities. This new task was crucial in that regard. Not only did I oversee all the medical training in the hospital, but also it became my responsibility to teach the field medics. The greatest need for their abilities was developing in a distant place called Vietnam.

The conflict in Southeast Asia had been escalating: By 1964, military personnel leaving their tour of duty in Germany would sometimes receive orders for Vietnam. Ironically, though we were members of the U.S. armed forces we knew less than the general public at home about what was going on there. The Army newspaper was of limited use, there was no daily American newspaper that we read, and we were not fluent enough in German to read the local newspapers. I was ignorant of events concerning our buildup of troops, though I was aware of increasing hostilities. However, I didn't question the American involvement. I was a soldier. My job was to be obedient to the mission, and if my government, in its wisdom, said we were needed to help the South Vietnamese people protect themselves from a Communist takeover, I believed it.

I was not expecting to be sent into the war zone. At the beginning of 1964, just before I left for Germany, Defense Secretary Robert McNamara told the House Armed Services Committee that the "bulk of U.S. armed forces in Vietnam can be expected to leave by the end of 1965." By the middle of the year, we had approximately sixteen thousand troops assisting the South Vietnamese forces-a relatively small number. The United States military had field medics with its units, but no hospitals, and there was no expectation that our involvement would ever include medical facilities. Therefore, nurses were not needed.

In Germany, we heard little about the fighting, but we imagined the worst for our comrades in Southeast Asia. Though I felt I was not going to be called to duty there as a nurse, my perception was that the soldiers who were sent to Vietnam were as good as dead.

In my new position as education coordinator, I designed courses to teach medics field techniques that would be useful to them in Vietnam. Even though many of us had not yet served in combat, we knew the types of casualties that would need medical treatment and the special conditions of working on the front line. Stabilizing a wounded soldier in the field is always the first, crucial task for a combat medic. We taught them to put needles in one another's arms, how to start intravenous lines to replace fluids that had been lost, and how to prevent shock. They applied field dressings to wounds to stop bleeding and prevent infection. They inserted nasogastric tubes through the nose into the stomach to prevent stomach contents from being regurgitated into the lungs. I had a sense of urgency that the medics had to learn as much as possible then, so they would not have to learn on injured soldiers in Vietnam.

In the military, your work is more important than personal or family issues. Because of the global nature of the military's business and the constant rotation of people from post to post every few years, you develop a strange mix of feeling important, because of your rank over others, and at the same time expendable and anonymous, due to constant reassignment to other posts and jobs. This flow in and out of places makes all arrivals and departures less significant. When you're transferred, you start all over again, making professional relationships. It's a good skill to have, but when a friend from a past assignment coincidentally arrives, it's cause for celebration.

That happened two months after I arrived in Germany, when Judy, my buddy and former roommate at Fort Benning, was assigned to Nuremberg also. The news delighted both of us and we decided to be roommates again and moved to an off-post apartment. Immediately we found a place to share in an old German building near the hospital. It was a quaint, two-bedroom apartment on the third floor. The tiny kitchen had barely enough room for the stove and a small table. The charming slanted roof extended to the dining and living room area, so we frequently bumped our heads on the ceiling. Our heat came from an oil furnace. We had to carry huge, five-gallon drums of oil up two flights of stairs. The smell of heating oil permeated the apartment and our clothes all winter.

In addition to living only one block from the hospital, we were across from a wonderful bakery. Each free morning we would stop there for fresh, rolls, which we considered a special treat and very continental. In America you could have milk delivered to the door however, in Germany you could have cases of beer brought regularly to your apartment. This we arranged as soon as possible and delighted in the prestige we felt this service brought us. It also made entertaining much easier, and Judy and I loved arranging special dinners and get-togethers in our apartment.

Judy soon had a steady date, Don, and as their relationship became more serious and they announced their engagement, Don's and my friendship strengthened as well. We frequently double dated at the officer's club or had a bridge playing evening with them until they married and Judy moved out to their own place.

I met Harvey in August 1964. I'd been in Germany for five months, enough time to feel comfortable with my work and establish a good circle of friends. Frequently, Judy and other friends would set me up on blind dates. The only recollection I have of these unmemorable evenings was that I was as tall as, or taller than, my poor dates. I wasn't a particularly good conversationalist when I wasn't interested in someone. That quiet aspect of my personality coupled with my date's uneasiness at being with a taller woman made these evenings exercises in polite boredom. Since my goal in the service was to excel, not to marry, when a friend said he knew a surgeon who knew a lieutenant who wanted to meet a tall girl, I agreed with reluctance.

So I went out on a blind date with Harvey Hawken. For the first time, when I opened the door, I had to look up to someone. Harvey was six feet; six inches tall, weighed more than 230 pounds, and was definitely not a pushover. I think he was as shocked as I to meet someone so tall. Standing at the door in my high heels, I nearly looked him straight in the eye.

He was from a rural area just south of Seattle. He'd gone to the University of Washington on a track scholarship, joined the ROTC program, and was now a second lieutenant in an armor battalion. He was a professional soldier. It was a role he proudly cultivated, as did I. We found each other familiar, and amazingly comfortable, even from the beginning. Our families were similar both being conservative, Lutheran, and middle-class. We were both firstborn children, each of us with three siblings. There were three boys and one girl in each of our families. We had both skipped fourth grade. We were both more than six feet tall. We were both college graduates, had serious, intense natures, and wanted to excel in things we did. Also, without modesty, I can say we made a good every looking couple.

For the next four months we spent every free moment together. The military functions we were expected to attend almost doubled because not only was I obliged to be at my own unit's events, I also had to go to Harvey's. He belonged to the combat arms unit, and their parties were the most rowdy I had ever attended. The standard goal at these blasts was to see who could get the most drunk while still standing. As the evenings progressed and the liquor flowed, the behavior disintegrated to new lows. There were guys who ate champagne glasses to draw attention to themselves.

As a woman I was in the minority, and the macho, glass-eating, drunk, men were obnoxious, but I had my rank and my six-foot-six escort, and I was not bothered. I never experienced the abusive or contemptuous treatment the women at the 1991 Tailhook convention in Las Vegas had experienced. I view that behavior of men toward women as fundamentally an abuse of power. It's only since my own investigation and discharge that I have been able to see that the real source of my protection in the male military world was that, as a nurse I was not perceived as a threat to any man's position. Now, as I and other women step out of "inferior" roles and compete with men, we become more frequent targets of male hostility and subtle abuse.

Nevertheless, back then the emphasis on drinking alcohol that was equated with manliness and was a problem in the military because it meant that most parties ended up as drunken fiascoes. The commanders never saw this behavior because the officers were always reserved and professional until after he had left (although it's hard to believe he didn't know about it since he too had been raised in the military tradition). As part of protocol, the commander would leave early so that the "boys" could behave unrestrained "fun". Getting drunk was not my idea of a good time. I could certainly hold my own and was not about to lose control so that would be taken advantage of. I felt as though I had to keep on guard to protect myself from physical advances and to keep restraint on my own relationship with Harvey. I was raised to believe that sexual encounters should be preserved for marriage—a restriction I intended to follow regardless of the behavior around me.

Fortunately, Harvey didn't push the limits very much. Because I outranked him, he was teased a lot by his buddies, but he took it very well, tossing one-liners back at them without getting defensive. He also handled the sexual innuendos nicely. He told me several times that his friends thought that he had "scored" with me, and wouldn't they be surprised to know that we hadn't been to bed yet. He said that not to put pressure on me but to separate himself from the immaturity of his friends. I respected him for that. We shared basic values about the sacredness of marriage, and I felt more at ease with him, knowing he honored the same boundaries and behavior that I did.

During time off from work we took day trips from Nuremberg to visit the surrounding areas. We went to the East German border and stared at the guards poised to shoot anyone who tried to escape from their side of the fence. In Munich we attended the pre-Lenten festivals, which were unbelievable beer parties under huge tents and with lots of "humpa-humpa" music. Harvey also began collecting beer steins, which gave us a wonderful excuse to visit gasthauses as his collection grew to more than two hundred steins. And, of course, we made frequent trips to Bonn to visit Aunt Lajla and Uncle Adolf, who graciously welcomed him.

Harvey was a camera bug, so on trips to the countryside he took more pictures of mountains and hills than anyone I had ever known. He loved natural landscapes-the curve of a river through the countryside, the outline of a stand of trees against a distant hill. He talked about the beautiful lakes and forests of his home near Seattle and sought similar terrain as we traveled in Germany.

From August through December, seeing Harvey in the evenings and weekends was as natural a part of my schedule as work at the hospital. We were a couple. People expected to see us together. By then, both of my best friends, Judy and Deanna, had married and moved in with their new husbands. I lived alone, and spent time with Harvey. He was a very personable, easy friend to everyone he met. When we showed up almost nightly at the officers' club, people would comment on how great the two of us looked together. The encouragement from all around us was not very subtle.

But Harvey never mentioned the possibility of marriage, though he wrote several notes to my mother telling her how fond he was of me. And I didn't want to consider marriage because I viewed it as a loss of freedom. I had no role model to demonstrate that a woman could be a wife and pursue a career. My mother hadn't. In marrying, she lost her autonomy, became subservient. Marriage meant losing all the things I enjoyed and had worked to achieve. Even though Harvey and I didn't discuss it, always being together, having our married friend tell us we made a handsome couple-all that pointed to an expectation of marriage, and I was beginning to feel trapped.

Harvey has a very strong personality. Like his physique, it's very imposing. It seemed to me that as long as his expectations were met, things went smoothly. But if something he didn't like happened, I feared a major confrontation. I sensed that even those first months together. Though I felt he was taking me for granted, that no matter what the event, he would expect me to dutifully be his date, I didn't feel I could talk to him about it. So I bottled up my feelings of being irritated, discontented or discounted, and was obediently available all the time. In those days, that's what a woman was supposed to do. Any magazine or film told me that. And I was used to taking care of others' wants and needs,

Yet there were times when I felt I couldn't breathe around him. Reconciling his constant presence in my life with my own needs seemed impossible. The only solution I saw was to stop seeing him; then maybe I'd get some breathing space. But that meant a confrontation, which I did not want. Finally, in January, he developed a muscle spasm in his back and had to stay in the hospital for several weeks. This gave me an opportunity to escape.

I'm not proud that I told him I wanted to stop seeing him when he was on his back in the hospital. But it seemed my best opportunity to get some distance in order to think things through. I didn't have the courage or didn't feel I had the right to do it until he was in the hospital. Disappointing him because of my needs was very difficult. On his second day there, I came into his room, listened to how he was feeling and how he'd be off his feet for a couple of weeks. Then rather suddenly, I told him I needed time alone.

I said, "I don't want to see you anymore. I am not in love with you, so why don't we just back off our relationship?"

He seemed crushed. It pained me a great deal. He insisted I not do this. I needed time alone but compromised when he persisted. I said that I did not want to see him for thirty days. And then I left. I got time off from the hospital and went to the Bavarian Alps for a few days by myself.

It was a great relief to be alone in the mountains, walking, thinking, and reading. I had time to reflect on the last months. I never expected to be married, only to continue my military career unattached. I wanted to become Chief Nurse of the Army Nurse Corps and a general, and that mattered more to me than becoming a wife. So, while it was a very hard thing to disappoint Harvey by not seeing him, it felt like the right course. I didn't feel committed to becoming his wife.

When I got back to work, the harassment started. Though Harvey honored my thirty-day moratorium on seeing him, I felt he conducted a rigorous campaign to get me to change my mind. I was astounded by his persistence. It seemed to me that he courted me from a distance in ways he never had while we dated. I got calls from his friends, who said, "What are you doing to Harvey? He can't work, he can't eat." My friends and colleagues said he called them. I'd come home from work and there would be flowers at my door with notes saying he was counting the days until my self-imposed separation was over. I'd go to my car in the morning, and written in the frost on my windshield would be the words "I love you."

I couldn't tell how much of this was because he wanted me, and how much was because he wanted to get his way. I hadn't intended to provoke him to be more attentive; I simply needed time alone to understand my own feelings. Whenever some reminder of him would appear, I blushed with his attention, and felt relieved no one was there to witness my response. His displays of attention were embarrassingly public; I'd been brought up to be a very private person, and I was frustrated by the continuous intrusion and bombardment and involvement of friends.

I didn't know what to do. Even though he didn't call me directly, I felt pressured. I wasn't able to analyze the situation. I had no models of how to balance my needs against his, and I couldn't talk to anyone about it. Both Judy and Deanna were married, and I saw them only with their husbands. Besides, my parents had taught me that feelings are private and must be kept that way. It has been a struggle all my life to share intimate thoughts with anyone, and back then I was so young and immature, it was unthinkable to break my silence with friends and tell them of my doubts. As for talking with Harvey, I couldn't do that either. Women didn't confront men, at least not in the world I inhabited. So I just went about my work, stepping around all his attentions.

But then, the heat increased. He called and politely, even sweetly, asked to see me when the thirty days were over. I couldn't turn down such persistence and intensity, and agreed to have a quiet dinner with him in my apartment. So the very first evening after the moratorium ended, he came courting. He arrived in splendid military attire, dressed in his most pressed and polished fashion, looking more as if he were coming to an inspection than to a dinner. In his arms were flowers for me: the whole courting business with a vengeance.

Then, at, dinner, he asked me to marry him. I was stunned. I looked at him absolutely dumbfounded. I wondered to myself what on earth I was going to say to this. After a minute, I said to him, "I need to think about it." We finished dinner and then we went to my weekly bowling league tournament as planned. Now I was in turmoil. During the tournament, I struggled to figure out what I was supposed to do or say. I didn't believe I had any options. If someone had said to me back then that my decision about marriage should be based on what I needed, I would have replied, "Well, I need to do what I'm supposed to do." My role as a daughter, woman, and nurse was to be there for other people. My family, school, the military, and the media reinforced that.

In addition, there was Harvey's commitment to win me over. Before this, no one had ever gone to such trouble to convince me to do something. My decision seemed to matter to him. I felt that not seeing me for just thirty days had sent him into a state of desperation and pain. If I agreed to marry him, I believed I would make him very happy; if I turned him down, I feared he would be devastated.

I tried to put the jumble of feelings and "shoulds" in some kind of order. Harvey and I had spent a lot of time together, and I felt comfortable with him. We had a foundation for our relationship. We looked good together as a couple-that was important, or everyone said it was. I wasn't sure what love was, but I did care for him. So as I thought about Harvey's proposal, his bombardment of attention, and his pain when it wasn't returned, I decided maybe marrying him was what I was supposed to do.

We got back to my apartment after bowling. I said to him, "Remember that question you asked me earlier? The answer is yes."

He said he was delighted!

And I certainly got caught in the moment and acted pleased. But I wondered what I had just committed myself to. I had felt trapped before. Now I believed my autonomy was gone. But, I thought, perhaps that's the way my life was supposed to be.

Looking back, I find it hard to explain my passivity in those years. I approached marriage with a blind optimism and superficiality. Harvey and I both came from very traditional families, both of us confirmed in the Lutheran church. No relative of ours had ever gotten divorced. All we knew was that when you married, you married for life. I assumed that once we decided to marry, we'd live happily ever after. It was real storybook stuff-but it was a view of life, relationship, and marriage shared by our friends and families.

I did believe, however, that my own career dreams were ended.

Moments after I agreed to marry him, I sighed and said, "I guess I'll never make it to be Chief Nurse and the first female general." Remember, in those days, women with children under the age of sixteen could not serve in the armed forces. Naturally, marriage meant children, and that would end my military career. I would have to return to civilian nursing (if I worked at all, and I wanted to work). I was losing control over my own life and, at the same time, agreeing to the most "normal" thing in the world. I felt both those contrasting forces; it was the price a woman paid. Though I was ambivalent about getting married, it meant doing what I was supposed to do and was a cause for happiness. Everyone around me would confirm that view in the following days.

As Harvey beamed with his victory, we called Judy and Don. They were thrilled with our news and insisted we come right over to celebrate. They told us they had been so certain we would announce our engagement that they had a special bottle of wine waiting on ice for months. It was one-thirty in the morning, but they broke out the wine and we toasted the future while they were still in pajamas. I carried the black cat emblem from that bottle for years as a memento of the evening.

Our next decision was when and where to get married. The dilemma was that our parents and friends lived on opposite sides of the United States. Harvey's family was in Seattle, Washington, and mine was in Bethesda, Maryland. But all our mutual friends were with us in Nuremburg, so we compromised by inviting everyone to Germany for the wedding. Of course, I was concerned that my father's frugality would prevent my family from traveling across the Atlantic to attend, but fortunately he was to present a research paper at an international meeting in Frankfurt in August. My plan was to pay for my mother's ticket and schedule the wedding for the day after my father's conference ended. How could they refuse that offer?

The next day, I called my mother. For months, I had mentioned Harvey's name as my escort in letters to my family, and he had written twice to introduce himself to them. For my parents, just that was enough to indicate a special relationship. My mother was pleased though not surprised, to learn of our engagement. She was encouraging and very respectful of my decision. She wouldn't dream of asking me anything specific about my feelings or plans but did offer us warm congratulations. When I described my offer to buy her ticket and have the wedding coincide with my father's trip, she was delighted. We also decided they could combine the trip to Germany with a return to Norway: they hadn't been back since we emigrated thirteen years before. Harvey and I then arranged to travel to Oslo to be with my parents and family for part of our honeymoon.

We also agreed to have a military wedding and scheduled it on the one-year anniversary of our first date. Unfortunately, Harvey's parents decided they could not afford the time or the money to make the trip overseas. We were both disappointed but saw no other solution.

There was plenty of time to plan, and I enjoyed choreographing all the details. Harvey's tank battalion was often away on field exercises and would also be gone for weeks just prior to the wedding. So that left me to make virtually all the arrangements.

I decided to make our wedding an excuse for the biggest, most perfectly executed party the Americans in Nuremberg had seen in a long time. In fact, it turned out to be a series of parties all over the military post and the city. If all went well, its highlight would be the bride and groom's ride from the church on Harvey's tank and subsequent helicopter ride to the hospital where the reception would be at the Officer's club.

From our engagement in February to our wedding date in August, there was plenty of time to get cold feet. I did. Of course, I kept it to myself and continued making arrangements. Then, when my concerns persisted, I called my mother. Discussing personal feelings like this was very unusual for us. She listened to how I feared losing my financial freedom and my autonomy. She said these doubts were natural, and not to take them seriously. She told me I was doing the right thing and that another opportunity for marriage might never come along, and so urged me to go through with it. I didn't question her advice but was reassured and went forward with all the plans. Even in hindsight, I feel I made the decision as best I could, given what I knew at the time.

I came up with some great ideas to make ours a unique ceremony. However, they meant departing from tradition (something I also found appealing), and either Harvey or my mother forbade them. I wanted chocolate, not the boring customary white wedding cake. Both my mother and my fiancé said no, so I gave in and ordered a white one from the bakery. Like Harvey, I wanted to wear my dress-blue uniform, but my mother refused to let me even think about it. She had always wanted a dainty, delicate daughter but instead got a tomboy, so I thought I could at least be married in a beautiful white gown and play the role according to my mother's expectations. My bridesmaids' dresses matched my dress in design but was in contrasting light blue that looked elegant with Harvey's dress-blue uniform.

The week of the wedding, I drove to Frankfurt to welcome my parents to Germany. I wanted my mother to come back with me to Nuremberg while my father attended the conference. However, he was against it because he hated to be alone. But this time I didn't accept his no. I did some fast talking, arguing that I was my mother's only daughter and it was more important that she be with me during this special time than with him. It worked. It was one of the few times I ever convinced him to reconsider a decision. Pleased with my victory, Mother and I returned to my apartment in Nuremburg and completed all the arrangements together.

Harvey's unit was still out on a training exercise in Graffenwoehr so one night I took Mother to the Officers' Club alone. It was one of the most amazing evenings we ever spent together. My mother charmed everyone. She eagerly joined in the banter and handled the sexual innuendos my male friends tossed her way with wit and sophistication. I couldn't believe it! I'd only seen her around my father's conservative, stuffy scientist colleagues. But here, particularly in this predominantly male, macho world, she captivated everyone. I was delighted. After this I also relaxed more in social situations, and began to use my own skills at verbal repartee with male friends.

The wedding day was a splendid success. Harvey returned only two days before the ceremony, but Mother and I had taken care of the last minute arrangements. Even the weather cooperated for the big blast. The parties and champagne began before we headed to the church.

I wanted the ceremony in the military chapel to be as private and traditional as possible. No cameras were allowed. It was carefully orchestrated and went beautifully. The best man was Matthew Rothert, Harvey's good friend and fellow officer. A tall, handsome Southern gentleman, he had the gentle accent of his native Arkansas and treated me with all the propriety I could imagine. My former roommate and close friend, Judy Morris, was beautiful as my maid of honor. And Deanna, my drinking buddy was one of the bride's maids.

After our vows, the soloist sang" Trust and Obey." I chose it for its pretty melody-and the lyrics reflected my belief that by marrying I was giving up my identity. By saying "I do," I became Mrs. Harvey Hawken and Lieutenant Hawken, giving up my name and myself. But I didn't think of those things in the beauty of the moment, among the kind guests who only wished us the utmost happiness.

Outside the military chapel, a squad from Harvey's company lined the walkway in their class D uniforms-khaki with combat boots-with their bayoneted rifles. As we left the church, heading to the receptions that were to last the night, Harvey and I ran down the path holding hands, past the gallant honor guard with their crossed rifles, up a moveable staircase that had been built for the occasion, and onto his tank. We felt invincible and grand on the tank as we waved and drove off to the cheers around us, though immediately we had to duck to avoid low tree branches we passed under. We made it to the general's helicopter without any injuries, lifted off for a view of the city, and buzzed around for a while, waiting for our wedding guests to depart for and meet us at the hospital officers' club and our reception gala. Eventually we flew to the hospital, as planned, and landed in front of it. Hanging out the windows, wondering at the spectacle we presented climbing out of the helicopter, the patients and staff waved and cheered. The blades kept turning as I stepped out of the helicopter, my long dress and veil swirling up in the violent draft. Finally, Deanna's husband, Ron, (who greeted the chopper) had to put his arms around me to keep my veil and train from flying off while we made our way to the car.

The reception was wonderful. Family and friends from America, Norway, Switzerland, and Germany celebrated with us. There were cousins and friends I hadn't seen in years. We stayed at the reception until the end of the party, not wanting to miss a moment. Even when the reception was over, many of us returned to our apartment to continue the celebration of our wedding.

Harvey and I were going to Norway for our honeymoon, but it was hard to leave our friends and family after the reception. Not only did I hate to say goodbye to the marvelous friends who had made the day and evening such a delight, but also I was reluctant to begin my new role as a wife. I wasn't quite sure what to expect.

Eventually we said our farewells and drove all night to Kiel, the northern port in Germany. Then we boarded a boat to Oslo. Our first night of marriage was spent driving the car and our second night was on the ship in bunk beds, but our first night together as man and wife was a lovely experience.

The next day, having arrived in Norway we drove to a secluded valley in the mountains called Eggedahl. Here we spent four days in a winter cabin that belonged to family friends. Though it was August, frost covered the ground both morning and evening. There was no running water, so each time we slid the hundred yards to the outhouse and sat down on the box, we froze parts of ourselves not used to being so unprotected. Perhaps the setting was romantic, but I couldn't help feeling embarrassed and awkward without amenities or privacy around my new husband. Days were spent reading, walking in the glorious countryside, roaming around with the camera, and fishing. Harvey loved to fish and I loved the water. He announced that since it was our honeymoon he wanted to go fishing. We got a boat and he put his two lines over the back of it and designated me as the one to row. I'm quite right-handed and hadn't perfected my rowing skills. With my dominant hand rowing strenuously away, I had the boat turning constantly in a circle. Harvey's two fishing lines kept getting tangled up. This made him quite unhappy and he let me know it. I dropped the oars and said, "If you don't like what I'm doing, then do it yourself!" The silence that followed was brittle. I vividly remember feeling demeaned. I felt he had an arrogant expectation that I would give in to his demands, I heard it expressed in an angry, parental tone of voice. Previously in our relationship, he'd been accommodating to me, but now it seemed he assumed I'd quietly do whatever he wanted and exactly as he wanted. It was our first husband-and-wife fight. Already I was finding it difficult to yield to his authoritarian style. Somehow we got back to shore and made it through the rest of our honeymoon, but not without tension.

When we returned to the world in Oslo a few days later, I still felt trapped and my emotional bruises from that first conflict hadn't healed. My parents were hosting a formal dinner party for Norwegian friends and family. Since I was returning from the primitive mountain cabin, I decided to look particularly nice for this gala event, and so got my hair done in town.

Emerging from the beauty salon, I felt quite elegant. But when I walked in the door of our room, Harvey took one look at me and became irate. He said he hated the styling I'd chosen—it wasn't *natural*; it wasn't what he was used to. His rage filled the room. He demanded that I comb it out and get rid of the curl.

I stood there, disbelieving. "No," I said quietly but with absolute conviction. We had been married less than a week. I was hurt by his criticism and I was mad, His will was as strong as mine; we were at a stalemate.

Of course, it was my mother who intervened again. She took me aside and told me that for the sake of peace, and all the guests who were coming to the party, I should do what Harvey wanted. I loved my mother and recognized the importance of the evening and so I backed down. Removing every trace of my lovely hairdo, making it straight and simple, I capitulated. I felt again I'd lost a little bit of my own rights for the sake of peace. Harvey calmed down, I smiled and greeted the guests, and the evening went smoothly. The food and company were marvelous, and Harvey was officially and generously welcomed into the family.

But the memories of our two collisions of will were imprinted in my mind. They were trivial events on one level, but revealed a need to control that I hadn't seen so clearly in Harvey before. I feared he expected and would demand that if there were any disagreements between us, they would be resolved by my giving in. I believed Harvey wanted a marriage like my parents' and his parents'. I had been raised with the same expectations, so I wasn't surprised, but still I felt bad. I felt humiliated. And I wondered if this feeling was normal-but I had no one to ask.

Our honeymoon continued with two weeks of traveling. We didn't fight again and settled into a relaxed rhythm of sightseeing. The mountains and forests of Norway inspired Harvey, and he talked about his dream of our returning to his home state and creating a life together there. We shared many qualities-our belief in hard work, our perfectionism, and our love of the military and its values. If he wasn't contradicted or thwarted, he was very kind and generous. I learned to avoid doing, saying, or being anything that would challenge him, and so things went smoothly and we enjoyed each other.

When we returned to Nuremberg and our work, I set about reorganizing my third-floor apartment to accommodate both of us. First of all, I had to learn to cook well enough to prepare a meal. This meant boiling water for vegetables and cooking a steak simultaneously, so that they were all ready and still hot at the same time. It was a feat of timing I had never attempted before. Those first weeks of domestic life were miserable. The meals were trials and errors and we were both grateful for the complete dinners offered at the Officers' Club.

I did take one risky, uncompromising stand as a new wife. I announced I would never iron his fatigues. It was a real departure from my normal obedient and accommodating behavior, and Harvey was a bit surprised that I had the guts to do it. But he didn't object. I sent the fatigues out to the military cleaners because, among other things, they needed enough starch to allow the pants to almost stand-alone.

But during those first years as we settled into married life, most things didn't change. We were two professional soldiers. We existed for the military. Someone else told us what to do, where to go, where to live, and because our professional lives were so busy, our personal lives took very secondary roles. Our career milestones took precedence over everything.

In Germany, I challenged military regulations and policy a second time and won. This time my promotion to captain was announced in the newspaper, but when the official orders were posted my name had been deleted. I learned a clerk had inadvertently left my name off the list. I wrote to Personnel asking why I should be penalized for a clerical error, and they backdated my promotion, and adjusted my record and pay accordingly.

Then there was a third challenge to policy. This time it was created because the military had just allowed women to be married and in the military so there were no clear regulations regarding distribution of quarters or housing allowance for married women. As single officers, Harvey and I, each received an allowance for living expenses off-post. When Harvey and I married, I lost mine because I was considered his dependent. Yet I was still an officer and should be entitled to some housing allowance. It was not as common then for two officers to marry, and when we pointed out the inequity of this regulation, the Army finance department changed the policy. We both ultimately received housing allowances just as unmarried officers would receive.

While the incidents themselves were relatively minor, these two experiences were very important to me. In the Army, where regulations are to be followed with unquestioning obedience, I discovered there is flexibility.

Specific circumstances can be considered. Commanders have discretion to respond in ways contrary to the written regulations. Just as when I first disobeyed an order to leave my patients unattended and report to "alert," I learned there is room to challenge a policy and win. These events also taught me that the military *takes care of its own.* Later, when I confronted the discriminatory regulation that bars homosexuals from serving, I assumed this flexibility would work in my favor.

Both Harvey and I were nearing the end of our two years of duty in Germany and waiting to get our next assignments. I received my orders first, ordering me to Fort Lewis in Washington State. Harvey was delighted. He wanted to be stationed in his home state more than anywhere else because that was where he wanted to live after the military. Though my family was in the East, I didn't dream of questioning Harvey's choice. I'd been taught that a wife follows her husband, and it didn't occur to me that I had a right to a preference separate from my husband's. If he wanted to live somewhere, I did, too. However, there was just one little glitch.

Harvey's orders arrived a few days later. He was being sent to Fort Lee, Virginia. I knew that the military would be more likely to change my next locale to match Harvey's than it would be for them to change his orders. Consequently, I suggested to the assignment department that I would like to remain in uniform but could do that only if my husband and I were stationed together. The Army accommodated my request and changed my orders. We both were transferred to Virginia in the spring of 1966.

We arrived back in the States to find the country enmeshed in the war in Southeast Asia. Several months before we left Germany, I had a troubling argument with my cousin Lille Mag that foreshadowed the turmoil I was to find back home. She was opposed to U.S. involvement in Vietnam. In fact, she called it aggression and suggested America wanted to occupy Vietnam. I was shocked by that analysis. I tried to convince her that we were only there because our ally, South Vietnam, had requested our help. We were defenders of freedom, not aggressors. Quoting from the German press, she vehemently disagreed. I remember discounting her views by telling myself they only represented the German bias against Americans. But now, at home, I heard some Americans saying the same things.

Since I'd left the United States in 1964, there had been a tremendous increase in American military personnel in Vietnam. At the beginning of 1966, there were more than 180,000 servicemen and -women there, and General William Westmoreland was calling for another quarter-million troops to be deployed in the coming year alone. U.S. troops were now authorized to take the offensive, and significantly more casualties were being reported. Still, I did not question my government's statements that we were there to ensure democracy and self-determination for the South Vietnamese people. I trusted my President and commanders, and believed they knew best and were doing what was right in a complex situation. I did not doubt them. I felt to do so would diminish the lives that were being sacrificed. It would only be many years after the war had ended that I could reflect on what had happened and question that blind belief. At the time, though, I believed and trusted American intervention was just and right.

Returning home, we heard the voices of protest against the war on the news. But we did not waiver in our belief in our government. Our friends and colleagues were unified and committed to serving our country in battle if necessary. That was the view of everyone we met when we arrived at our new post at Fort Lee, Virginia.

Fort Lee was the training center for the older Quartermaster Corps, currently known as Supply and Service Corps. Harvey had transferred to the Supply and Service Corps from the Armor Corps when he decided he would not become a career military officer.

I reported for duty at Kenner Army Hospital, on the post. Initially, I was the relief supervisor and later head nurse of a newly opened respiratory care ward for recruits. Then I was moved from a clinical position to one of teaching and supervising when they asked me to develop a training program like the one in Germany to prepare medics to go to Vietnam.

We lived off base in a sparsely furnished two-bedroom apartment. There were two full-size beds, one in each bedroom. Since the beds were not long or wide enough to comfortably accommodate both of us in the hot, humid weather of the Virginia summer we maintained separate bedrooms. Though I didn't realize it during my marriage, looking back I can see that while we shared our lives and were deeply committed to each other, I never felt at ease being intimate with Harvey. It was more comfortable, in a number of ways, to have separate bedrooms.

Much of our off-duty time was spent with my parents in Maryland or with college classmates and friends in Virginia. However, it didn't feel like a calm, normal life, no matter how hard we tried. The Vietnam buildup was moving ahead with intensity, and all of us had a sense of grim foreboding.

Then one day it happened. Harvey's unit was on orders and told to prepare for deployment to Vietnam. They were not given an exact date but we knew that he would be leaving within months. That same night we were at a cocktail party at my parents'. We were strolling around, drinking and talking about his orders. Suddenly, I began to cry.

Harvey put his arm around me, hoping to ease my feelings of panic and dread. He was my husband, my best friend, and he was being sent to war. I knew only one thing could make his going to Vietnam bearable.

Regaining my composure, I said, "There's no way I will stay here wondering what's happening to you. I don't want to sit at home waiting for someone to come knocking at the door with *the telegram*. I want to volunteer to go, too, so we'll both be there together."

I was never before so desperate for his permission. After a moment, he agreed. We both were relieved and frightened, but whatever emotions we would have from now on, as we fulfilled our military obligations, we would share them equally. Or so we thought!

The next week, I went to the Army Nurse Corps headquarters in Washington, D.C., and volunteered to go to Vietnam. By now there were so many troops over there, new medical facilities were being built and nurses were needed. Many of us volunteered. It was my duty, and going as a healer, I did not consider that I would be in danger. The Nurse Corps assured me I would go if and when Harvey went.

Now we waited for our orders to be deployed to Vietnam, and continued our duties at Fort Lee. As military people, our whole circle of friends were expecting to go and at the same time fearing it. But those fears were never discussed. And Harvey and I held to the fact that at least we would be there together as they'd promised. In December 1966, we finally received our separate orders to leave. Our February departure from the United States was to be from Travis Air Force Base, in California. But something went wrong with our plan to serve in Vietnam together. Several weeks after the original mobilization orders, Harvey's orders were canceled. We waited for mine to be canceled, too. They were not. But I did not ask for them to be changed. It was unthinkable to allow my personal life to interfere with this most important duty-serving the wounded men in a war. I had joined the military to heal soldiers in battle; once I got orders sending me to that duty, it was hardly appropriate to request they be canceled. Now I would go alone.

Harvey decided to accompany me to Travis Air Force Base. We made arrangements to stop for a week in Washington State on our way. This was also the first time I would meet my in-laws. Harvey wanted us to buy land near his childhood home, so we would have something to dream about and connect us to Washington during our year in Vietnam. From the first day I met him, he'd talked about returning to live there. He wanted land with a view of a mountain called Mount Rainier. I'd never been to Seattle, but he was my husband and it was his choice.

We stayed with his parents-my first opportunity to meet and get to know them a little. Each day we looked for property to buy. The day before we had to leave we finally found land that matched Harvey's dream: eight acres of trees with a creek running through it and a view of the snowcapped Mount Rainier. Our final day was spent signing papers for the purchase. The land truly would give us something to plan for during our year in the war zone.

During that week, as I made ready to leave, we were in a strange position of hoping Harvey would soon be sent to the war as well. During the next days we were numb. We showed no emotion as we made arrangements for both of us to go as far as Travis Air Force Base in California, where I then would board a plane for the long flight to Vietnam. It was a journey my training as a nurse and choices as a soldier had led me to, but I embarked on it with one overriding concern: Would I be a good enough nurse?

CHAPTER 6

. . . .

Vietnam

In my memory the men in the beds are always the same—though they were not there at the same time. The beds always occupy the same positions in the ward, but they are at a skewed angle, not the neat, spaced rows of reality. Then I see their faces. The images come randomly, unexpectedly, unsummoned. Not only was I unable to save them all, I don't remember their names. There were so many. We were too busy. When I go to the Vietnam Memorial, I don't know whom to look for. I cannot tell you who we saved and who we failed. It was the ultimate betrayal.

. . . .

Like most vets I know, I rarely talk about Vietnam. And almost never with people who weren't there. What could I possibly say? If you were there, no talking can add or help or change anything. Tay Ninh, Mekong Delta, Hamburger Hill, and Tet—you just have to say the name, that's enough. If you weren't there, no words will make you really understand. If you weren't in Vietnam, you just don't get it. Just like, if you've never been discriminated against, you don't get it.

But recently I've come to realize that healing can even occur with the attempt to understand. Words can help.

All of us who served in that war have both a Vietnam unique to ourselves and a shared experience that bonds us together. Each experience was as individual as our own fingerprints, and as similar as our hearts that have lost so much. We distinguish those different, yet all one, Vietnams by a thousand things: what job you did, whether you volunteered or were drafted, were an officer or enlisted personnel, believed or doubted, felt doomed or hopeful, saw combat or worked with the injured and dead, and the most important time of your life or the worst (or both), were inspired to achieve or driven to despair (or swung like a pendulum between the two).

Probably one of the most important distinctions is the period when you served there. The Vietnam of 1965, when only 16 percent of the total battle dead was draftees, was very different from the Vietnam of 1970 when draftees made up 70 percent of all combat fatalities. Or, if you were there when 50% of all the casualties of Vietnam occurred. Often, during discussions with one another, veterans find that their feelings or memories differ. Inevitably, this discrepancy is resolved by asking each other, "What year were you there?" "Where were you assigned?" In different years, the number of troops serving and dying was dramatically up or down, the support at home deteriorated as journalists showed the fighting more graphically than had ever been done before. The music of the time—both a cause and effect of feeling—went from the sincerity of folk to the cynicism of rock. And each year the availability and use of drugs and alcohol by troops increased, making the Vietnam of 1970 wildly different from that of 1967.

My Vietnam lasted from February of 1967 to May
1968. It was the period of rapid buildup of our forces
and the most massive casualties of the entire American
presence in the war. The year 1967 began with 380,000
US troops in Vietnam and ended with half a million
there. During my first year in-country, fighting increased
tremendously. American casualties for 1967 alone were
9,353—greater than our total casualties from 1961 to
1966. In my second year, 50 percent of all the casualties
for the entire war occurred. Among the tragic time of
1968 was the infamous Tet offensive, a month of vicious
fighting in almost every city and province throughout
South Vietnam. Even the U.S. embassy in Saigon was
overrun and held for hours by a Viet Cong suicide
squad. Though the offensive was stopped and the enemy
casualties were extraordinarily high, it profoundly shook
our confidence. You arrive as one naïve person and leave
as another casualty of war.

Vietnam was not like previous wars. Military leaders
had no front lines to mark on the maps. So they counted
bodies to judge the success of a mission. These numbers
of dead and wounded were put on mimeographed flyers
and placed on the dining tables in our hospital mess hall
each evening during Tet. Their purpose was to keep us
informed through military intelligence and to prevent us
from reacting just to TV news. We took the Army news
as gospel. We read the numbers and looked for trends.
Was it getting worse or getting better? The body count
invariably showed we were winning. It boosted morale,
demonstrating through numbers our Allied success in a
war of hills, hamlets, shadows and tunnels.

I served in Vietnam as a healer. I did not see combat,
I saw the results of it. But like everything in that war,
my work was a mix of contradictions. I helped save
some men with such massive injuries that I could only

wonder if they hated me for it. When we did make them 100 percent better from their medical diseases, we were the agents that propelled them back out into combat and possible death. When we could not save them, I was there with them when they died.

When I got on that plane at California's Travis air Force Base in 1967, waved goodbye to my soldier husband and headed toward my second war, I believed that the leaders of our country and our Army were all knowing. I had to believe that or I could not justify the death and maiming that would surround me for fourteen months. One thing that I knew with absolute clarity then and that remains true now is that the men and women who served in Vietnam did so out of duty, courage, love, devotion and patriotism. They were and are our very best.

We didn't know how long it would be before Harvey would be sent to Vietnam. Remaining behind was tremendously difficult for him. And soldiers or not, there were tears rolling down our cheeks as my plane took off.

I spent the twenty-four-hour trip to Bien Hoa in meditation and reflection. There were three women and 130 men aboard our plane. Mary O'Neill, Susan Dunn, and I sat near one another but I don't think we talked the whole time. We seemed lost in our own thoughts, I was not worrying about my own safety—as nurses we knew that whatever might happen to us, it would always be a hundred times worse for the men.

It was surreal—I had no preparation for what was to come: no idea of where we were going, what war was going to be like, what to expect, or what our living conditions would be like. With brave humor, I wrote my parents during the flight how much I was looking forward to not having to cook for a whole year. And indeed I was. But otherwise, my uncertainty deepened as the trip progressed.

My parents and my brothers had supported my decision to volunteer for Vietnam; in our family, once a decision is made by one of us it is respected. Later, when I called my parents to say that Harvey's orders had been canceled and he was staying behind, they assured me they would act as Harvey's family in my absence. The only time my mother revealed concern was when I left Washington, D.C. I went to my parents' home, hoping Mother would come with us to the airport. She refused. Seeing us off, she said was too stressful. She didn't want to be seen crying. So we said our goodbyes at the house.

During the flight, I also wrote to Harvey. I missed him and the comfort his companionship gave me, though we both expected that his unit would be deployed to Vietnam soon and we would be reunited.

But more than anything, I was going to face my biggest challenge as a healer, and this thought overshadowed all others. I worried about what I would face as a combat nurse. Most likely I would be treating injuries I had never seen before. My one consolation was that others had preceded me (or so I thought). Others knew what to do and would teach me whatever I needed to know.

No one had to tell us when we entered Vietnamese airspace. We knew and it was eerie. It was the middle of the night, pitch-black and an entire country lay below us, but there were no lights. The plane had also turned off its lights, inside and out. We seemed to be floating into a black hole.

Suddenly in the distance a huge flame shot into the sky. But instead of falling back down to earth, it remained there, suspended with undiminished power. At the time the bright, piercing light subsided, only to be replaced by another burst. As we got closer, the sharp flames increased. It didn't take long to realize just one thing could make such a violent dance of light: an ammunition

dump was exploding. It was the start of the 1967 Tet—
the Vietnamese New Year—and an enemy offensive had
begun.

As our plane approached Bien Hoa airfield, we not
only saw but also heard the rapid, pulsating explosions.
Touching land, the plane shuddered with each blast.
Soon a young lieutenant from the base boarded the plane.
Seeing our anxious and bewildered faces, he greeted us
with bright confidence.

"Don't worry folks," he said, "we're not going anywhere
without an armed escort."

His assurance didn't give me a lot of comfort. Among
other things, he was a "butter bar" and I was well aware
of how much they knew. Not only that, since I had been
promoted to captain just before I left Germany, I felt this
lieutenant was talking down to me. However, with the
ground shaking beneath us and the sky exploding above
us, I had to admit he had war experience and I did not.
When he asked us finally to follow him to a waiting bus, I
did so without a word.

We filed onto the bus with our bags. The rush of the
heat from the tarmac, even at night, enveloped us in its
oppressive embrace. Here we were, calmly taking our
seats, while around us the night sky was pierced with
fingers of fire. And now it became clear we were going
to travel outside this "safe" air base, leave its perimeter
protected by lights, barbed wire, and armed guards to
journey out into the dark countryside on a bus that only
had screens over its windows for security. Just then,
another lieutenant jumped on board and welcomed us to
Vietnam with a one-sentence briefing I will remember as
long as I live: "You will come to believe that this exercise
is really the Unwilling leading the Incompetent into
something that is totally Useless."

I couldn't believe what I was hearing.

I had been working for the success of this mission for many years, even before my arrival. In Germany and at Fort Lee, I had trained medics for Vietnam. Then, when Harvey received his deployment, I'd volunteered to come. I believed the Vietnamese needed our help to remain free. But here was an officer saying, in effect, American soldiers didn't want to fight and the Vietnamese soldiers couldn't fight and the struggle itself was futile. This was an incomprehensible and self–defeating thought. I rejected it. There had to be a reason that we Americans were sending our young into battle. That reason was to maintain the freedom of our South Vietnamese ally, who wanted us to be here. The lieutenant's words were not the welcome I had expected.

We traveled without incident in the darkness to our temporary quarters at the 95th Replacement Station, which turned out to be adjacent to Long Binh, the Headquarters for the military in South Vietnam. It was located just twenty miles northeast of Saigon. Though it was only a short drive from the Bien Hoa air base, we were exhausted by the time we arrived and collapsed into our bunks. When we got up the next morning, the brilliant sun illuminated what had been in shadows and I now felt as if I were in a waking dream. Sights, sounds, and smells enveloped us in a totally new, foreign world.

Mary, Susan, and I were housed in small wooden hooch. Resembling a cabin with few amenities, it contained cubicles with bunk beds and a screen over the window. All I could see, looking out of the window, were more than fifty acres stripped of all vegetation. This barren ground was covered with small huts, tents, and lots of personnel and vehicles. Defoliating the lush jungle was one of our weapons against an enemy we often couldn't see or distinguish from friendly civilians. As the sun rose and people began to stir, the dust, heat, and humidity hit each of us. We could hardly move.

After breakfast in the mess hall, I went back with the other women to our quarters, passing a guard booth by our hooch. I hadn't understood the nuance of its position until then. The guard was for our protection, as women, from the GIs. After months in an all-male world, these men were so horny that any time they saw a woman there were catcalls, whistles, applause, and invitations. These advances didn't consciously intimidate or threaten me, but I certainly felt on display and uncomfortable. It was only years later that I heard about the rapes that took place in Vietnam. At the time, there was such a stigma about getting raped that the victims kept it to themselves for fear of retribution.

Also, within a few days of my arrival, I became head nurse of the medical ward and six months later of the neurosurgical ward, and since I was the other nurses' "boss," I didn't feel it was appropriate to talk with them about their private lives, and no one reported anything to me in my official capacity. All I knew was that each of us was wooed with vigor, constantly propositioned for sexual liaisons. Most of the men couldn't imagine that we were not available to them as sex objects. Perhaps they were still assuming that women joined the military only if they were whores. Despite all this attention, I told myself I was safe from physical attack. I refused to believe there was any real risk, assuming that my rank and my marital status protected me. That was probably not true looking at it in retrospect.   Married female officers were assaulted-though I never was.

In the States, my orders had directed me to go to the 3rd Field Hospital in Saigon. I arrived with my white hospital uniform, but this dress now seemed inappropriate for wartime duty. However, right after I landed, my orders were changed. This happened frequently in the war zone-usually without warning or explanation. We assumed it was due to the ever-changing nature of the escalating conflict. I had to wait five days until I received a new assignment, to the 24th Evacuation Hospital at Long Binh, located near my temporary quarters.

Meanwhile, the other women and I decided to get acclimated to the country and to the war in practical ways. First, we cut one another's hair as short as possible. Then we gratefully changed into jungle fatigues and boots. Now our uniforms suited our environment and duties. Our most interesting excursions during the first few days were trips to the Special Forces camps. These Green Beret soldiers worked directly with the Vietnamese civilians, including the Montagnards who lived in the highland region of Pleiku in central South Vietnam. The Montagnards were tribe's people who were considered some of the most loyal and trustworthy warriors in the country. The Green Beret soldiers worked with local populations to conduct search-and-destroy missions. They were seasoned combat vets, and when they offered to show us around their compound and teach us how to protect ourselves, we were grateful. We would get out of the hot, boring dust bowl of the replacement station, and we could take a look at life in the countryside.

Traveling by open jeep through our own security gate and then onto Highway 1 was incredible. This two-lane "highway" was the main line of transportation through the country. Clogged with humanity and vehicles of every kind, it was a parade of cultures. American military equipment and personnel traveled alongside Vietnamese who walked or rode on bicycles or three-wheeled scooters, called lambrettas. Buses also jammed the road, carrying many times their capacity of people, baggage, and animals that hung out from the doors and windows and perched on the top. People drove with insane disregard for their own or anyone else's safety. As we traveled the highway, the perilous nature of our venturing off post soon became evident. Here we were, American women in uniform sitting in an open jeep, totally exposed to any sniper interested in using us as targets. Although we had a military driver, we lacked any real protection. After several miles, we finally went off the road and into a field, then onto another, less obvious military compound. The gate was guarded and the entire perimeter was surrounded by concertina wire-layers of barbed wire wrapped like a gigantic Slinky. About twenty Vietnamese bare-bottomed kids running around their meager huts were outside the protective wiring. The Special Forces troops were housed and headquartered at the main building inside the impenetrable fence. The stark contrast between the living conditions of the Americans and Vietnamese was like that between whites and blacks on the plantation in the South before the Civil War.   However, I soon noticed the Americans living in that military compound had fewer amenities than we did in our barren hooch.

For our first week in country we spent many hours each day at this camp as we waited to receive our permanent assignments. It was better than doing nothing in the replacement station. In fact, our Green Beret hosts gave us an excellent introduction to our new world, at war, in combat. We practiced firing weapons and leaned about the medical care of wounded civilians.

I was surprised at how difficult it was for the Green Beret medics to get supplies. No one knew exactly why, but the chain of medical supplies did not adequately provide for them. Perhaps it was thought that they could get whatever they needed from the local communities because they worked directly with civilians.   But of course, they couldn't.   Later, when I had extra medical supplies on my ward, I always gave them to the Special Forces medics who came scrounging. They had no direct source of supplies and were desperate for help to treat their wounded.

The practice of bartering and scrounging supplies I witnessed here was common throughout Vietnam. Everything, even equipment and vehicles, was obtained this way.   The Vietnamese stole 25 percent of all U.S. supplies that came into port for their own black market.   Given such shortages, finding other ways to get necessities was a part of the system of survival and it revolved around the skill of each unit's sergeant. His reputation and proficiency were based on how well he scrounged. Since all of this "procurement" occurred outside regular channels, as officers we quickly learned to make our wants known in the appropriate fashion. If an action was necessary to carry out our military mission, then a direct order was indicated. But if we wanted to obtain something not because it was necessary but because it would be nice to have, the informal route was better. So, instead of filling out paperwork, you said to a sergeant, "Gee, wouldn't it be nice if we had a sink, a desk, a stethoscope." Then suddenly the equipment would appear. It was also customary, and important, not to question how these items were obtained. (Years later, when the Watergate and Iran-contra scandals were revealed, it wasn't surprising to me that the system was the same. All a superior has to say to a good military man is "Wouldn't it be nice if..." and magically it happens.)

After five days in-country we had become acclimated to more than just the temperature. I was getting used to operating in this new context of personal fear and threat. Wearing my fatigues and helmet was normal, and I'd learned how to use weapons. Returning to our hooch each night in the open jeep, I sat shotgun. As we sped through the darkening countryside, past the lines of traveling civilians, I held an M-l carbine. It was a wonderful little weapon, its lightweight making it easy to handle. Perched on the jeep, my leg hanging out as I held the weapon, I'd say to myself, "If somebody shoots, I'm going to shoot back." Of course, I had no idea of the ramifications of that—who I might be shooting, or if I would really fire. But I said it to myself nonetheless. Thankfully I was never in a situation where I had to pull the trigger. It was the only time in Vietnam I carried a gun. Health-care workers were forbidden by the Geneva Convention Agreement to carry weapons while on duty in a hospital. But it was a lesson in how quickly I could adapt to this new world.

Finally, I was given my permanent assignment and prepared to report for duty. I was assigned to the new, four-hundred-bed 24th Evacuation Hospital, my home for the next fourteen months. It was at Long Binh post, just a couple of miles from our replacement station, and I was driven there by jeep. Its site, too, had been defoliated. Red dust filled the air. The sand and metal Quonset huts were overwhelming. Long Binh would become, by the end of the American involvement in Vietnam, the largest U.S. military facility in the country.

The chief nurse, Lieutenant Colonel Angie McCloud welcomed me and immediately showed me to my living quarters, an eight-by-ten-foot room in one of the buildings adjacent to the officers' club. The window extended the full length of the outside wall, from about eight feet off the ground to the ceiling, and was covered with a mesh screen. This screen prevented bugs and larger, unwanted creatures-rats, snakes, soldiers-from coming in. The inside walls of each room also extended up eight feet, and the rest was open to the rafters. Voices and sounds from each room traveled freely though this open area. My room had a metal cot and a wall locker.

Adjacent to our building was a tent city for all male officers and enlisted personnel. The women's quarters were plush by comparison.

After dropping off my duffel bag and footlocker, I was given a tour of the hospital. It was so new that not all of the wards had been opened yet. Two columns of Quonset huts were set up parallel and across a quadrangle from one another. Walking through the facility, we finally opened the door of one of the buildings and looked in at the emptiness. I didn't know why I was being shown this barren Quonset hut but I remained silent until Lieutenant Colonel McCloud spoke. "Captain Hawken, this is your ward. You are the head nurse, your ward master and several of your personnel are here, fix it up and be ready to accept patients this afternoon

That was it. She walked away to her other pressing duties.

My ward was to be the new medical intensive-care unit. It was strange being assigned a medical ward, for I had expected that in war the patients would all be combat and trauma casualties. However, I discovered, that is not the case. Less than one third of the casualties in a war zone are from trauma; the other two thirds of those we treat in the hospitals have illnesses or diseases caused by the environment or exposure to parasites. I initially felt disappointed, but also relieved, at this assignment. I suddenly realized I had little idea of what I was doing, but then so did everyone else.

The ward looked like a giant tin can, cut in half-length wise and placed on the ground with the open cut end down like a turtle shell. It was stark, and had the closed-in feeling of a bomb shelter. The floor was concrete and the curved walls and ceiling were corrugated metal. A few windows were cut through the metal and covered with plastic. There were doors at either end. Stepping inside, you looked down a long, narrow interior, about the length of a quarter of a football field. We began preparing for patients. We made two rows of cots separated by a six-foot aisle down the middle of the ward. Thirty beds were lined up like soldiers, about three feet apart, with nightstands in between for personal belongings and medical supplies. Down the length of the ward, hanging from the ceiling were metal bars on which were hung privacy curtains. Usually the curtains were open, but if a patient required it, they could be pulled all the way around the cot. Halfway down the ward was a nurses' station. There was one private cubicle for either a female patient or a male patient with an infection.

Typical of Vietnam facilities, there was no internal plumbing. We took a honey bucket-a stainless-steel receptacle-from cot to cot and emptied the contents of catheter bags into it and carried it to the outdoor latrine. Then we washed and disinfected the bedpans and urinals in an area just outside the ward. Ambulatory patients used the outhouse, which was about one hundred yards away: a ten-holer. It serviced several wards as well as staff at the same time. Fifty-five gallon drums where cut in half and placed under the holes as collecting bins. Every morning the American soldiers who were prisoners in the stockade removed the drums and took them to the far end of the post, poured on diesel, and set them on fire. Each day the black smoke of burning excrement and fuel filled the air. It was another fine contribution that the war made to the environment.

Adjacent to the latrine was an outside shower. Since we didn't have running water, each day a truck filled a container on the roof of the wooden shower facility. Water in each stall was turned off and on by pulling a string attached to valve. You really needed three hands to take a shower, but frequently your teeth served you well.

It also meant that there was less waste of water because it was not running all the time. Water temperature was determined by when you took the shower. During the day, when the temperature was 120 degrees, the shower was that hot. In the evening when the temperature dropped to 80 degrees, the water did also and we froze. Regardless, it was an incredible luxury compared to what the men in the bush contended with-weeks without a shower or clean water.

As soon as we had arranged our ward, the patients began arriving. Many of them had malaria. Though everyone had to take pills to prevent it, they did not work for all types of malaria and infection would occur. Patients' body temperatures would get so high we were concerned they might develop seizures or suffer brain damage, so our first task was to get them as cool as possible. But often their high fevers made them delirious, very weak, and unable to get out of bed, so we all struggled to bring down their temperatures by draping alcohol-and water-soaked towels over their bodies. Then we placed electric fans to cool them. This was effective but uncomfortable for the patients, so we hated to do it, but it was necessary. As soon as their fevers dropped and they were able to walk, they preferred to cool off in the shower.

The medical ward was always filled with sick young men. The most common medical problems besides malaria were typhus, dengue fever, pneumonia, skin infections and fevers of unknown origin (that meant we couldn't figure out the cause) The ward was colorful because the house medical officer, Bruce Boklan, had a marvelous treatment for the jungle rot that the men often got from walking on patrol for days at a time with wet feet, wet socks, wet boots. Their skin would literally begin to rot. Painting potassium permanganate on the men's feet killed the fungal infections and added stunning magenta color to the ward. Sixty purple feet protruded from the beds.

I got up each day at about 0600 (6 AM), got into uniform and went to the mess hall for a breakfast of reconstituted eggs, milk, toast and potatoes. Officers sat together and talked. It was a quiet time, getting ready for the intense pace of the day ahead. By seven o'clock, I was at the ward. The staff assembled and we began with a half-hour report by the night staff on the status of patients and what had occurred during the night shift. Then, as head nurse, I gave each nurse and corpsman his or her daily assignment and we got to work. There was a different tempo on the medical ward as compared to the neurosurgical intensive care unit where I later became head nurse.

The most important thing about the medical patients was to obtain a diagnosis and then treat them appropriately. Hydration, monitoring their vital signs, keeping the fever under control was key to their return to duty. Contrastingly, the care on neurosurgery was much more structured because the patients were critically ill and unable to communicate and usually was post-operative (had undergone neurosurgical procedures). Patients were monitored every fifteen minutes to four hours, depending on their condition. They were bathed and fed, their dressings and IVs changed, and we assisted the doctors on their rounds. Usually we worked twelve-hour shifts, with a dinner break before we ended at 7:00 p.m. At night I often went to the officers' club to socialize.

Several times a month there would be red alerts-when enemy mortar and artillery shells would fall near the hospital compound. Doctors, nurses, enlisted personnel-anyone not essential to the wards-would put on their helmets and boots, go to the fortified bunkers, and spend the evening hours together. I always took my guitar and led sing-alongs to pass the time and distract us. One of the neurosurgeons, Don Patrick, joked that we only had time to be afraid between songs. Some people would play cards; there were cocktails and much laughter. In the war zone, we all developed a sense of immortality-it was necessary to keep us going. While I was there, we never experienced a direct hit, though the administrative building did sustain an attack after I returned to the States.

Evening was the only time available to communicate with my family back home. Harvey and I didn't write-we made tapes for each other. Each night, just before I went to sleep, I listened to his latest tape and made one in response. Because the walls of my room didn't go up to the ceiling, and sound traveled, I got under the covers with the tape recorder. I told Harvey about the details of my day. We shared our dreams about the home and farm we'd build on our new property when we returned from Vietnam. I promised him I was safe and faithful. In some ways, we got closer to each other with our daily monologues and were able to be more loving and caring than we had in person. We fantasized about our romantic reunion when his unit finally arrived. Each day I sent off a new tape and received one in return. I missed his companionship, and the tapes were very comforting.

Our married life so far had been a series of tours of duty. In Germany, we said our more normal life would begin when we got home. Returning to America, we faced the challenge of the escalating war and almost certain assignment to Vietnam—and again put daily life on hold while we prepared ourselves for possible combat duty. And now with me in Vietnam and him in Virginia, we talked only of reuniting. Later, when Harvey arrived in Vietnam, we again looked ahead to when the ordeal would end and we could begin our normal life together in the States. There was, I see in retrospect, always a reason to put our relationship on hold.

My mother and I corresponded every week or so. On Mother's Day, about three months after arriving in Vietnam, I called her as a surprise. She thanked me for the call, but I could tell from her voice that something was wrong. Finally she asked me never to call her again from Vietnam. She explained that calling made my presence in the war zone so real to her and that it was too upsetting. I didn't call again and I missed hearing her voice.

Patients rarely died on the medical ward. This was a luxury during wartime. But we saw and cared for so many sick young troops. These were seventeen- and eighteen-year-old boys risking their lives in a war none of us really understood. What was particularly hard was helping them get well and looking forward to their discharge from the hospital, and then suddenly realizing they were better off being sick and in a safe place. We were sending the healthy back to combat. I hate to think of how many we had "cured" only to die at a later time, in the field.

That painful realization hit me my second month there. One of my patients had recovered from malaria and was to be discharged from the hospital soon. He was healthy but the day before he was to leave he came to me and asked for a priest. When the priest arrived, the young soldier requested the last rites there on the ward before he returned to battle.

I was devastated. Until that moment, it had just not registered what war meant for these young men. Suddenly everything became more serious. I worried more about Harvey arriving safely.

Looking back, I realize that after this I never again wrote to my parents about my patients or what I was doing. From then on, I only wrote to tell them I was fine and to talk about the weather. I began to shut down emotionally so that I wouldn't feel guilty about returning patients to duty and possible death. The mission of the Army Medical Corps is "to preserve the fighting strength." And we did.

As I closed myself off from feelings, my focus became even more intense on my work. I had superb help in this. Dr. Bruce Boklan, my medical officer and mentor, was bound and determined that I was going to be a thinking practitioner. He was a teacher and a healer. From the first moment we started receiving patients he made sure I learned basic field medicine. He wanted nurses to understand the medical evaluation, the diagnostic techniques, and the rationale for all the laboratory tests. I learned more during the six months I worked with Bruce than most internists would in years of practice in America.

On April 30, almost three months after I arrived, Harvey landed at the port of Qui Nhon. His entire unit was shipped over with its equipment and then sent immediately to Da Nang, just fifty miles south of the demilitarized zone that separated North and South Vietnam. We were almost four hundred miles apart. He couldn't get a pass to come to see me even though an Air Force colonel friend of mine, Dick Coombe, had flown to meet his ship and had talked with his commander. Dick had arranged for Harvey to be flown to Saigon so we could spend a few days together. But Harvey's commander, for reasons we never understood, wouldn't allow it. So it was up to me to do the traveling. I was able to get a seventy-two-hour pass to visit him, and, through Dick's intervention, began my long journey north. To assure I was escorted properly, Dick wrote a letter of introduction for me to carry to each airfield operations officer I met traveling to Da Nang. I didn't have any specific arrangements to get to Harvey, just Dick's letter, my own resolve, and the reality that many things happened during the war outside regular channels.

First, I was driven the few miles to Bien Hoa airfield. Though not scheduled to fly, I walked into the flight room and showed them Dick's letter. They looked at me, looked at each other, and then said a chopper would take me to Saigon. Hurdle number one was crossed. With the same luck, persuasion, and the generosity of pilots, I got from Saigon to Pleiku. On the last leg of the trip from Pleiku to Da Nang, I was sole passenger on a large Chinook aircraft. The weather was hot and " muggy, and there was the unmistakable smell of old blood throughout the craft. Its previous mission was carrying dead soldiers out of combat zones. I could feel around me those recent, silent passengers, and I grieved for them.

Touching down in Da Nang was like returning from a dark world. Before I could regain my usual composure, Harvey appeared. We hadn't known when, or even if, I would arrive at Da Nang, so he'd been waiting for hours in the humid hanger nearby. We had both eagerly anticipated this moment for months. But now it was very awkward and strange. Standing there before me wasn't the husband I'd been looking forward to seeing, but another soldier in fatigues, and since arriving in Vietnam, I'd been trying to stay away from soldiers in fatigues. As he put his arms around me, I stiffened and felt a terrible need to keep distant. I'd become guarded and closed, not only to survive the pain of working with so much suffering, but to protect myself from the unwanted sexual advances and threats of the men. Being touched, even by my husband, made me feel my personal space was being invaded. Rigid and unresponsive, I froze, caught in confusing impulses. It seemed as though Harvey did not understand my stiffness. He said he was hurt, and reminded me that he was my husband, that I was safe with him and I could relax. I was able to soften a little, but couldn't completely shake off the self-protectiveness I'd developed.

Our first night together in dingy, single-bed quarters at Da Nang was not the romantic reunion we'd envisioned. Harvey found himself with a wife who had changed. As head nurse of a ward in a combat hospital, I had been performing with a level of authority and self-confidence he hadn't seen before. I didn't automatically defer to him, as I had in the past. But while it seemed difficult for him at first, I hoped that our being together now, in the place that had so shaped me, would allow us to be more understanding of each other in the future.

The difficulties of that night were overtaken by the enjoyment of the next day. From morning till night, we relaxed and swam at China Beach. Floating on air mattresses in the South China Sea, delighting in the warm rays of the sun playing on our bodies, we also listened to the artillery shells exploding on the mountain-affectionately called Boom-Boom Rock-that overlooked this idyllic beach. You develop a fascinating illusion that nothing can happen to you. If you don't feel invulnerable, you won't be able to move. At the same time, you know subconsciously that every moment you're tempting fate by enjoying life and being out there. It's a constant, unresolveable tension. So you just experience those contradictory feelings and keep living from moment to moment, taking pleasure when you can, appreciating the fragility of life in such a world.

After three days together, Harvey and I said goodbye, confident that very soon we'd see each other again. The illusion of omnipotence allows you to get through these difficult, uncertain times. Now that we were both in Vietnam, we assumed the next hurdle of being stationed nearer each other could be overcome easily.

Returning south to Long Binh was hectic. Unable to travel back as quickly as I had expected, I arrived a little late. The only transportation I'd been able to get was a huge Green Giant helicopter that normally carried out loads of casualties from a firefight. It finally touched down on the landing strip at my hospital about 0815 (my leave was up at 0800). Naturally, just the sound and sight of it descending brought the litter bearers and medics running out of the emergency room to meet what they assumed were wounded soldiers. Instead they saw me climb sheepishly, tan from my days of swimming. Since I was fifteen minutes late for duty, I gave them an embarrassed smile and ran to the ward. Pretending I'd never been gone (much less late in arriving back), I resumed the pace of work as though I hadn't taken a break at all. It was easy to do because our work and ward camaraderie was, by now, more familiar than the "normal" life I'd briefly experienced with Harvey in Da Nang. Throughout my tour of duty, each moment I took off to relax or swim or do anything but work on the ward felt like stolen time. But as head nurse, I made my staff take time for themselves—though each of us felt guilty when we did.

Despite our youthful confidence that we'd meet again soon, Harvey and I didn't see each other for several months. His unit, a Supply and Service Battalion, was reassigned from Da Nang to Tay Ninh, near the Cambodian border. Harvey's commander believed Harvey and I had caused this move of the entire unit so we could be closer. Of course, that was ridiculous. But the commander's suspicion continued and he wouldn't give Harvey permission to visit me, although we were only forty miles apart. The mentality that the enemy was everywhere caused inappropriate fears and behavior. There was a constant distrust of people even on your own side.

One night, Harvey was able to stop by my hospital on his way to Tay Ninh, and I introduced him to my ward staff and some of the nurses who lived in my hooch. We spent the evening together, sharing stories, food, and drink at the officers' club. Unfortunately, the following morning I overslept. Worried I'd get teased by my staff; I came on the ward as unobtrusively as possible. I was relieved to see everyone diligently at their duties, hardly lifting their heads to acknowledge my late arrival. I went to my desk. There, on my chair, was a pillow. At first, I was confused and looked around, not quite getting the connection. Then it dawned on me. I blushed, looked up at all the faces watching mine, picked up the pillow, turned and threw it at my ward master. The whole ward-staff and patients roared with laughter.

Soon after that visit, we got very lucky. Through some fluke of scheduling, Harvey's unit moved a third time, this time to my post. Not only was fate kind to us, but my progressive chief nurse believed that married couples should live together-even in a war zone where there were no accommodations for couples-so Harvey moved into my room in the nurses' quarters.

There was only one problem. Since none of our rooms had walls that extended to the ceiling, there wasn't complete privacy. All of us could hear noises from adjoining rooms. One of the few advantages was that when someone needed assistance, all she had to do was call for help and it appeared. Uninvited rodent guests were common in our quarters, and Harvey was immediately enlisted to combat this invasion. When someone screamed, he'd run to her room, and then stomp on the rat. He soon became everybody's big brother.

When Harvey moved in with me, my routine didn't change very much. I still went to breakfast in the hospital mess alone. Harvey had to eat with his unit, so every morning he got in his jeep (named Grethe) and drove across the post to join his comrades. He had a desk job overseeing the flow of supplies and worked long hours, too.

We did, however, have evenings together. Almost every month we got a package from our real-estate agent who had sold us our property in Washington State. She sent a letter highlighting local events, included newspapers, maps, and even photographs of our land as the seasons changed. We spent nights making lists of what we wanted in the house we would build and how we'd develop the surrounding acres. Other evenings were spent at the officers' club or entertaining members of my staff and buddies from his unit.

By now, I had let down my guard with Harvey, but I still felt the need for some physical distance. At the time, I told myself that the fatigue, the emotional numbness, the danger involved in working in a combat hospital was not conducive to physical intimacy, and we both believed things would change when we got back to normal life. Harvey and I now didn't share feelings with each other as much as we had on the tapes, but it didn't occur to me to question why. We worked hard, and whenever we weren't on duty, we were the gracious married couple to all of our single, lonely friends.

Inevitably, living as a couple in the small, almost communal nurses' quarters became awkward. I was very sensitive to how lucky I was to have my husband with me when married soldiers were separated from their spouses. I was concerned that my situation might make other nurses feel more isolated or lonely. Of course, in our room we heard voices and sounds in the night, but

I never thought anything of it. Harvey tried to convince me that there were sexual liaisons taking place in the rooms adjacent to ours. I said that this was impossible. It absolutely could not be happening. I believed nurses would never engage in sexual interludes if they were not married. Harvey was as adamant in his insistence as I was in my denial. Throughout my fourteen months in Vietnam, I steadfastly held to my view. It was only after we returned to America and I learned that some of my colleagues had become pregnant while we served together at Long Binh that I was forced to realize I'd been wrong. My innocent ideas about people and relationships were becoming tempered by reality.

But whatever was or was not happening in the other rooms, it seemed inappropriate for us, as a married couple, to be living in the nurses' quarters. With Harvey's connections in Supply and Service Corps, he was able to get materials and men to build married quarters for us. We got approval to locate the hut on the hospital compound, near the perimeter of the housing area. Harvey and his crew began this construction project with great enthusiasm. His skill at scrounging, along with his ability to work long and hard, made him popular.

After the usual delays and obstacles, two rectangular huts were erected end to end with enough room for five married couples to have a ten-by-twenty-foot space each. This allowed every couple two rooms. One was a bedroom, with enough space for two cots, a dresser, and footlockers. The second was a living room, where we ended up with a stove, coffee table, chair, and love seat of traditional military quality. As inventive as he was industrious, Harvey also built an indoor sink from a basin with a hole in the bottom and a hose that ran outdoors to drain. He jerry-rigged a twenty-gallon coffee container to be our water source. I had hoped to avoid cooking for the duration of my Vietnam tour, but Harvey's mastery at scrounging bestowed on us a huge refrigerator. The generator was strong enough to keep it running and cold but couldn't provide power for the stove at the same time. Since the stove looked good but never worked, we devised an outdoor barbecue by cutting a fifty-five-gallon drum lengthwise, filling it with charcoal, and using the shelving from the refrigerator for the grill. This way I could create everything from exotic meals of toast and Norwegian fish balls in curry sauce for just the two of us to parties featuring steaks and lobsters that Harvey was able to divert from a general's kitchen.

We also used this outdoor barbecue to cook feasts for my ward staff. After our wonderful dinners, I would get out my guitar and all of us would sing folk songs and reminisce about the good old days before the war. And we shared our own countdowns-a common ritual in Vietnam during times like this-when we compared exactly how many days each of us had left before rotation back home. Our need to have social time together outside the ward was so important we even found a way to entertain during monsoon season. Placing one jeep on either side of the grill, and then balancing doors on the roofs of the jeeps, we were able to provide cover for the guests and the grill. On one of his trips to visit us, Dick gave us a housewarming gift. It was a wall banner that jovially announced COMBAT PAY AND GRACIOUS LIVING GO HAND IN HAND. However humorous we found it, I also appreciated that despite the fact that our quarters were pieced together from discarded junk, they were truly gracious compared to what many others in Vietnam endured.

We filled our social lives with as many ordinary tasks and enjoyments as we could possibly arrange in such an extraordinary environment. It didn't block the pain or loss, but it helped us get through the days. And even though we all had twelve-to-fourteen-hour shifts at least six days a week at our own hospital, there was still time to volunteer to do more. One look at the conditions in the countryside told us any assistance we could provide civilians were needed.

The nearest civilian facility was Cholon Hospital in Saigon. To get there we went by open jeep down Highway 1, joining the human parade of cyclists, lambrettas, and walkers. By now I knew enough to be truly frightened. I'd heard many stories of U.S. soldiers who had been injured, and even killed, when a civilian had tossed a grenade or other explosive device into a jeep. Our only protection was luck and diligence-making sure as we slowed down through villages that nothing and no one came near our vehicle. Fortunately, we made our way each week to the Vietnamese hospital without incident.

I knew that U.S. AID nurses had been at the hospital for nearly three years, teaching nursing and patient care from a Western perspective, and that they needed help. When a group of us from the 24th Evacuation Hospital began our volunteer work, we believed that Western medicine was best and could be applied to this civilian community. Yet, as we encountered the traditions and beliefs of this ancient Asian culture, we began to realize how much we ourselves had to learn. Walking into the four-story civilian hospital was a shock. Hundreds of beds less than two feet apart occupied every inch of the vast rooms. There were two and sometimes three patients in a bed. Usually they would be placed so that people with the same leg amputated would share a bed with their heads at the opposite ends. Each patient's entire family, from children to grandparents, hovered around the bed twenty-four hours a day with their food and belongings.

We weren't prepared for the way medicine was practiced in this culture, either. When we first arrived and went to check in with the Vietnamese nurses, they were taking naps or working in some remote area of the hospital. The nurses rarely attended actual patients-that work was left to the families. When a doctor in the hospital ordered a medication, the nurses would give the prescription to a family member, who would get the prescription filled in the city and bring back the medicine to the nurse. But then the nurse would dispense the entire day's dose to the family member all at once. It was the relative's job to see that the patient got the right amount at the right time. Unversed in the requirements of medicine, the family member sometimes gave a patient the entire daily dose of medication at one time.

As we toured the facility, we noted the lack of sanitation and patient monitoring. Since our American neurosurgeons were teaching the Vietnamese surgeons certain operations, we thought it appropriate that we provide follow-up nursing care. While the staff expressed an interest in our assistance, after weeks of working with them it was clear our efforts were essentially useless.

The Vietnamese had never heard of footboards to prop up the feet, after surgery, to prevent foot drop and contractures. They did not turn the paralyzed patient so bedsores and infections were common complications after surgery. They were not familiar with the technique of logrolling a patient off his back after surgery to check for bleeding without disrupting the surgical site. They did not use sterile equipment or sterile water to irrigate urinary catheters. There was no such thing as running water or supplies. After the years of war and the millions of refugees, there were not enough of these medical necessities to go around.

Nevertheless, week in and week out we went to demonstrate and try to follow-up on what the neurosurgeons were doing. But not much changed. Finally we thought that perhaps it would help if some of the Vietnamese nurses could see what went on in an American hospital. So I made arrangements for about ten civilian nurses to come and spend a day with us at our hospital. Each Vietnamese nurse was assigned to work with an Army nurse in a different area. By noon the Vietnamese nurses were exhausted and wanted their customary midday nap. There was nothing to do but accommodate them, and for several hours they all slept while we continued with our duties. But even when they returned to the wards in the afternoon, they did not have the stamina to complete a typical American workday.

After six weeks of traveling to Saigon during our off-hours, we reluctantly terminated our attempts at teaching. It was clear that the type of care we were providing was based on Western practice for Western patients. Their medicine suited their two thousand year-old agrarian cultures. It could not save a man maimed by high tech weapons. We could do that, but once the patient survived, then what? A war-injured paraplegic cannot work in the rice paddies. To think we could suddenly appear with new ways of doing things, with radical (to their minds) philosophies about medicine, and expect to easily impose our standards was wrong, though in our ignorance we tried. The difference in our two cultures was made even more apparent when I took care of Vietnamese patients on my own ward. For example, his family brought in a nine-year-old boy, paralyzed when struck by a stray American bullet. After his surgery and treatment, the family was called back to take him home and begin his rehabilitation. Though he was a paraplegic, he could become wheelchair independent with a little help. But when his family arrived and saw his condition, they refused to take him home. They'd expected us to make him walk again which was impossible-and so left the hospital without him. I was dumbfounded. On reflection, I began to understand that in a rural village, where subsistence is difficult, physical labor is required in fields or rice paddies, and this family had no way of imagining how their child could contribute on crutches or in a wheelchair. Also there were no rehabilitation facilities in Vietnam. And overriding all these practical realities was their cultural belief that if a person was not whole, he or she was better off dead. We were finally able to get the boy to a civilian hospital, but I feared his chances were not good. Almost half of all people with spinal-cord injuries die of complications. Dependent on a medical system ravaged by war, he would have quite a struggle to survive.

All of these difficulties came together most profoundly when we treated prisoner-of-war patients. You have to remember the type of war this was: a conflict with American and Viet Cong, North and South Vietnamese casualties. By means of the medical evacuation helicopters, the wounded were picked up and transported to hospitals for care within minutes of receiving their injuries. That meant that sometimes a hospital received casualties from both sides of the conflict. When I first arrived at Long Binh, before we had a separate ward for POW patients, an American soldier woke up from surgery in the recovery ward, looked over and saw a Viet Cong soldier beside him. The American bolted up in his bed, reached over and tried to kill the Viet Cong patient. Medics rushed in and stopped the attack.

The problem was obvious, and soon the POW ward was opened. This provided some isolation and protection for everyone. Now, however, others often ostracized the American nurses taking care of these POWs because they were "caring for the enemy." It was their job, not necessarily their choice. But the hatred and prejudice that war inspires in people regardless of their altruistic beliefs regarding equal treatment for wounded and suffering patients created this bias. Why waste our precious time and supplies on the enemy while we were caring for and losing Americans? A strong sentiment throughout the war, it stayed with me even after I returned home.

Perhaps this immediate resentment-at time's hatred-toward all Vietnamese was so lasting because we could never tell who was the good guy and who was the bad guy. Even the Vietnamese women each of us hired for three dollars a week to clean our rooms, wash and iron our uniforms and clothes, were not to be trusted. Although all Vietnamese were frisked before entering and upon departing the military post, there were times those same employees planted booby to detonate after they had left. You had to distrust every civilian, event children. It was that kind of war.

Ultimately, I realized that this two thousand-year-old culture probably knew what was best for its people—best because it could be supported by the beliefs and the practices of its people. It's very hard to remain dispassionate when we see things occurring that are counter to what we, as Americans, believe are basic to our way of being. However, I think the important thing I learned is to take life as it comes, and not try to change those things that are impossible to change. Cultures endure because they serve their own people and environment.

One of the most difficult parts of being in Vietnam was hearing about the antiwar demonstrations at home. I had joined the military because I believed in America and all it stood for. Maintaining a strong democracy required that people would be willing to defend it. I offered my service. Yes, I had also received a lot of benefits for being in the military, but anyone could get those same benefits if they chose to join.

As a military person, my job was to obey lawful orders, and going to Vietnam was one of them. It was very difficult to see people flee to Canada in protest against the war. I didn't understand how anything but cowardice could make citizens run from their own country to avoid serving. When I watched antiwar demonstrations on TV in my quarters after a twelve-hour shift in the ward, what I saw were people trying to save themselves. I couldn't see anything in their behavior—on the streets screaming at police, carrying vicious signs—that showed me they were action out of principle.

The demonstrations against the war and the direct attacks against servicemembers returning from Vietnam were very painful to see and endure. Those of us in uniform had given up a lot to follow the orders of the President, our commander-in-chief, to serve our country, and yet the country berated us and made us feel like villains. Only once during my tour, on Memorial Day in 1967, was there an event that supported us in Vietnam. It was a parade in New York City that was broadcast to us by the Armed Forces Network. Afterward, nurses and corpsmen worked in the ward with tears of gratitude that some people back home cared for what we were doing.

Celebrities did come to visit us and offer their support. However, some of these visits seemed very self-serving, for the benefit of the stars themselves and the people at home rather than for the servicemembers on the front lines. When Bob Hope came in 1967 there was so much hoopla over arrangements for the TV crews and cameras that the media appeared more important than the entertainment for the troops.

By contrast, Martha Raye came to visit and she was fabulous. She had been through several wars, seen many casualties, and suffered injuries herself. As a nurse, she had also received an honorary commission in the Army Nurse Corps, and now held the honorary rank of colonel. She would have wowed us by reading the phone book-her charm and power were that great. She brought us *Hello, Dolly!* and when she came out on stage at Long Binh, twenty thousand troops stood and gave her a welcome that they must have heard in Hanoi. I will never forget her opening remarks: "The people back home demonstrating against the war are not fit to polish your boots." We agreed and loved her.

During my fourteen-month assignment, the 24th Evacuation Hospital rapidly grew to its full size. It became the center for neurosurgery, orthopedics, maxillofacial surgery (treatment of jaw and facial injuries), and ophthalmology, in addition to offering general surgery, urology, internal medicine, physical therapy, radiology, and other standard services. It opened in early 1967 with 200 beds and a staff of 30 doctors, 60 nurses, and 225 enlisted personnel. By the end of the year, more than 9,000 patients had been treated and the bed capacity had increased to 400. From the air it looked like a vast web of low Quonset huts radiating out in every direction and surrounded by a deep perimeter of barbed wire that was punctuated by guard towers and gates.

In this extensive medical empire there was one ward that was avoided. Staff who didn't work there wouldn't go near it and sometimes made jokes about its personnel and patients. They called it the "vegetable garden," and just stepping in the door, you understood how it got this name.

It was the first ward of its kind in Vietnam and its proper name was the neurosurgical intensive-care unit. Its patients had head and spinal wounds. Many had received other injuries and amputations, but all were there recovering from brain and spinal injury. Usually they were unable to speak or move on their own.

As this new ward was set up and began receiving patients, I was head nurse of the medical ward. I too, avoided it, but for different reasons. From my student days, I'd thought of neurosurgeons as the most arrogant prima donnas of all physicians, and I didn't want anything to do with them. Neurology was also my father's area of expertise, so I wasn't going near it.

That's why, in August 1967, when the chief of neurosurgery, Don Patrick, came into my medical ward and asked me to step outside with him for a minute, I was not particularly happy about interrupting my duties. He walked outside and I followed him into the dust, dirt, and heat.

"Grethe," he began, "the head nurse of our ward is returning to the States. Being head nurse of the neurosurgical ward in the most complex nursing position in the hospital. The other neurosurgeons and I think that you are the only person to fill the position. Would you accept the position of head nurse?"

My answer didn't require much thought. "I like where I am." I said.

But he was not deterred—stubbornness was another trait of neurosurgeons. He flattered me—always an effective strategy. He promised I would face extraordinary challenges and make important contributions—always-powerful attractions. And, finally he offered to teach me everything he could.

I looked at him sternly and said, "I'd love it."

Days later, I became head nurse of the neurosurgical unit. When I stepped onto that ward, my personal Vietnam again changed. It suddenly became very quiet, very still. Don's description of what I would find was accurate. This ward was different from any I had worked on, anywhere.

Here was where medical technology and the helicopter's ability to evacuate even the most horribly injured met. In other wars, most of the patients on this ward would have died where they'd fallen or as they were taken out. But in Vietnam we had the extraordinary work of field medics and the Dust-off pilots. "Dust-off" was a term used for the helicopter that by 1967 could be on the scene of a battle or assault no matter how deep in combat it was, to bring out the wounded and fly them to the nearest hospital. The Dust-off crews went in regardless of the danger to themselves. The average time from injury to operating room was only twenty minutes. The distinctive sound of their rotor blades meant hope for wounded men and, for nurses, the arrival of casualties.

Unlike the medical ward I had just worked on, all the patients came to this neurosurgical ward after having been wounded. The Viet Cong and North Vietnamese Army troops used AK-47s and AK-50s, which fired round after round of bullets at great velocity and distance. Fragmentation grenades, incendiary grenades, claymore mines were thrown or hidden not just in combat zones-for all Vietnam was a combat zone-but in villages and on paths, and were tossed into passing jeeps and buses. When these weapons exploded, they destroyed everything around them. They made bodies into mincemeat.

That's how our patients got to us. What struck them down was random and savage. What they needed to survive was meticulous surgery, extraordinary nursing, and their own determination to live.

There was an outward serenity to the neurosurgical ward. But that was only on the surface. Underneath the quiet order, the patients' struggle to survive and the staff's intense work continued around the clock.

From the first day, I loved the challenge of running this ward. First you learn to watch. These silent rows of patients lying perfectly still with head dressings may look the same to the untrained eye. The intravenous fluid bottles hang on poles that punctuate the neat rows of beds. There's no verbal communication between patients and staff. Many in the beds are unconscious and most have a tracheotomy tube in their throats to allow us to suction secretions out of their lungs and prevent pneumonia. But after you watch and work with the patients, every fifteen minutes checking their level of arousability, blood pressure, and respirations, and after you perform the mundane tasks of feeding, bathing and turning them, you begin to learn that touching itself is caring and communicating.

A neurosurgical nurse must give to the patient without ever being sure the patient is aware of being cared for. You read letters from home to patients who show no visible sigh of understanding what is being said. You write letters for patients who must slowly struggle from one word to the next, helping them make their letters understandable to their families back home. The hopelessness that floods over the soldier with an inoperable cervical spinal wound can be overwhelming for both the patient and the staff. The child-like condition of a patient with brain damage causes profound spiritual and emotional stress for everyone. All of this work, this care, requires that you use heart and head in equal portions

I learned more about hope in the neurosurgical ward than anywhere else. Though it was called the vegetable garden because the patients were frequently mute and comatose, to those of us who worked there the smallest response or movement from a patient made us ecstatic because it signaled an important potential for improvement. If after a week of coma a patient could even grunt in pain—that gave us hope. The flicker of an eyelid, or the squeeze of a hand from a young man who had been motionless before—that gave us hope. The long struggle to finally say a single syllable meant that this soldier might learn to speak again. These signals of determination and life were occasions for joy.

But our mission had another powerful and sometimes tragic constraint. We were an evacuation hospital. This was a war in a foreign, hostile country. So we not only had to stabilize our patients after their surgery; we had to prepare them to be evacuated to a hospital either in Japan or back home. They couldn't stay with us indefinitely. In those early years of the war, we didn't have the technical means to airlift out someone who was not able to breathe on his own. Of course, if we could get our patients on a plane headed for a hospital in Japan, it was like sending them off to a blessed land where, we could tell ourselves, they'd get better. But those on respirators, needing the help of a machine to breathe, could not be airlifted out. We had three or four days to get them off the respirator and breathing on their own. That is the time it takes brain or spinal cord swelling to recede after surgery and functioning to return. If we were not able to wean them off the breathing machine by then, it meant they couldn't breathe independently, and there was nothing more we could do. They could not be sent home and we knew they would die.

I remember most vividly one such young man because he looked so young and was so innocent. I can still see his face and hear his voice pleading for help. He was only seventeen or eighteen years old, blond and blue-eyed. He had a neck injury with a gaping wound in the back of his head. A field medic must have been right beside him when he was hit because at that moment he stopped being able to breathe on his own. In some respects, it was amazing he had survived long enough to get to us. But with unrelenting dedication, someone had been with him the entire time, manually pumping air through his mouth and into his lungs. We called this "bagging" because it was literally a special breathing bag that was used. Some medic had bagged him within minutes of his massive injury, and continued this determined, delicate process as he was put on a helicopter, flown out of the combat, taken off the transport, and rushed into surgery.

He came to us a quadriplegic. Though he was stabilized, he couldn't move his arms or legs, and his injury was so high up in his spinal cord that he could not breathe on his own. We placed a tracheotomy tube in his throat and hooked him up to a large respirator called a Drager. The methodical clunking sound of this machine meant another breath of life had been pushed into his lungs. The delicacy and severity of his injuries also required us to put him in a Stryker frame instead of a bed. This special turning frame is like a rotisserie, allowing the patient to be turned from back to front without any movement of the spine.

Through all of our work on him, he was awake. But he couldn't, talk or make a sound except when he exhaled the air the Drager had pumped into him. That breath passing back out over his larynx could allow him a word or phrase. As soon as he discovered this, he called out

"Help me! Help me!" But there was nothing more we could do.

Day and night, each time the machine gave him the power of a breath, he implored, "Help me, help me." His rhythmic cry permeated the ward. He barely slept. By the fourth day of his unceasing struggle, I not only agonized for him, but for the other patients and my staff.

We tried several times to see if he could breathe on his own but he couldn't. There was such damage to his upper spinal cord that he would never breathe independently again. Trying to ease his burden in any way possible, we finally placed him on a regular bed so that he could lie on his side, see more around him, and perhaps, I hoped, feel less isolated than he had on the Stryker, where he could see only the floor or the ceiling. We also took him off the Drager and placed him on a much quieter respirator that could be used while he was in a bed.

But he continued calling out, "Help me, help me."

Every day the neurosurgeon in charge of his case would look at his chart and say, "Let's give him another twenty-four hours." When those twenty-four hours were up, he'd say, "Well, let's give him another twenty four." After four days of this, there was no improvement in this young soldier's condition. And still, with each breath he cried out for us to do something.

Finally, his neurosurgeon came on the ward, reviewed the situation, and turned to me. "Nothing more can be done. Go ahead." He paused, looking down at the floor. Quietly, he gave me one last instruction. "Do what you can to help him." Then the doctor left.

Now we slowly reduced the rate of the breaths the machine would give him. He became sleepier, and although still responding and pleading for help, he was not in as much anguish. The breathing rate was gradually reduced until he lost consciousness and the machine was turned off.

I had seen so much suffering and violent loss that his quiet death represented a sort of peace. We all felt both profound sorrow and relief. He had died quietly. We no longer had to hear his cries for help-although I hear them still.

It was my job as head nurse to take care of everyone on the ward. If an order was given by a doctor to turn off a patient's respirator, it was my job, not anyone else's. It was under these circumstances that I learned to watch everyone and everything very carefully, not only my patients but also my staff. I had eight nurses and sixteen corpsmen and thirty patients. I made sure that no one was feeling too much despair or frustration or loss. Of course, I couldn't make it go away, but it was my job to see that my staff as well as my patients were taken care of.

I found over the weeks and months that when anyone died on the ward, I hated to have his face covered by a sheet. I thought it bad for morale because it was a symbol of failure. The sheet prevented those around the man from seeing the peacefulness of his death and excluded him (for I believed his soul was still present) from the humanity around him. Also, a part of me felt that if a man's face was not covered, maybe he was not really dead and there could, just possibly, be a miraculous recovery.

Although driven by feelings I knew to be irrational, I changed the ward policy. We cared for the dead soldier's body and prepared it to be picked up by Graves Registration as before, but would not cover his face until he had left the ward. And I preferred to care for the body of each dead soldier myself. This was my way of saying good-bye and of grieving for the loss of each life. I have continued that ritual through my clinical practice since Vietnam.

During the Tet Offensive of 1968 we received massive casualties. From January 30 to February 5 the hospital admitted 401 patients—taking in more than a hundred on February 1 alone. The operating rooms worked nonstop and surgeons were available to sew up only the most critical wounds. Therefore, the nursing staff took on some of the doctor's tasks, including suturing some patient's wounds. The ammunition dump was again attacked at Long Binh, producing explosions that went on for days. Everyone pulled together, working extra hours with intense commitment. For a healer, Vietnam during Tet was the best place to be, and the worst.

One of the most memorable events on the ward occurred with a young man named LeRoy. He had suffered a catastrophic head injury. Nearly half his brain had been destroyed. He also had a tracheotomy, an opening in his throat, which required re-exploration several times to keep his airway open. No one could be evacuated with skull fragments in the brain because there was too great a risk of developing brain abscessed from the bacteria, during the journey home if any pieces were still in the brain. So LeRoy had three separate operations to remove remaining bone fragments. His condition was so critical that he had been placed at the far end of the ward with those expected to die. But LeRoy didn't die. He survived for days, then weeks, breathing on his own, yet never responding in any way. After three weeks in and out of surgery, it was time for him to be evacuated out of Vietnam.

I believe that the sense of hearing is the last to go before death. So I went to tell LeRoy he was leaving Vietnam. Though he had not once responded to touch or voice, I bent down to him and said quietly, "LeRoy, we're going to get you ready to be evacuated to Japan." Suddenly he opened his one remaining eye and looked directly into mine. He had understood. Encouraged, I continued: "You'll first go to Japan, be there for a few days; then you'll be sent to a hospital close to home." With the one hand he could move, he gave me the high sign. I fought back tears of joy.

We all did. Here was one of those who were expected to die and yet because of his youth and vigor he survived to be evacuated. This taught me that even in the gravest situation there could be hope and healing.

It was in the neurosurgical ward that I fashioned the philosophy I still maintain. All that death, all of the maiming, all of the loss there has to be a greater good, but it cannot be found by looking back. Always look forward.

Working on these young men, trying to put the pieces back together, you can't allow yourself to imagine them as they were the moment before their injuries-the father, the son, the scholar, the athlete. You think of their lives beginning at the point of their devastating wounds. Then, any response is improvement and provides hope for tomorrow. You cannot get preoccupied in what might have been if this terrible brain damage had not occurred. That type thinking is futile for patients and for the staff.

My life's philosophy is based on the belief that there's always a purpose, always a way of adapting, of taking what you have and making the most of it. You can only find it by looking ahead. I did that after my divorce, and during my investigation and discharge by the Army. You cannot dwell on what might have been. Life begins now and goes forward from this point.

As our individual tours of duty came to an end, we developed what we called a short-timer's attitude. It lasted the entire last month before our departure date,

which for me was in May 1968. Although I continued to
work with the same intensity and commitment, I realize
in retrospect that I subconsciously began disengaging
from those I worked with. Our life together had been
so intense for over year, and now, suddenly, I would be
leaving and perhaps would never see these people again.
Camaraderie had developed among us of a depth that
can be reached only when people are in life-threatening
situation and survives together. There was no graceful
or gradual way to leave my colleagues and friends who
stayed behind to complete their tours. Inevitably, this
wrenching sense of separation and isolation continued
until my departure from Vietnam.

Harvey and I talked often and specifically about what
we'd do when we returned to the States. Several months
earlier, he had requested reassignment to Germany. It was
denied, and so he had decided to get out of the military.
That would allow us to settle down and begin building
our dream estate in Maple Valley. We also wanted to
have children. So, although I loved the military and knew
that having a child would automatically put a halt to my
career. I began my first pregnancy during my last months
in Vietnam. I stopped malaria pills in February to avoid
any risk of damaging the fetus. Tests verified that I was
pregnant but we kept that a secret from everyone but my
close colleagues and staff.

Just prior to our departure, my ward staff gave me
a farewell party and shower. The pink baby outfit later
proved to be the wrong color the infant, but I was deeply
touched. My favorite gift was from Clem Markarian, a
nurse on my ward. He knew that ever since my first days
in-country, when I had visited the Green Beret camp
and seen the beautiful crossbow and arrows made by
the Montagnard tribe, I had wanted one. So, during the
spring of 1968, he had taken helicopter from Bien Hoa

and flown two hundred miles to the mountainous region of Pleiku. 1t was a very hostile area, with lots of Viet Cong activity. Somehow he was able to obtain the bow and arrows as my farewell present. I will always remember his thoughtfulness and the risk he took in getting it. Today the crossbow and quiver of arrows hang above my fireplace.

As we said our goodbyes I was struck with what we had accomplished together. We were a committed team who relied upon one another's skills, strength, and devotion. Our particular ward received citations, I recommended many of my staff for Army Commendation Medals, and near the end of my tour, my commanding officer, LTC, Dr. Robert Lever, awarded me-as he did many others-the Bronze Star. But achievements like ours were common in the medical corps in Vietnam. Thousands of people served as I did, enduring loss and pain as I did. In the military we look the same, act the same, and, in many ways, experience the same. Each person I met and worked with gave me the gift of strength as they put issues of personal safety after the duty of caring for patients. It was an ethic we all shared.

But soon it was time to go to the airport and start our journey home. Toughened by the hardships of Vietnam, I was surprised how lonely and frightening it was to actually leave. Sad, eager, and anxious, Harvey and I waited at Bien Hoa Air Base for the plane that would take us out. The nearly 120-degree heat was nothing compared to the constant sound of rockets and rifle fire around the perimeter of the air base. We had a terrible feeling that we would be shot down just as we were taking off. We stood in line to climb up the stairs to get onto the charter plane that was to take us home. Walking up the stairs we felt like easy targets and wondered to each other if it would hurt when we got shot. Hearing rifle fire as I approached the cabin door, I rushed in and around the corner. Finally we were all safely settled in the plane. There were no instructions from the pilot, just a quick message that the takeoff would be rapid and abrupt. He asked us to bear with him, a request I was delighted to grant. As the plane taxied down the runway, I expected to feel a bullet or a shell halting our escape. It was by far the most rapid ascent I have ever experienced. No one said a word. No one breathed. We kept going straight up, until finally the airplane leveled off. We'd made it! Everyone took a breath, and then a roar went up in the cabin. One hundred and fifty soldiers cheered. We were on our way home.

But Vietnam was not that easy to leave. In many respects, I didn't really come home from Vietnam until one particular visit I made to the Wall in 1987.

There's something that happens at the Vietnam Memorial when you walk down into that slash of earth and black granite. It begins as you look at the names. Each name represents a life. A before but no after. For me, it is overwhelming because any one of them could have been a patient, and so the list represents all our failures.

On this visit, in 1987, I was there alone and in uniform. I'd recently been promoted to colonel but this was before my own investigation. Vietnam was still yesterday for me, so I wasn't really home yet. My war memories overwhelmed more recent events in my mind because of my unresolved feelings: I was proud because I'd been there as a healer, I felt guilt at having survived without physical pain, and I struggled with shame because we'd lost so many.

Before I went to the Wall itself, I headed to the tent for the POW/MIAs that stood on the grass to the side. I walked in, and sitting at a table there was a hardened, grungy old sergeant. He got up, came around the table, and stood before me.

Looking directly into my eyes, he said, "Welcome home."

Just those words, from this Vietnam vet who understood because he'd been there, and suddenly the facade that goes with being an officer, of being in control, left me. And finally, after so many years, the tears came.

"You know," he said, "it's okay. Colonels can cry, too." He put his arms around me and we wept together.

After that, I went back down to the Wall, glad to be alone. It was too much. How to understand the meaning of all the sacrifice? What had happened to my patients? Which of them were listed on this testament of devotion and loss? I will never know. And so I struggle with this feeling that I betrayed them. Not only did I fail to save them all; I don't even know their names.

Mother and me. It's 1942 in Nazi occupied Norway
when she used me as the gun running decoy

With my brother Jan Wilhelm in
traditional Norwegian dress, 1947

My first uniform. I'm fifteen years old, on the Arcade
Pontiac semi-professional fast-pitch softball team. 1957

Mother, me, brothers Tom and Jan W, father holding
Paal, at our home in Washington DC, 1959

Getting sworn in to the Army 1961

Receiving my 2nd Lt commission, with
Major Anna Cost, my recruiter, 1962

Hanging out with buddy, 2nd Lt. Virginia Lewis,
Camp Bullis, Fort Sam Houston Texas, 1963

With Harvey, just getting off the helicopter after
our wedding in Nuremberg, August 14, 1965.

Welcome to Vietnam during Tet Feb 1967, when the ammunition dump has been sabotaged and exploding.

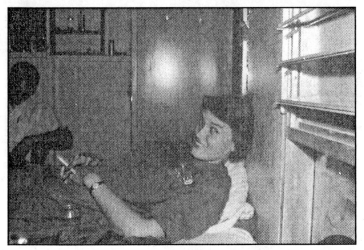

Resting in the hooch, VN 1967

24th Evacuation hospital and housing
for staff, 1968, Long Binh
(in foreground)

Awarded Bronze Star from hospital commander
LTC Robert Lever, Long Binh, 1968

Grethe & Matt 1969 Seattle Ferry

By 1977 Major Hawken had 4 sons

CHAPTER 7

. . . .

Perfect Life, Fragmented Person

Everything stopped. I held this helpless little creature who was also a part of me. It was almost as if we were both captured in time. Just the two of us. Immediately, I knew my world was no longer my own. Now that I was a mother, my life was trivial in comparison with this other, new person's existence.

. . . .

Harvey and I flew back from Vietnam together. Sitting in the plush seats of the airliner, we enjoyed our first-in-a-year fresh milk and talk and the sense it was over. But what was beginning eluded me—just as any understanding of what we'd been through eluded me. That would take years to capture. For now, I was happy to have gotten out of Vietnam alive. I felt the survivors' relief as well as guilt at feeling relieved. It seemed Harvey experienced the same thing.

We landed in New York. We were home, but I didn't feel at ease. Everyone spoke our language-and yet I felt out of place. Driving to my parents' home in Maryland, I knew there were no snipers on the road, no possibility that grenades would be thrown at us. Still I was on guard. I jumped at sudden sounds. A car backfiring made both of us flinch. And the approach of a traffic helicopter reminded me of the shapes and smells of maimed and broken bodies, the urgency of crisis. The fast-food restaurants we stopped at were friendly and filled with choices—but the choices now seemed frivolous. This world used to be ours. Just fourteen months before, I'd taken it for granted and enjoyed its routine pleasures. Now it gave a kind of offense. While in Vietnam, we'd counted the days until we could return. To this? Yes, to this. But it would take time to appreciate why.

My thoughts went back to all those soldiers still in Vietnam-going on patrols, plunging into tunnels, rushing through operating rooms. And yet now all around me the free people of America went on about their lives oblivious or disapproving of our sacrifice there. For the second time in my life, America felt alien.

One terrible truth about war is that it's more exciting than peacetime. When you're there, you want out of it. But when you get out, you miss the intensity. You're disoriented. The camaraderie is gone. If you've been a warrior, the trip back is almost impossible. For a year your job was to increase the body count, but now you return to a society where killing is unacceptable. To this day I see that struggle to come to terms, to come home, in some of my patients at the Veterans Hospital. Back then (1968), neither Harvey nor I had to make that horrible transition, because both our identities in Vietnam-Harvey's as a supply officer and mine as a healer-were transferable to peacetime society. But for the former warriors, the trip back was far more difficult. And all of us returning from Vietnam faced the challenge of rejoining a country in conflict over the war we had risked our lives in, and absorbed with concerns that seemed petty to us.

Fortunately, the welcome commotion of a family reunion brought us a respite. Harvey and I arrived in Maryland and were immediately drawn into rowdy conversations with my brothers. During my time in Vietnam, I'd received very few letters from them-Jan had written once, and Tom and Paal had sent only occasional notes. We'd become distant after I moved away to college, then went to Germany and got married. But now we all felt a bit more precious to each other, I think. Both Jan and Tom, my two older brothers, were quick-witted and playful. They didn't let me pull any older-and-wiser-sister posturing on them. Paal, a very polite nine-year-old, helped serve guests and, just as we had done as kids, kept track of those who had had the most drinks.

Jan had fallen in love and married a wonderful woman, Kit, while I was overseas. Now I got to meet and enjoy the person that had filled the one letter he had managed to write me; bright, tough, and matched Jan's humor barb for barb. We caught up on all relationships-Tom was the gentle clown of the family, and Paal, who I barely knew, was eager to hear tales of war.

My parents were thankful for our safe return, but kept their distance from us. They didn't ask questions or offer advice. I suspect absorbed with their own flashbacks to another time, another war. Harvey and I, though polite, were not talkative. A few times my mother commented that we seemed always on guard, and carried a tension we hadn't had before. She didn't say it critically—it was a compassionate observation. She'd been in a war. She knew it would take time for us to feel safe again.

One evening my parents invited their friends to a homecoming party for us. We were asked to show our slides of Vietnam. Everyone got their hors d'oeuvres and drinks, settled into chairs to watch and listen. Harvey turned on the projector and we began. But the images did not capture the real horrors of poverty and war. These were just pictures. Our audience couldn't see how the living were maimed and they couldn't feel the silence of the neuro ward. They didn't see the children searching through garbage heaps for food, the civilian huts made out of aluminum beer cans discarded by Americans, the fields where crops were replaced by bomb craters.

My parents' friends asked questions. Looking back, I realize they were innocent enough inquiries. Yet, at the time, they angered Harvey and me. When someone asked, "Did the civilians want you to be there?" I felt impatient and irritated. I wanted to yell, "Americans were dying because the Vietnamese asked us to be there." That's what I believed to be true. But here, in the States, the newspapers doubted that reasoning, and some of these people accepted that view. I wanted to say to them, "If you weren't there, we can't teach you." But I didn't. I was polite and became very quiet, and though my mother changed the subject and made everyone feel comfortable, she could tell I was upset.

Harvey and I seemed to feel the same way. Being in Vietnam and returning together gave us a deeper bond. Now we said to each other it was us against the world. Only we (and our military friends scattered around the country) truly understood the necessity for the war. It would take almost twenty years for me to question that view.

Though not an easy visit, it was a good one. My family distracted me a little from the confused and sad feelings left over from Vietnam. At first, I prided myself on how easily and well Harvey and I were adjusting to this culture shock. But I had to admit that as I encountered questions about the war by misinformed friends and relatives, I became abrupt and distant. My jumpiness continued. Out shopping or walking, I found myself scanning the surroundings as if expecting an attack. My responses were more suitable for Saigon than suburban Washington, D.C. Finally I realized that our return from Vietnam would take more than a plane trip and a reunion dinner.

But we were fortunate. Though they asked questions we found painfully uninformed, my family and their friends respected us and our service to our country. Harvey and I never suffered the rejection or criticism that many veterans endured when returning to the country that had sent them in harm's way. We were met only with well-meaning ignorance. But that itself was alienating and a shock.

Increasingly, antiwar demonstrators around the country were taking to the streets. The music we came back to was more cynical than what we'd left, the drugs more prevalent, the hair longer and dirtier, the language more obscene.

What saved us, I think, was our property. The eight acres of trees and creeks we'd bought prior to leaving for Vietnam was there, waiting for us in a corner of the Pacific Northwest.   Our memories of it were idyllic. While we were in Vietnam, we treasured the letters from our real-estate agent with news of the goings-on in the community and maps to help us plan. Our land served as the repository for our dreams all through the months in Long Binh, and now we were free to begin building our perfect life.

After a couple of weeks on the East Coast, we drove cross-country to Washington State in our Porsche. In Germany we'd traded in my Karmann Ghia and Harvey's VW hatchback and bought our first Porsche. Even with the added cost of shipping it to the States, when we return to Fort Lee, Virginia, the car was much less expensive to purchase in Germany. When Harvey was ultimately deployed to Vietnam, he traded in the car for a new one we'd pick up when we got back from the war.

Driving to our property in our new toy, Harvey was happy and excited. I was miserable. Now my pregnancy was giving me a first-hand education on what a woman endures to have a child. I was ill constantly, in part due to morning sickness though I also suffered from motion sickness. The only thing that helped in any way was eating. So I ate or slept for the entire trip, missing much of the scenery.

Our destination was Maple Valley, Washington. A small, still-rural community twenty miles southeast of Seattle, it served as a forested buffer between the more industrial town of Renton, home to Boeing, and the beginning of the foothills of the Cascade mountains. This part of the country was ruled by water, and that comforted my Norwegian soul.

To the west, Puget Sound served as a saltwater passage to the Pacific Ocean and hugged the downtown perimeter of Seattle. On the east edge of that city, forty-mile-long Lake Washington provided a serene border of clean, deep water. The entire area nestled in a rich valley between the Olympic and Cascade mountain ranges. The high peaks trapped clouds, forcing them to release their water before they could travel on. So it rained or drizzled a lot—feeding the great forests and myriad rivers that wove through the largely undeveloped land. One of those rivers had a small tributary that meandered through our property, down through Renton, and eventually on to Lake Washington.

Our journey back to our place, which had begun almost a year and a half before, ended on an early summer day in May 1968. We followed that tributary of water up to our land, got out of the car at the county road, and started walking. We'd finally arrived. Here we would create our future: a homestead, a family, and a farm.

The land was just as we'd left it. We made our way to the rise of a knoll in the center of the property. From here you could see the surrounding terrain on every side. Forty-five miles to the south, Mount Rainier arched its white and craggy way into the sky. This was the exact place we had decided-during the evenings of planning in our hooch in Vietnam-to build our house. We stood there, silent, surveying what we owned. To Harvey it was beautiful in its starkness. And to me it was beautiful, but only in its possibilities. Looking at the second-growth Douglas fir and scrub alder trees, the blackberries and swampy marsh where the small creek dribbled into a web of cloudy pools, I thought it was a mess. But it was our mess. And both of us saw in these untouched acres our solution. Here we wouldn't need the world, only each other: there were the pastures for the cattle we would raise for our own food, the creek that we'd divert and enlarge into a pond to stock with fish that we'd catch, the rich soil reclaimed from the marsh for our own gardens and vineyards. In the center of it all was the ridge of land where we'd build our large house for our soon-to-be-large family.

Vietnam was here with us, too. It was in our desire to go it alone, in our need to get back to the land, and in our belief that we could do anything we set our minds to. We felt invincible. We'd survived the war. We could handle anything. It would be a perfect life. Harvey and I loved work, loved challenge, and loved to impress the world with our accomplishments. And we loved the land. It would provide continuity. But since it was only land-raw, untouched-we couldn't live there just yet. We had to excavate for the septic tank and install the pipes, gravel, and pump for the drain field. We needed to dig the ditches to run from the country road up four acres to the building site. Only then could we put on a singlewide trailer that would be our home during the planning and construction of the structure itself.

We were doing all the work ourselves, and it would take us a few months to get these basic systems in place. With great generosity, Leona and Howard Hawken, Harvey's parents, took us in while we made our property habitable.

We had few possessions, so our move into Leona and Howard's basement was achieved quickly. The only certainties in our lives now were our land and our child, who was due in November. That gave us seven months to get ready for the baby.

On returning to the States, Harvey got out of the military. The decision had taken years. In Germany, he had begun to question whether he would make the Army his career. His decision to leave the service had come partly out of his yearning for home. He said he'd take any job at all if only he could live in the Pacific Northwest. At the time, I was preoccupied with our status as officers and was rather snobbishly appalled to hear him even joke about stepping down in position, but that's how much the Northwest meant to him. With the constant rotation of active duty, he knew that he couldn't rely on being stationed at home for any length of time. So when he was stationed in Germany he had begun the process of separating from the military by requesting a branch transfer from the combat arm, Armor, to the Supply and Service Corps. Harvey's initial obligation incurred when he was on the ROTC scholarship at the University of Washington. With his three years of active duty that obligation was fulfilled. He also reverted from being a potential career officer to an indefinite status whereby he could leave the military at any time. When we were assigned to Vietnam, all those decisions about remaining in the military were put on hold.

As his tour in Vietnam came to an end, Harvey requested reassignment to Germany. Despite his yearning for home, from our vantage point in Vietnam and looking back at our previous experience at Fort Lee, we knew we did not want to endure another stateside assignment. But overseas you represented America in a foreign land, and particularly during the Cold War, with tensions so high between the Communist countries and the Western democracies, there was a sense of military anticipation and purpose. Additionally, after experiencing the life-and-death responsibilities of serving in a combat zone, we knew that stateside duty would be a boring and mundane repetition of "everything by the book." In a peacetime Army, people are more easily bored and get caught up in petty bureaucracies and protocol, and we didn't want our lives limited that way. However, Harvey's request for reassignment to Germany was denied. So he decided to resign his commission and end his military career.

On our return, Harvey left the Army and was happy to be out. But what next? His B.A. had been in forestry, and he decided to get a master's in forest products. He was accepted for graduate school at the University of Washington, to begin in the fall of 1968. Until then, he was pleased to have the summer to throw himself totally into working on the property.

I was still on active duty and was assigned to Madigan Army Medical Center in Fort Lewis, near Tacoma, Washington. My separation from the military would occur in six months, or one month before my baby was due. Unlike Harvey, I wanted to stay in the military. However, that was impossible because of the regulation that said, in effect, motherhood was incompatible with military service.

I had been slated to be head nurse of the intensive-care unit at Madigan. When I arrived for duty and informed them I was pregnant and my days in the military were numbered, they were not happy. They reassigned me as assistant supervisor for evenings and nights-the "ramp tramp." Each night I walked the seven and a half miles of corridors to check all twenty wards in the hospital. It was my responsibility to make sure everybody got to work and there were no major problems with either staff or patients. After making a rounds of one ward and its staff, I then went on to the next ward and made the same analysis. A glorified messenger and a jack-of-all-trades, I was also the person to oversee any crisis during the night and was on a paging system that notified me of any emergency.

In many respects, it was a good job to have after the intensity of Vietnam because it allowed me to keep some professional distance. I managed staff and wrote reports. My removal from direct-care duties became even more important than I first realized. As I settled to my new job, it was obvious (and worrisome to me) that I had changed rather dramatically on returning to the States.

The remoteness and irritability that I'd struggled with in Maryland after returning from Vietnam, continued. And now I had it even at work. It was so unlike me. Never had I been easily angered or frustrated–not as a nurse or officer in any of my positions before or during Vietnam. But now, suddenly, I had a very short fuse for dealing with trivia like paperwork, military protocol, and filling out reports. This "living under the flagpole" as we called it in the military–the constant jumping through 'stupid bureaucratic hoops' to do a simple task–felt like a waste of valuable time and talent. I had just spent fourteen months dealing with life-and-death decisions, never needing a doctor's order to provide routine patient care. The stateside pre-occupation with trivia drove me wild.

Throughout the hospital I saw that regulations as well as traditional roles and practices prevented nurses from doing their jobs efficiently and well. If a patient asked for an aspirin at two o'clock in the morning, the physician had to be called for authorization, which course caused the doctor to be quite annoyed at being awakened at such an unearthly hour. Yet patients who needed or demanded something always went to the nurse to complain. We were caught from every angle. The nurse caused every problem identified by the patient, the physician, the housekeeper, and the family. At every turn, I felt that whenever anybody in the hospital needed someone to dump on, the nurse was the recipient of that impulse.

These were very uncharacteristic feelings for me. In the past, I always found solutions to frustrations at work and believed that getting angry was allowing myself to be victimized. But now, none of that helped. I was often angry, and though I tried desperately not to show my feelings, they still surfaced. Why had I changed? What was different? How could I reclaim my even-tempered self? It was a painful mystery to me until some colleagues came to my assistance.

Other nurses who had preceded me home from Vietnam had had similar experiences adjusting. They explained it wasn't the present that was making me so upset; it was the after-effects of Vietnam. One colleague in particular, Major Mary Kuhn, was helpful. She had been back for over a year. I told her how difficult it was not to get angry at physicians, at patients, and how I was not typically like that. She assured me that all I was experiencing was the normal transition to peacetime duty. She saw it in every nurse who returned from

Vietnam, and had felt it herself also. The key to recovery was to settle down and try to reclaim civilian priorities- which in nursing meant dropping back into a more subservient role. In a combat hospital, the nurses were trained and expected to do much more. In Vietnam the doctors often joked that their job—when they weren't doing surgery—was to come around and ask the nurses what they'd already done so that the physicians could write the orders for those procedures after-the-fact. But back home we had to forget all that. We had to get back to the civilian or peacetime way of doing things, where nurses' jobs were very restricted. Major Kuhn told me it was a process that took about six months to get through. She called it a recovery phase (this was years before the concept of post-traumatic stress disorder, and there was no regular counseling or assistance to returning vets to help with our reentry). Her advice helped, but I still found the daily stupidities of hospital protocol and the societal role of nurses burdensome.

Perhaps our reentry was more difficult because, in those days, we didn't discuss whether we'd served in the war. We felt that sooner or later everybody in uniform was going to go and there was nothing special to talk about. It was just one of your rotations. In the military everybody takes a turn. So instead of sharing what we'd experienced, we kept it all in, tried to repress the memories, grieved alone.

Madigan received a number of casualties from Vietnam. They were primarily patients with amputations, on the orthopedic ward. Because we didn't talk about the war, we didn't share the camaraderie that we do now when we Vietnam vets meet. Then our memories were still too raw. As nurses we felt, "We've made it back on our own two feet, while many of these poor guys didn't." Just that. When patients with fresh wounds arrived, we couldn't give one another emotional support because we were all so needy.

Juggling these adjustments to peacetime life, working every spare moment on our property, Harvey and I failed as good houseguests at his parents. During that summer of 1968, living in his parents' basement, we didn't offer to help our hosts or attempt to fit in with their expectations. We told ourselves that their home was "just" a place to eat and sleep. But those were rather essential activities, and we, in our selfish immaturity, took them for granted. When Leona told us we couldn't smoke in the house, we were insulted—completely insensitive to her needs and how offensive smoking could be in someone else's home. Harvey and I had few possessions, so we didn't appreciate their value to others. After a day digging, raking, and hauling in the mud, rock and brush, we tracked in a trail of dirt on their lovely carpet, oblivious to the damage we caused. Leona was working as a middle-school counselor, had her own job and family to manage, and here she was suddenly dealing with two twenty-six-year-old kids camped out in her basement. Considering how obnoxious we were, she was very gracious during our three-month intrusion.

The moment we announced our water lines were in and working, Leona said brightly, "Well, then, it's time for you to move out." She'd had enough. But we weren't ready for this gentle suggestion that we leave, and again felt quite offended. Now I cringe at our audacity and thoughtlessness. Fortunately, it didn't cause any lasting strain in our relationship.

We moved to our own place feeling put-upon because we had to leave at least forty-eight hours before we were ready. We'd bought a ten-by-fifty-foot trailer and placed it on the area behind the knoll where our house would be built. The trailer was new, nice and fresh—I'd never lived in a place that was new before. It had that wonderful raw smell of glue and new carpet. It was special because it was ours, and we were determined to keep it spotless.

From the first day, Harvey and I rigorously set out to make our place perfect. Entering the trailer, we took off our shoes, and so did guests. We built a porch and an overhang to provide an entry from the ever-present rain. I raked muddy, rocky acres into gentle, smooth slopes for our surrounding lawns. From our windows we could appreciate the slow but daily progress: another ten yards of blackberries cleared, another two dozen trees planted along the driveway, another lump of muck turned into a bed of ivy. It might be just a trailer now, but we treated it like a mansion.

Harvey and I worked very well together. My pregnancy slowed me down a little as the summer turned into fall–I raked more than hauled or lifted. Otherwise, we shared equally in our tasks. I can remember only one major disagreement during this time.

One of our few possessions was a TV that we'd bought in Vietnam. It became Harvey's companion during my evening shifts at the hospital. I'd come home after work at one-thirty in the morning, and he would be installed in front of the TV. I'd worked all day at the property, then gone to Madigan, and come back exhausted, and he'd want me to watch television. His addiction got so bad; he hardly acknowledged my presence when I came in at night. If I tried to talk to him, share a bit about my day, he would get annoyed. How dare I interrupt his TV? It got progressively worse–he began to turn it on and sit before it during the day, and this, when we had so much to get done, finally drove me to complain. One Saturday I told him with uncommon intensity, "I wish the damn thing would explode." He was quite surprised, but couldn't rouse himself from his chair. The next day, while the TV was on but he was outside, it didn't exactly explode, it sort of whimpered and went dead. Delighted, I told him the TV had blown up. He gave me a peculiar look that said, "Did you do something to it?" I went on about my chores, smiling. It broke the pattern for him. And after a few days of wonderful peace and quiet, we jointly decided not to get it fixed or replaced.

That was the summer of 1968. We didn't get another TV until 1979. For eleven years, we didn't watch news, sitcoms, dramas, or sports. And working several jobs, living in the country, raising children, we didn't go to movies, listen to the radio, and subscribe to magazines or newspapers. We withdrew, dedicating ourselves to our family and land, going outside to the world only to do jobs that enabled us to support our idyllic isolation in the country.

We missed a lot. Perhaps that's what we wanted. Of course we had a vague awareness of the antiwar demonstrations. But something in us, possibly set in motion by our unresolved feelings about the war, wanted isolation from all that. It meant we also missed the reexamining of women's roles and the growth of the feminist movement in the late 1960s and '70s, as well as the environmental movement and the slowly emerging activism for homosexual rights. At least on the surface it would appear that we missed all that. But no. Our quarantine of the news of social upheaval ultimately failed. The changes in roles and values of the 1970s that caused a shudder throughout American society-captured in part by the decade's popular cliché' "getting in touch with yourself"-would eventually confront us too.

If everyone else was getting in touch with their feelings, Harvey and I were getting things done. My baby was due in November (1968). We had all the major projects underway on our property and were prepared for the winter rains and occasional snow as parenthood approached.

On September 30, 1968, after seven years as an enlisted woman and officer, I was separated from the military. Harvey lasted in graduate school for six weeks. The content of his classes seemed irrelevant to him, and the jobs he envisioned this degree would allow him to pursue didn't really inspire him. He'd gone into the master's program in Forest Products because it seemed a logical progression from his undergraduate work. But his real talent and interest had been more captured by landscape design and construction. He was very unhappy reading and writing about trees. When he was assigned a research paper on the prickly pear (a type of tree), it reached a point of no return. Just months before he'd been working in Vietnam with half-million-dollar budgets, with equipment and men, and now he had to pretend a particular pear was important. He was frustrated. His unhappiness was so profound, I readily agreed he should leave school and explore other careers. He did, and for the next year, embarked on a series of self-employment situations, the longest lasting of which was selling cleaning products.

In fact, Harvey was on one of his cleaning-products presentations the night I went into labor. I was home alone when I began to have a few funny feelings in my uterus. I thought, "Gee, I don't know if this is something..." Then, all of a sudden, there was this gush, and even though I'd never experienced it, I knew my "bag of waters" had just broken and I was going into labor. So I took a shower, packed a few things, and lay down on the couch with a towel under me just in case there was more fluid coming. Not knowing how long it would go on, I waited for Harvey. It was eleven at night. The definitely labor-like feelings continued, but I thought I could wait until

Harvey's return, which I assumed would be any minute. But Harvey didn't get home till two in the morning. The moment he walked in the door, absolutely exhausted, I said, "We've got to go to Madigan" (the Army hospital). He looked at me as if he were about to collapse, then drove me to the hospital. He began the fifty-minute trip driving a little too fast, until I asked him to slow down, which he did. By the time we arrived the contractions were about five minutes apart.

Since this was my first pregnancy, the doctors at the hospital decided to give me a spinal block to relieve some of my discomfort and also gave me a painkiller. I felt spacey but still in pain. At one point Major Hersey, one of the supervisors I'd worked with at Madigan when I was on Active Duty, came in on her rounds and sweetly asked me how things were going. In my now-not-very-collected state, I wanted to tell her, "Well, what do you think? I'm in agony here!" Thankfully, I was able to keep my mouth shut—out of the military, even in labor, it would not have been appropriate for me to talk like that to my former superior officer. Then I remembered my own experience years before as a young nurse in OB (obstetrics), judgmentally dismissing women in labor as "wimps." As I suffered on the table in that delivery room, I wanted to call out to my younger self and implore, "This really does hurt!" If I hadn't been suffering so much, I would have laughed at myself. I never had pain like that before. It was very difficult to keep control, but I didn't want to be a wimp. The medication I'd received dis-inhibited me, as it was supposed to, so it was hard to control myself and not cry out. A moan did escape me now and then.

The contractions seemed to slow down and it looked as if it would be some time before I actually delivered, so I told Harvey to go home and get some sleep. I was very pragmatic-he was exhausted and I could handle this. He turned around and went back to Maple Valley and bed.

Just after he left, the nurses noted that the baby had reacted badly to the medication I had been given and to the caudal anesthesia. The baby was in fetal distress. They medicated me with Pitocin to accelerate labor and finally had to use forceps to help bring him out. I anxiously waited for the baby's cry. As soon as I heard his wail, I knew he was okay.

They cleaned him up and put him in my arms. Up to that moment, this nine-month process had been an ordinary obligation or, when I was particularly uncomfortable, a nuisance. I disliked being pregnant. I resented what it did to my body and how it interfered with my activities. But now, when I held my son for the first time, all of those feelings fell away. Here was this precious new life. And we were profoundly connected. It was an experience completely unlike anything I'd ever known. There is only one word for what I felt: awe.

Of course, those first minutes after delivery he was ugly, but then I thought, "He is mine, how could he be ugly?" I tried to call Harvey to tell him what a beautiful baby we had, but he was asleep and didn't answer. Next, I phoned my mother in Maryland. It was one of the few times since I'd left home that I'd wished she wasn't so far away. She greeted my news warmly and told me that my father was also delighted I had a healthy son.

The baby was put in the nursery and I was given a room down the hall. The hospital was quiet and the hallways empty. Still, I couldn't sleep. I got up and walked before I should have. Even though, as a nurse, I should have known better, I thought the usual precautions didn't apply to me. I was tougher than other women. But the sensation in my legs wasn't back, so I almost passed out when I got up and started down the hall. Still, I was dying to have a cigarette and go to the bathroom. On my way, I went to the nursery and looked in at him. Again, I felt that this was something extraordinary-not a routine event. Not at all. It was so outside of anything I'd ever experienced, I couldn't believe this had really happened. I kept going back and forth throughout the night just to peek in: to look, to see if he was real.

When I held him and fed him in the morning, I felt I had received a gift of love. Here was this totally helpless creature who needed me.

My life had changed.

By midmorning I was able to get Harvey on the phone, and he returned to the hospital to meet his son. He was equally delighted and proud.

We had two major differences of opinion about our son and child rearing. In both cases, I did something unusual. I stood up to Harvey.

The first involved naming the baby. Harvey insisted we continue his family's tradition of giving male children forenames beginning with H, so that their initials would be HHH. We had not found a name we both liked that began with H. For days, the baby had no name. Finally, I asserted my view (I thought the whole thing silly, but wouldn't say that). I said, "It's really a shame to name a kid just for the initials." Harvey relented. We named our son Matthew, after the best man at our wedding. It was a major victory. I rarely confronted Harvey, though here, with an important decision, I'd stated my case and won.

The next disagreement concerned breast-feeding. Harvey believed it was the mother's unquestioned responsibility to breast-feed. My upbringing and style was to bottle-feed. Harvey was adamant, insisting I do it the "natural" way. Now, with the hungry child in my arms, our philosophical disagreement took on a more urgent tone. I was tired, the baby was crying, Harvey was demanding I not use a bottle. Irritated, I told him, "If you want to breast-feed, you do it. I'm not going to." That ended our argument. Later, after resting, I was able to discuss it more rationally. Again, I departed from our normal dynamic. I stood my ground, explaining that if I breast-fed the baby, Harvey would never see either one of us because it was a very private matter and I wasn't about to do it in public. I'd take the baby and go into my room, and Harvey would be excluded from any involvement in feeding. It was difficult for him to accept my strong feelings, believing as he did that a mother must follow certain rules. He unhappily relented, realizing he had no real control over the issue.

Another rule that Harvey believed defined motherhood was that the mother must not have a job outside the home. For the first nine months after Matt was born, I stayed home, devoting all my time and energy to the property and the baby. It was a challenge learning about being a parent. We weren't very social-in part, because I didn't want to expose my infant to any germs, and I wasn't too eager for people to visit for the same reason. Too rigid and protective, I also sterilized everything that Matt came in contact with until it occurred to me that children were successfully raised long before human beings knew about sterilization. When I stopped running my house like an intensive-care unit, Matt continued to survive—in fact, he was quite healthy. It must have been the daily cod-liver oil.

From the beginning, I spoke only Norwegian to him. It seemed right. He would be introduced to half his heritage and become bilingual just by my talking to him. It was a practice I employed with each of my sons, though initially Harvey's mother was unhappy about it she came to be very proud of her bilingual grandchildren.

And yet, poor Matt. He was our first child. We were both fresh out of the military, and we made sure this little fellow knew discipline, order, proper behavior. He had to be perfect—like everything else in our lives. I also felt that children were brought into an existing family and became part of it; the entire family was not supposed to be turned upside-down just because there was a new baby around. So, we had strict rules around our house. Matt was raised as a military kid.

During that first winter, we were snowed-in a few times, and both Harvey and I loved the quiet isolation-just our family, secure and alone on our place. That feeling was short-lived, however. Harvey had a series of jobs that didn't work out. Primarily, they were pyramid-style businesses-like Amway-that promised independence and wealth if he invested his own money and time. He did, working long hours and draining our bank account, but money just wasn't coming back in. Our finances became increasingly meager and unstable. Soon Harvey developed a bleeding stomach stress ulcer. Now his rule that as a mother I was not to work outside the home seemed crazy. He had an ulcer. We had no money and I wanted to work. My frustration at abandoning both the military and nursing made me grouchy and resentful. It was a waste of my education not to work, particularly when Harvey was ill. Around the house, I was ill tempered, which I didn't like any more than Harvey.

Harvey finally acquiesced. Almost a year after Matt's birth, in October 1969, I began working two nights a week as a night-duty nurse at a rural hospital in Snoqualmie, at the base of the Cascade mountains, twenty miles north of our home. I was delighted to go back to nursing, even if it was the most rudimentary kind of work. I was doing what I cared about: helping patients, using my skills and training, contributing to our family's financial health. At the time, I never dreamed this job would ultimately take Harvey and me in opposite directions.

Soon after I began nursing again, Harvey's fortunes changed for the better. He passed the exam for the Washington State Patrol and began his training as a cadet. It was an excellent choice for him, as the culture and duties of the job were similar in many ways to those of the military. It offered structure, order, discipline, and fast cars. The only drawback was a requirement that after his academy training he would be stationed in Chehalis, 120 miles south of our home. He came home to work on the property on his days off, which didn't necessarily correspond to mine. The career opportunity made it a necessary sacrifice.

When Harvey moved down to Shelton to begin cadet training, parenting was my primary responsibility. To accommodate my schedule at the hospital, I would take Matt to his grandmother's on my way to work each night. He'd sleep there, and I'd drive the hour to the hospital, work my shift, then, in the early morning, drive back to pick up Matt and bring him to our mobile home. Once he was safely in his room with the gate up, I'd take a nap. The days were filled with chores on the land and playing with the baby. Because our income was limited, we cleared the land ourselves-chopping down acres of blackberry bushes and other scrub vegetation. We dug up boulders and rocks, preparing the soil for Harvey's ambitious landscaping. We shaped and planted the pastures, dug ponds and made the small creeks feed into them. Life had a quieter rhythm. Pleased to be working again, happy with my child, and rewarded by the steady progress on the property, I felt my testiness disappear.

In early 1971, I changed employers and moved to a new position at the Veterans Hospital in Seattle. I was still on part-time night duty, though working with more responsibilities.   Now I was working on a combined medical and surgical, ear, nose, and throat, and research-and-rehabilitation unit. I was also back with military expatriates. This was more to my liking than the unfamiliarity of obstetrics and civilians at the hospital in Snoqualmie.

At one point I injured my back moving a bedridden patient. During my medical evaluation I had several X rays and was given muscle relaxants to control the muscles spasms. I didn't know I was pregnant. When I found out, I was in turmoil. I knew there was a chance the X-rays and medications might cause damage to the fetus since it was such an early stage of pregnancy.

Abortions had just been legalized under some circumstances in Washington State, and a few clinics were doing them. Harvey was still in Chehalis, so we discussed this on the phone and he understood my concerns. There was no definitive way to determine whether the fetus was malformed, but there was a possibility. It was a terrible dilemma.

With sadness, and concern because I didn't know what I should do, I sought medical advice regarding having an abortion. I went to a physician who listened to my history and my fears. He condescendingly told me, "Women have had X-rays and been on medications for eons. Don't worry about it, the fetus will be just fine."

Still, I knew there was a risk of fetal abnormality, and my concerns persisted. A few days later, I started bleeding. I had another decision to make: I could put my feet up, go to bed, and try to keep this spontaneous abortion from happening, or I could continue with my plans for a shopping trip to Portland. I got in the car and drove to Oregon, did my errands, and drove back. When I got home that evening, I aborted. This confirmed my suspicion that there was something wrong with the fetus.

Believing things happen as they are supposed to, and for the best, I felt relief—but a tremendous sense of loss.

I was really enjoying working again, even just part time. Soon an opportunity came that enabled me to work full-time. My aunt, Aagot, was searching for a new living and working arrangement. In her mid-fifties, she was at a transition point in her life. Aagot was an independent, bright, accomplished woman who always pursued fascinating jobs that took her to new cultures and new places. She'd never married, happily insisting, "I'd rather be a hobo." But this hobo did remarkable things. She was trained as a Montessori teacher and later as a laboratory technician—a choice of career influenced by the fact that the Norwegian government paid for that training if you were the daughter of a doctor. After World War II she worked for her brother-in-law (my father) in his laboratory, but soon wanted to do more than create slides and collate data.

After a series of unsatisfying jobs in America she began working in Montreal in the 1950's with Dr. Roy Swank, a prominent neurologist and specialist in multiple sclerosis. Dr. Swank focused on the role of nutrition in slowing and reducing the severity of the exacerbations of this debilitating disease. Aagot, as his assistant, helped their patients maintain a stringent low-fat diet. As this treatment modality gained support, Aagot traveled throughout the world collecting statistics, researching diets in cultures with a low incidence of MS, and following up with patients. When Dr. Swank moved his clinic from Montreal to Portland, Oregon, she went with him. But by 1963 she got the itch to travel again and, joining the Peace Corps where she worked with a health group in Colombia.

During her years in Portland, she regularly traveled for vacations to the Oregon coast, and bought a lot in

Lincoln City, on which she one day hoped to build a home and retire. When she returned from the Peace Corps, she didn't yet have the financial means to do retire. She'd been living at my parents in Maryland and working in childcare as a nanny. However, she and my father didn't see eye-to-eye on a number of things, including her drinking, and Aagot wanted out of that contentious situation. She then moved to Lincoln City to start the building of her retirement home, but she still needed to earn and save more before she could comfortably retire. So we asked her to come live with us and help with Matt and developing our property.

Aagot arrived in Maple Valley in July 1971. She shared a bedroom with Matt. Though the trailer was getting crowded, we noticed it less because we were working outside as much as we could.

I was delighted to have her join our homesteading project. Vigorous, curious, and devoted to children, Aagot worked in every capacity. Her presence also encouraged me to practice our mutual Norwegian language and culture. Aagot and I divided the chores. We must have picked millions of rocks together. She and I were equally obsessive about every project we took on. We'd dig rocks out of the acres around the house site, and rake, pick and rake some more, hour after hour until the land was smooth.

Both Aagot and I are devotees of sunbathing-Norwegians always are. As soon as the clouds parted, we'd strip off our clothes and let the sun bake and brown us as we picked raspberries, mowed the lawns, and then skinny-dipped in the ponds. Just in case anyone approached from the distant road, we carried sack dresses over our tools to throw on in a flash.

Aagot lived with us for six years, and the birth of three more sons. We were two generations of Norwegian women, brown and happy, the children at our feet, planting grass, ivy, and seedlings. And always, as the family grew, the planting, building, farming, cooking, and cleaning all revolved around the boys. Norwegians often have extended-family networks like that. With Aagot's presence, Harvey and I could both pursue careers while raising our sons.

In the late fall of 1971, Harvey returned home from his two years as a cadet and living in Chehalis. It was a difficult adjustment for me—eased, I suspect, because I had been working full-time night duty at the VA hospital since Aagot had arrived.

Harvey's work schedule, as a State Patrol Trooper, rotated between days and nights. With each of us on nights and rotating schedules our time together was reduced. But even so, I missed my autonomy. I had loved being alone with Matt, being the primary parent, cook, and farmhand. Looking back, I see that I didn't miss Harvey during the years he was away. But when Harvey moved home—well, it was difficult. Not that I said anything. These were dangerous feelings-and didn't fit into my utopian vision of a perfect family and farm. Since there wasn't tension with Harvey—in part, perhaps, because we rarely saw each other-and we had so much to accomplish to get our house built, we again put our relationship on hold.

I took on more work, nurtured my son, and got spiritual sustenance from the land. Now that Harvey was home, he, too, put all his extra time and energy into completing the plans for our house and shaping the surrounding acreage. On the few days we had off together, we drove around and looked at houses on the market to get ideas for our own. At the same time, Harvey was completing the landscaping-he didn't want to begin building the house until he was happy with the basic design of the land around it.

He wasn't just planting—he was reshaping the terrain. And he was a perfectionist. The main feature of his elaborate landscape design was a series of ponds connected by the creek. A bulldozer dug the first crude shapes; then Harvey finished the contours by hand. It took months of hard labor. The areas surrounding the water were to be sloping lawns punctuated with stands of trees and rhododendrons. After the scrub and rocks were removed, and the dirt was raked, Harvey felt the areas still were not smooth enough to plant the grass. So he took an old, full-size mattress spring, tied a wheelbarrow full of rocks on top of it for weight, then attached a body harness—one end to the bedspring and the other around his waist and over his shoulders—and dragged it across the land. I asked him not to abuse his back and hips like that, but he said this was the only way he could get the land as level as he wanted it. When complete, the lawns were beautiful. Though he never complained, his back and hip problems increased, and he eventually required surgery to relieve some of the pain.

In 1971 the military regulation forbidding women with dependents from serving in the military, that had caused my separation in 1968, was changed. I knew I would resume my military career. But should I go back on active duty or join the Army Reserves?

The more I worked in the civilian world, the more I realized how stifling the active military could be in terms of ingenuity, growth, change. It's a system that prides itself on its traditions: rigid, aggressive, and male-dominated. Because it doesn't tolerate change easily, women have had a difficult time breaking the barriers. Superiors are entrenched in their positions of power. The status quo is protected and perpetuated.

I questioned whether it would be healthy to be in that confined world again both in my thinking and in my actions. When I was younger, I loved and needed that outside direction. But now on active duty I would lose all say in my professional and personal choices. I would not only be told what kind of work to do but through rotation of assignments, I'd be told where to live. And, too, when I studied the different roles the military played in a changing world I questioned as never before.

I saw that the Reserve Forces contributed tremendously, despite the fact they were not in a full-time military setting. With the Active-duty forces, the federal government is sponsoring a day camp for the million people that are in the ranks except when we are at war. The soldiers in Armor Corps get their toys and play war. They shoot at one another, and the worst thing that can happen is that there is a tragic accident. The rest of the time they're learning the game of war. It's a little bit like playing cowboys and Indians, only now the toys are bigger and more expensive. This situation has evolved since World War II, when there was a real need to protect our country. Preparedness was and is essential. But with evolving technology, the nature of preparedness has changed. In the interim years between the "big" wars the question becomes: How do you maintain and train the troops? There are field exercises and war games-that's what they call them. During those times, troops work eighteen and twenty hours a day, and it's a tough regime. Most of the time, however, they aren't in the field. What do they do? Maintenance. They learn how to clean the equipment and they do the maintenance and they eat and they sleep and they party and then there's another war game and then it's time to rotate to a different place. It's a repeating cycle.

Of course you have to have a standing army, a ready force able to move at a moment's notice, but it's not moving all the time. And unless there is a specific mission, like a Somalia or a Bosnia or a Grenada or a Panama, the troops have an awful lot of downtime. There's no question that we need a strong, effective military. But not everybody in the Army has to be in that ready state. That increases the value of the reserve forces and the National Guard. By and large, the Army Reserves are made up of support units. Sometimes they are combat forces but usually they are hospital units, supply and service providers, backup personnel, petroleum and transportation services, and military police.

Those in the Army Reserves are civilians who for forty days out of the year—fifteen days in the summer and two days each month—put on a uniform and do soldierly exercises during drill weekends. The rest of the time they learn how to be productive members of civilian society. But Reservists are not highly thought of by the active Army because they are perceived to lack full dedication to the military. But what is overlooked by the active military is that reservists have full-time jobs out in the world, have families and are part of their communities. They may not have the same military skills as those who are on active duty, but they certainly offer their professional talents to their country and are just as ready to put on the uniform and put their lives on the line as active-duty personnel.

It seemed to me that to be a civilian and an Army Reservist was to have the best of both worlds. In December 1972, four months pregnant with my second child, I joined the Army Reserves and became nursing supervisor at the 50th General Army Reserves Hospital at Fort Lawton, Washington. I loved being back in the military. The clarity of roles, the shared values of discipline and order, the uniforms and teamwork and defined goals—there was no other place in which I felt so right. For the first time since my marriage, I felt that my dream to become a national Chief Nurse might one day be realized.

In May 1973, my second child and son, David was born. Harvey was helping an old friend coach the high-school track team and wasn't at the hospital for the delivery. I was disappointed, and played the martyr, saying to myself that if it wasn't important to him, I didn't need him to be there. During this delivery, I refused to take the disinhibiting medications or spinal block. Matt, my first son, had reacted to them and gone into fetal distress-I would never risk that again just for my own comfort. I also wanted to be alert and participate fully in this birthing experience.

David was a happy baby. His older brother accepted him and looked after him, playing an adult role to his little sibling even though he was only five. Now, with two small children in the family I took the summer off to tend to the garden and can vegetables and fruit for the coming year.

After five years of saving money, planning our house, and preparing the site, we began to build. We took our drawings and lists of what we wanted in a home to a designer who translated them into a working blueprint for the builder. A contractor friend of Harvey's was hired to put up the basic structure, while we helped in every way we could. Construction began in the summer of 1973. I made all the meals for the crew so they wouldn't have to leave the site. All of us—except the baby—helped.

I had realized that I was no longer challenged by my job at the VA. Aagot's arrival had already helped me reclaim my military career while still being a mother. But I also wanted to achieve more professionally. The frustration I'd felt working as a nurse when I returned from Vietnam lingered. The roles and duties of staff nurses were limited. I could look forward only to the same range of responsibilities year after year regardless of how hard I worked, and how good I was at my job.

Now taunting me was the idea of medical school. I decided to give it another try. This time I would make it happen, I would become a doctor. I studied long nights in the trailer after working outside all day. I took the medical school entrance exam, but my score was too low for me to get into a program I respected. I regrouped and dealt with my bruised ego and decided to apply graduate school. Aided by generous letters of recommendation from the neurosurgeons I'd worked with in Vietnam, I was accepted and offered a traineeship at the University of Washington School of Nursing.

Back in school, I began to realize how dangerous I'd been professionally the last few years—I didn't know what I didn't know. Much had changed since I'd received my last academic training ten years before. There were new discoveries in anatomy and physiology, new theories of pathophysiology, and new treatments that I hadn't learned while performing the duties of a staff nurse. The more I learned, the more I realized there was to learn. Nothing is more exciting than that, and nothing more humbling than realizing you don't know it all.

I started graduate school in 1973, surviving financially on the GI Bill, my traineeship in nursing, and my Army Reserve pay. I was simultaneously taking the advance military training I would need for promotion, so time was precious.

As our house slowly took shape, Harvey helped with the construction by working on his days off—he was determined and obsessed, pushing himself beyond his physical capacity. I did all the staining on the exposed cedar siding and interior wood. Both of us continued to play the roles of superman and superwoman. Those roles actually felt natural to us—and since we were equally driven— we cheered each other on.

On David's first birthday May 1, 1974, we moved from the trailer into our beautiful new home. We had five bedrooms and three baths, on two stories. The ground floor opened onto a huge lawn that sloped down to the man made "lake". Our vision had been realized—we had our gorgeous home surrounded by a working farm, rolling lawns, and beautiful landscaping.

My parents had never seen our home and had met only Matt once. By 1974, I was pregnant with our third son, Andy. I thought it was a good time for them to visit. But my father could not take the time away from his work, and my mother rarely left my father to fend for himself. Finally I was able to convince her to come out to meet David, see our home, and be there for Andy's birth. A month before her scheduled arrival, she, my father, and fifteen year-old brother, Paal, were on their vacation at their cabin in Canada. Their place was on a lake that they had to get to by boat at the end of Road's End. The seclusion and quiet was something they all loved.

My parents said the peacefulness reminded them of Norway. This particular trip came after months of concern over my father's health. He had developed persistent headaches and had seen a number of specialists. Finally he had a tentative diagnosis of cerebral arteritis and early hydrocephalus. The doctors suspected that an infection of the arteries of his brain caused the pain and might also mean that the normal fluid on the brain could not be absorbed as quickly as it should. This would make the brain cavities enlarge and cause a gradual loss of some functions, such as memory and balance. My mother had to take constant care of him, preparing special meals, limiting his physical exertion. That routine was more of a burden for her when they stayed at their place in Canada, because it was isolated and had fewer amenities. But, as always, she never complained, even though she herself was on medication for hypertension. My father came first.

On the last day of their vacation, my mother collapsed. She was washing her hair, bending over the bathtub to rinse out the shampoo, when a brain aneurysm ruptured. The blood vessel bursting in her brain probably killed her instantly. Friends rowed over across the lake to get my father and Paal, my youngest brother who was with them, at their cabin. Although she was dead my father tried for six hours to revive her.

She was too young. She hadn't had a chance to visit. That wasn't how things were supposed to happen. I never said goodbye. My father and brothers had the cremation and memorial service for her in Canada. Being seven and a half months pregnant, I did not feel I could make the arduous trip, and decided to meet up the family when they returned to Maryland.

The family grieved and celebrated her life, but I had to deal with her loss alone over the next years. My father's sadness was mixed with fear for the future. He had never managed the daily chores of life. That had been my mother's role. How would he take care of himself? How would his special diet and routine be maintained? Attempting to be helpful, I took him to the grocery store to shop for the foods he had always insisted my mother buy for him. He was shocked. He never knew their cost. They were too expensive; he would make do without them. But of course, for years my mother had managed to buy them for him on the fixed allowance he provided.

It was hard to be understanding of his great loss while mourning my own. And it was hard not to be angry with him. All her life my mother had catered to my father's health concerns, yet had neglected her own well-being. He was grief-stricken, and for the first time I could recall, he wept openly. He told me of trying to restore her to life. How, during those hours of doing CPR his sense of helplessness was overwhelming until he finally understood that her soul had left her physical body. I felt compassion for him, but we didn't talk about my own anger. Our time together ended without a resolution. We have never been able to tell each other what we feel. Instead, we seem to have always been jockeying for position with each other. I wanted his recognition as his oldest child and the only one to work in his field. But he was unable to give it to me because of my subservient position as a woman. Over the years, I have realized that there won't be a resolution to that, but my anger is gone and I can appreciate the love between us.

During the mid-1970s, two of my brothers, Jan and Tom were establishing their own, very different careers. Jan and his wife, Kit, now had two young children. They were building a beautiful home in suburban Virginia and he had recently become a vice president of a major construction company in Washington, D.C.

Tom had taken a different path. He had founded and was operating a nonprofit educational organization, the Norwegian School of Nature Life, in Park City, Utah. Its programs and philosophies were similar to those of a school in Hemsedal, Norway, of the same name, where people were taught how to pursue the "unselfish and simple life in nature." Tom had become interested in this work while attending Florida State University. He traveled several times to Norway and took courses at the Norwegian School of Nature Life as he completed his degree at the School of Physical Education and Sports in Oslo. Returning to the United States, he decided to begin a similar school here. The school teaches people how to live outdoors without abusing nature and offers courses in Nordic skiing and hiking as well as wilderness outings for young people.

My life in Maple Valley continued. Andy was born in 1974. Then Tom came along in 1976, shortly after I finished graduate school. Matt acted the adult to his brothers and, like me, he needed external validation constantly to feel he was good enough. The other boys weren't burdened that way. David excelled in any sport. Andy, from infancy, had a bullheaded "Don't tread on me" attitude. Always tough. Getting him to do anything-pick up toys, eat a bite of food-was a major battle. It got to the point where we had to decide which battles we were going to take on with him. And it's been the same ever since. More than any of the others, Andy had Harvey's stubbornness. And Tom, tenacious and sweet, was always picked on by his older brothers, so he cried loudly, no matter how far away his brothers were when they threatened him.

Just as Harvey and I had planned, our energetic, happy tribe had almost any activity they wanted available at home: swimming, fishing, playing, and working with animals. Aagot and I continued to speak only Norwegian to them and Harvey spoke only English-though he, too, was learning enough to understand a lot that we said. Their bilingual upbringing had a benefit I didn't originally anticipate. Because I also disciplined them in Norwegian, we could keep our hassles over authority and behavior private even with guests present. As a family, we were now totally self-sufficient. In our pastures, we raised our own cattle, and as the boys got older they took over much of this work as 4-H projects each year. We caught fish in our pond and got eggs from our ducks. All our vegetables came from our own garden. Two freezers and a huge pantry stored the year's supplies I washed, cut, froze, and canned. What we didn't grow ourselves-like apples and cherries-Harvey would barter for and bring home by the truckload. Then I'd can the fruit for the winter.

Over the years, we had planted an acre of raspberries. Our summer harvest was more than two tons of berries, which the boys and I picked and bagged. Harvey made outstanding raspberry champagne, and the kids sold the fruit and put that money in their own bank accounts. I also baked bread, made mayonnaise, and, of course, raspberry jam by the gallon.

By the mid-1970s, we had a large circle of friends from Harvey's work on the State Patrol as well as neighbors and other parents from the community. We entertained often, proud that everything served-food and wine-were homegrown and homemade. We truly had gone back to the land. We worked all the time and because we were striving to realize a shared vision, we were happy.

To our friends, we were the perfect couple. They admired how well we worked together and how much we were able to accomplish. The parties we hosted were the envy of our circle, and that was important to us.

In September 1977, when Tom was a year old, Aagot, now able to draw Social Security, decided it was time for her to take a trip back to Norway, then return to the home she had built several years earlier in Lincoln City, on the Oregon coast. After she left, I hired a woman to care for the kids at home as Aagot had done. But I would come home from work to find the kids crying and carrying on, their toys and clothes all over the place, and the kitchen a disaster area. It would take the rest of the evening to calm everyone down, clean everything up, make dinner, get the kids ready for bed, and be a cheerful mother and accommodating wife. After several weeks of this, I was cheerful and accommodating no more. We had a traditional marriage-I did not ask Harvey to help in the areas of housework and childcare, and he did not offer to assist. If I was going to work outside the home, it was my job to make sure the kids, the cooking, and the cleaning were taken care of. So I decided to take the boys to daycare in someone else's home early in the morning. The older boys, Matt and David went to school from there. Sanity returned, and they all benefited from being with other children.

As part of my graduate work, I developed the role of clinical nurse specialist in epilepsy at the Veterans Hospital in Seattle. I loved my job. Only part-time, it allowed me to also spend time with the boys, do farm chores at home, and continue in the Reserves.

During the last year of my master's program, the faculty adviser for my thesis, Pam Mitchell, received an invitation to lecture at the regional chapter of the American Association of Neurosurgical Nurses on the role of the nurse practitioner in treating epilepsy. Unable to attend them, she recommended me in her place. I was delighted and honored. Finally, here was a sign that I was considered an expert in something. In addition to preparing the lecture, I developed a very lengthy syllabus and handed it out at the beginning of my talk. Overkill but it went over well.

That lecture led to others at local hospitals, then to national and international symposiums. As my articles began appearing in journals, and my name was mentioned as a resource and expert, I felt I was realizing a dream of long ago. With this success, I began to feel that a Ph.D. was within my grasp. After several years of postgraduate work, I applied for and was accepted into the doctoral program in nursing at the University of Washington.

I felt Harvey viewed my professional successes only as absences from the home. He did not seem overly ambitious at the State Patrol. I saw his energy and passion go into landscaping our property, and I suspected he wanted me to have that same focus. I'd loved creating our estate but I got bored with maintenance. When our work at home went from completing our vision to just continuing the status quo, I turned more to my career for challenges.

I wanted both family and career. But I felt Harvey saw it as an either/or proposition: if I was successful professionally, that meant I wasn't happy as a wife and mother. I feared he had, over the years, become increasingly resentful as my career expanded. This made me sad and frustrated.

After all, I was no longer the young, unsure woman he'd married in 1965, or the wife isolated and homebound in 1969, or the night-staff nurse in 1973. During our assignment in Vietnam, my mother later told me, Harvey had written to her complaining that I took my role as head nurse too seriously and didn't defer to him as I had in the past. My autonomy lessened when we returned to the States, I left the Army, and we started our new life together. But now, completing graduate school, I had begun a challenging path as a specialist in neuroscience nursing; rejoined the military, I again contributed as an officer; becoming a mother, I had moved outside myself and experienced a different kind of love.

One event symbolized this profound shift in our lives. In 1979, Harvey refused to attend the annual raspberry festival we always hosted for University faculty and friend. It was a daylong event for people to come out to our home, enjoy a buffet I'd prepared, drink Harvey's raspberry wine and champagne, and visit in the arboretum-like surrounding. They also purchased raspberries from the boys. It was a special time for our family, and Harvey had previously enjoyed this event, but now he dismissed it by calling it an orgy for my "ERA friends."

This mystified me. I supported the passage of the Equal Rights Amendment (we were still without a TV and uninformed about feminists in the news, yet the ERA was "in the air" as it came to a vote in state after state), but I certainly didn't discuss it, much less work for it. As a military officer, a Veterans Administration and federal employee, I could not be politically active. That would be "conduct unbecoming" and therefore improper.

Harvey's fury against my "ERA friends" had nothing to do with the Equal Rights Amendment. And, of course, it had everything to do with it. But the key word was "equal"—not better or worse, not special or disregarded, but *equal*.

In the Nurse Corps, I didn't feel gender constraints (in 1966 men were allowed in but constituted only 10 percent of the personnel). I was given a job, I was expected to carry it out, and my relationships were based on its performance. By 1979, I was a lieutenant colonel and had been promoted from the medical-surgical supervisor to assistant chief nurse of the 50th General Hospital (Army Reserves). The purpose of our training was to maintain our skills as a hospital that could be activated at any moment to care for patients or casualties.

But, increasingly, Harvey didn't seem to appreciate that my work outside the home was important to me, to the people I served. It became so troubling, I remember once breaking my characteristic silence on all matters that were personal, and talking with a colleague at the university about my frustration with Harvey. I explained to her that my children were happy and doing well in school and sports, but that Harvey criticized me for the time I spent on my career. She revealed that she, too, found it difficult to justify to her husband doing anything other than housekeeping. My solution was to have no personal life or private time other than with my family. This didn't appease Harvey, but it eased my guilt.

Our long-planned dream of home, family, profession had become a reality. It was perfect. And yet ... something was wrong. I sensed it but couldn't name it. I felt as if I were being ripped apart. Yet why should I feel bad? Our life was perfect, our home was gorgeous, our children were wonderful, the military was rewarding. But still I had this strange, horrible feeling. When it came, I'd take on more-preserve more jam, plant more ivy, work on another research project-and become too busy to concern myself with feelings. There were my children, my patients, my unit, and my husband. But eventually, that feeling would catch me again–like a voice that said I wasn't good enough, or doing enough–and again, I'd take on more.

At home I fulfilled the role of farmer's wife and mother. The chores on the property had become monotonous and overwhelming. It was commonplace for Harvey to come up the driveway with the truck filled with apples at five o'clock in the evening, with the result that I would have to spend all night making fifty gallons of applesauce and still go to work the next morning at the hospital or the university. The next week it would be a truckload of cabbage, and we'd make a hundred pounds of sauerkraut. We would use it, after all. And Harvey did his share. But more and more I felt that we were slaves to the property. Harvey didn't see it that way. In his view, my professional work should be abandoned for the farm chores. Now I often wondered, "Where in the world are we heading?"

Our goals were different. Our interests were different. He seemed to be content as a State Patrol officer. I had professional ambitions and sought challenges. I felt he was threatened by my work, my future, and my income–

still it didn't occur to me to question our marriage itself. With the boys to consider, it was unthinkable. And there was one more part of our vision we needed to complete.

It was time to consider a last child-I wanted a girl. I said so to Harvey and he turned the conversation in a direction I hadn't anticipated. In a way, my questioning our marriage was precipitated by this conversation. He asked me why I wanted another child when I wasn't home for the ones I had. And he walked away.

It was and wasn't true. It was a terrible thing hearing his judgment of me and trying to decipher what more I could do as a mother.

Harvey was passed over for a promotion in the State Patrol (he was promotion from trooper to sergeant after our divorce). My military career continued to go well, while my workload at the epilepsy clinic in the Veterans Hospital and my lecturing increased. As a family, we prospered. As a wife, I felt increased distance and growing tension with my husband.

In the summer of 1979, I reduced my schedule at work and school-taking a partial "vacation." I was starting the doctoral program in nursing at the University of Washington in September and wanted some time to rest and think. It was really an opportunity to relax and enjoy what we had spent the last ten years creating.

It was wonderful to have more time to spend with the boys. My only obligations were chores on the property. Matt and David, with Harvey's help, took care of our four cattle. We had about half an acre devoted to growing vegetables. Our busiest time was the three-week harvest of raspberries every August. The kids and I picked twenty to thirty gallons a day—it was a horrendous job, but we went down the rows of bushes and filled the gallon plastic bags with berries efficiently and quickly.

Before the rigors of the harvest, however, I had some free time. As I reflected on all that we'd accomplished, I realized I didn't have any friends of my own to share it with. The people we entertained were couples. Harvey went fishing and hunting with his buddies. But I'd cut out that part of my life in order to have more time at home to devote to my family.

I decided to try to have a personal life. It might sound strange, but having a friend was a bit of a new experience for me. Randi-—my childhood playmate from Oslo, who visited me whenever her assignment as a flight attendant with SAS allowed-was a friend. But we rarely saw each other.

So that summer, I made an effort to get to know two colleagues to help round out my life. Frecia was my age, divorced, and in the doctoral program at the University, and Barbara, a psychiatric nurse specialist, was in my unit in the Reserves. We would have coffee or pick raspberries together in our vineyard and then talk over drinks and dinner on the deck. I enjoyed being with them, and socializing with friends meant that not every moment was being taken up by some chore or project.

I also began to sense a camaraderie that I didn't feel with Harvey. My own interests were changing and becoming vastly different from his. I missed having someone to share ideas with.

That fall, school started. During orientation, we were reminded that a doctoral program is costly—for the students and their families. To prepare us for the commitment ahead the lecturer quoted a statistic: 75 percent of all marriages don't survive one spouse's completing a Ph.D. I thought it was an interestingly high figure but denied it had any relevance to my own life.

One evening, as I did dishes after feeding the crew of boys, I got a phone call from Barbara. She told me she had breast cancer. She was to have surgery and would miss the next months of Army Reserves duty. As her military supervisor, I needed this information. But she was also a friend. I began to cry. My tears came both from empathy with my friend's fear and pain, and from a sense of my own mortality.

Harvey was in the kitchen When I got off the phone and told him about the call, he seemed angry. He said he wondered whether I would pay more attention to him if he got cancer. I was stunned.

In December 1979, Harvey strained his back again, as he had done in Germany years before. He went into the hospital for several weeks during the holidays. I continued with my plans for a traditional, formal Norwegian Christmas and now invited my own friends to attend, as well as family and neighbors. I particularly encouraged Barbara to come, though it was soon after her surgery. She did, and we all had a lovely time.

There had been times in the past in our marriage when I would grow distant from Harvey and not realize I'd done so. I'd be unusually quiet and preoccupied. He said he would feel I didn't give him my attention. Finally he'd blow up, angrily describe how I was distant from him and say, "Do you want a divorce?" I would think: Maybe that's not such a bad idea. But having no other home, or place, or family, I would put that thought out of my head and shift my attention back to my husband, and we would return to our normal routine.

But this time, when he returned from his stay at the hospital, I was more distant that I had ever been. And this time, I was aware of how I felt: I did not want to be even physically in the same space with him.

Harvey tried his old strategy. He blew up: I was the absent wife who cared more about her career than about her husband. But I couldn't go back to my old attentiveness as I had before. I couldn't deny that I didn't want to be with him. I couldn't pretend. And I couldn't decide to leave because this was my family, this was my home, these were my children. The conflict immobilized me. The tension between us increased. Underneath the façade of clinician, mother, officer, my guilt and hurt grew more intense every day.

One Saturday afternoon that winter, on my way home from Reserve weekend, driving as I had for the last ten years, past the same landmarks, to our dream estate, to our perfect home, I veered my car toward a telephone pole, thinking: I could hit this pole and end the pain. With a mental jolt, I jerked the car off the shoulder and back onto the road again. But I found it difficult to hold the steering wheel steady. When I finally pulled up to the house, I sat in the car and shook.

CHAPTER 8

. . . .

Family Crisis and Divorce

I was sitting in the car in front of Leona's house. I had picked up four year-old Tom, and Harvey came out of his mother's house, wanting to talk to me. I had my hand on the car window. I was wearing my engagement ring, and Harvey grabbed my hand and tried to pull the ring off, physically to pull it off, with Tom sitting right beside me. I got my hand back in, closed the window, and drove off. Tom looked at me like a protective parent. "Don't ever," he said seriously, "wear that ring around him again. "

. . . .

I had almost driven into a telephone pole. That's all I kept thinking as I sat in the car. When I finally stopped shaking, I got out of the car and went into the house. Harvey had never seen me like this. White-faced and trembling, I could barely explain what had happened.

I told him about my urge to kill myself. He was very concerned, and insisting that I get help, he called the counselor assigned to work with the State Patrol. Dr. Smith agreed to see me at his home in Redmond right away. Harvey gave eleven-year-old Matt instructions to watch the other boys for a few hours and we immediately got in the car. He drove the twenty miles and waited in Dr. Smith's living room during my first session with the counselor.

Dr. Smith asked me what happened to cause this distress. Still in shock, I tried to sort out my feelings. Harvey was the same, my children were the same, our home was the same, and my work was the same. But I had changed—I found it difficult to be with Harvey, and that caused an unbearable pain.

Dr. Smith suggested I see him on a regular basis for a while. I agreed, more numb and exhausted than anything else. I felt pulled in a thousand directions, wearer of a hundred masks. Were none of them I? Was I wife now? Mother? Nurse? Soldier? Farmer? The days went by without shape. I went to my jobs and performed my roles. And I went to the counselor. At Dr. Smith's urging, I looked back on my life for clues to my despair. I told him how I felt different from my peers in high school and college, and how I'd wondered if I was homosexual but had finally resolved-or was it denied-that feeling of being different by deciding it came from being a Norwegian in America. I had never discussed these feelings with anyone before. I told him the times in my marriage when I'd grown distant from Harvey, and that now I was withdrawing again. Being intimate with Harvey was unpleasant and something I tried to avoid. It had gotten to the point where I found it difficult to be in the same room with him and had begun to look for work-related reasons not to be home.

As we talked about my distancing from Harvey, Dr. Smith said he believed an individual's sexuality is on a continuum. He explained that there are times when all of us feel closer to or more distant from a partner or spouse. There are also times for each of us when we may feel more drawn to someone of the same gender and other times when we may not. My current feelings, he suggested, could be a phase. But I didn't think my feelings would change. It wasn't a matter of choice either: no matter how hard I tried, I was uncomfortable being with Harvey. I did not feel on any continuum. I was at a dead end.

Looking back now, I find it very difficult to describe my feelings of dread, pain, and confusion. I do know I didn't see myself as homosexual. My new friendships with women were just that: friendships. Married women didn't–in those days, in my circle—-have friendships with men, because that suggested a sexual attraction. Women had friendships with women, men with men.

In hindsight, I suspect that in having my own friends for the first time since meeting Harvey, I was able to experience what I didn't get in my marriage: shared interests and autonomy. I realized I couldn't keep ignoring my own needs. I knew I didn't want to be with Harvey, and I was convinced I would not be with a man again. But that was the extent of my certainty. It was an ending for me. Just that. A deadness. No feeling. And the thoughts of suicide persisted.

Barbara, a psychiatric nurse, knew the signs of someone in distress and was worried about me. She spent time with me, asked good questions, and let me talk. Like Dr. Smith, she was there for me in a crucial way-she was a lifeline.

Once during the winter and spring of 1980, she had to travel on business. Before she was to leave, she tried to contract with me that I would not kill myself while she gone. She and Dr. Smith were the only ones who knew I still struggled with this thought, and she believed that if I gave my word to her, I would not break it. I couldn't make that contract. But she was smart enough not to change her travel plans—that would have given me too much power. So she asked me to agree to call Dr. Smith before I did anything to hurt myself. I've often felt that her concern and intervention saved my life.

Several times during the months of counseling, Dr Smith asked to see Harvey and me together. We complied. Harvey was particularly upset, even enraged, when the subject of sexuality came up. By his response, he seemed threatened by the idea that everyone was on a continuum–had the potential for feeling close to someone of his or her own gender.

For me, the counseling sessions opened up avenues to explore the source of my unhappiness. For Harvey, they seemed frightening. Our marriage was being questioned, which meant it was at risk. He began a campaign to pressure me to get over this crisis and go back to an undistracted commitment to him. He had friends call me and tell me what a wonderful husband he was, what a perfect family and home we had. He went to my workplace and talked to colleagues, begging them to convince me to stay in the marriage.

Along with trying to pressure me, he was also trying to understand. Over the years, we'd met the dean of the Nursing School and her husband at social events. Harvey thought very highly of them. Here was a couple in which the wife had a challenging career and the marriage was strong and healthy. Without telling me, he made an appointment with the dean and her husband. He told them about our troubles. When he came home and explained he'd done this, I was dumbfounded. How could he embarrass us like that? And yet it also showed how desperate and lost he must have felt. I didn't get mad–he'd already done it, he was hurting, too, and angry words wouldn't help. I don't remember his telling me if the dean and her husband had been helpful. Years later, the dean told me how after their meeting with Harvey her husband had predicted that our marriage wouldn't last because of my need for professional challenge and Harvey's need for a wife to cook and clean.

At home, Harvey began marathon interrogations of me, and would talk, rail, and insist that I remain in our marriage. His campaign was more intense than his crusade in Germany fourteen years earlier when I said I didn't want to see him. There was more at stake now for both of us, and, of course, our sons' best interests were more important than our own. I was immobilized. Harvey seemed distraught. I couldn't continue this situation. I had to do something. But I wasn't sure that ending the marriage was the solution, because I still believed the problem was in me, not in the marriage.

As a clinician, when I receive a new patient who is suffering and has symptoms that defy easy diagnosis, I begin a deliberate process. First, I listen to the patient explain what is happening, what his symptoms are, what the concerns are that have brought him in for treatment. Then I observe anything and everything. The key to the illness can be hidden in the most ordinary activity.

I approached my own dis-ease (because I now saw it as a sickness, of soul) this way. To try to isolate my symptoms, I first separated out the parts of my life. Instead of running rapidly from one role to the next, I attended to one aspect of my life at a time. I spent evenings in town with friends. Then I focused, in turn, just on my work at the hospital, then on my career in the military. Each of those separate areas felt right. But when I got into my car to go home at night, the symptoms would start again. Did that mean the problem was in me, and work just distracted me from myself and therefore from my unhappiness? I could find that out only by being alone. I knew that going off by myself might very well increase my depression and self-destructive impulses, but it was necessary to understand the source of my pain.

So, feeling that nothing could be worse than what I was already struggling with, I took a week off from work, while Harvey was available to take care of the boys, and went to Aagot's in Lincoln City. I didn't discuss with Aagot why I was there. She knew me well enough to accept that if and when I was ready or needed to talk with her, I would. My dialogue was with myself. There, on the Oregon coast, I became a recluse.

I read books on human sexuality and psychology. Alex Comfort's book *The Joy of Sex* allowed me to finally admit to myself what felt unnatural and wrong. No matter how hard I tried to change my feelings, I couldn't: being sexual with my husband, even though I consented, felt like an invasion. Reading Nancy Mayer's *The Male Mid-life Crisis: Fresh Starts After 40* and Dr. Wayne Dyer's *Pulling Your Own Strings* taught me that each of us is responsible for our own happiness-and that there are alternatives. For the first time, I gave myself permission to feel. I didn't have to conform to what other people wanted me to be. I had rights, and an obligation to shape my life.

I walked on the beach. I slept and ate. I began to realize something very important: I wanted to live. By the time I packed to return home to my other lives, I knew the problem was in our marriage.

When I got back to Maple Valley, Harvey was more distraught than ever before. In the midst of rowdy hellos with the boys, the tension was extraordinary. But I felt it was crucial for the boys to return to a normal routine. I went back to work and school, and caught up with my patients' cases. I continued with my duties in the Reserves, and relished the discipline and camaraderie. I resumed my nights of cooking for the family, harvesting, maintaining the gardens and lawns. But inside the house, with Harvey there, I felt constant agony.

Finally, just days after my return from Oregon, he told me that he was no mother, that the children needed me, and that he would move out of the house, since I was better equipped then he to manage the farm and the lives of our children. He grabbed a couple of bags and moved to a friend's home nearby.

Suddenly, life was calm. I could focus my attention on my sons. By leaving, Harvey had unwittingly shown me the solution. It was an awful realization-but a relief to finally accept what I had to do. I loved my children, our land, and my work, the Army. Being with my husband was neither physically nor emotionally tolerable. I had to get out of the marriage.

Perhaps because Matt was the oldest, he asked the most questions, though all the boys were distressed. I told them that their father and I were talking and thinking and working very hard to find a solution that would be the best for each one of us. Again and again, I said they were not ever to blame themselves for what was happening with their father and me, that we loved each of them very much, that what we were doing was very serious and the rest of our lives depended on what we said, did, and planned. I asked them if they wanted to talk with Dr. Smith, and always made opportunities for counseling available to them.

One day while I was down in Oregon picking up the boys from their summer camp vacation, Harvey moved back into the house. It was a total surprise.

Now the worst part of our nightmare began. In counseling sessions, our attempts at communication dissolved into anger and accusations. Harvey said hurtful things trying to get me to give in to him. I knew he wanted a decision from me—the decision to remain his wife. But I was still immobilized. He pushed and pushed. We departed the sessions feeling worse than ever.

The nights were particularly difficult. We tried to shield the boys from our pain, but couldn't. Over and over I attempted to explain to Harvey how lost and lonely I felt, that somewhere in my life I'd stopped being a person and become part of a project—the estate. I tried to say this was about my search for my own life, and I begged him to see it not as his failure but as my need. When he expressed frustration or anger, I withdrew and said nothing. I was so wrapped up in my own struggle to pull away that I didn't interact with him. In retrospect, I suspect that made him even more frantic. He wanted to be included and I was excluding him. My worst fear was that the children might overhear their wounded father.

Though we lived in different parts of the house and didn't need to interact, we had a few confrontations in front of the children. At one point, three-year-old Tom told him to "not talk mean to Mother." When it was time for the kids to eat, I would prepare the meal and eat with them, whereas Harvey would lock himself in the bedroom. Later I would retreat to my bedroom, giving him some time in peace with the boys. Then I would put them to bed, and Harvey would begin his desperate, furious arguments with me. The next morning the boys would implore both of us not to hurt each other.

This situation was intolerable for the children. I called a women's resource center and asked for advice. They gave me the names of three attorneys who were family-law specialists. The first one I called was Harriett Cody. We talked and she suggested a meeting. During the first encounter, I realized that in practical terms I didn't know what I wanted—except that I loved and wanted to be with my children and had to end this torment with their father. Odd as it may seem, I hadn't considered what getting a divorce would mean. No one in my family or Harvey's had ever gotten a divorce.

With Harriett's guidance we began the legal steps to end the marriage. It was difficult to sue for divorce–what an extraordinary step for me to take–but it was unthinkable to subject the children to such anguish any longer. Harvey's attorney was a man known for successful, aggressive divorce litigation. So the legal part of our very personal journey began. Harriett drafted the divorce summons, and I had it served on Harvey on July 31, 1980. His birthday. It was mean. I see it now as the act of a wounded animal.

We both still lived in the house, neither one of us willing to relinquish our sons. It was up to the court to determine who would get temporary custody. Of course, I wanted my children. It was my only desire. It seemed essential that I retain custody.

Our first court date was set for August 15, 1980. The judge would hear evidence and arguments from both sides in order to determine who should have temporary custody of the boys.

One evening, a week before the hearing, Harvey said that if I would stay with him until Christmas, and if we were unable to work out our problems by then, he would agree to give me custody of all four children. I said I would see Dr. Smith with him for the next months to attempt this reconciliation, but I could not agree to live with him. He insisted we live together. He believed he could make everything all right and keep our lives from being turned upside down. Yet we'd been trying all along, and I could not subject myself and the children to more of what we'd all been through. His anger in front of the boys now included questioning my mental competence, my sexuality, and my abilities as a mother. Should I let this go on in order to avoid a custody battle? Every day the boys were hurt more deeply. Every day they lost more trust, more security. Five more months of that was unthinkable. We were already at the breaking point. I told Harvey I would not barter my sons.

My attorney proceeded with the custody hearing. I wanted the court to order Harvey to move out of the house so that I could restore some peace and security to the lives of my children. We would let the judge decide. As planned, we appeared before the court on August 15, each to argue for temporary custody. Harvey arrived wearing his State Patrol uniform. He was the perfectly dressed, spit-shined officer. I was a Ph.D. student and a lieutenant colonel in the Army Reserves, but I didn't think it appropriate to wear my uniform and medals. Harvey's cold confidence and control was in stark contrast to the angry behavior I'd seen just the night before at home. My own anxiety and pain were probably obvious.

My belief that I would win this sad, cruel contest kept me going through the custody hearing. In my affidavit to the court, I explained how important it was for the boys to stay with me. Tom, not yet four, was so upset, he refused to be left with our longtime baby sitter, and I had begun to take him everywhere, even to my classes at the University. I related similar incidents with each boy. As proof he should be the parent, Harvey submitted nineteen letters and sworn affidavits of support. It seemed he had gone to everyone, telling his story and soliciting a letter that attested to his fine character or encouraged the court to award him custody. There were letters from acquaintances, friends, and co-workers: owners of the feed store where he bought grain, the mechanic at the gas station where he serviced his patrol car, fellow state troopers, the president of the local meat-packing company. In these letters, our home and farm were described as the result only of his work, his vision, his money, and his love of his sons.

I had my record of military service and awards, my list of articles and lectures, my professional positions, my years as the primary parent when Harvey was away, my love of my children. But, thinking it unnecessary, I had obtained no letters. Traditionally, temporary custody was given to the mother. My record as a nurse, officer, and mother was very strong. Harriett and I believed that the depositions—mine and Harvey's—presented as evidence to the judge, along with my appearance at the hearing and my credentials, were all that we needed to win.

The hearing took under an hour. After our testimony, the judge shuffled his papers and said he'd reached his decision. He announced that Harvey would have temporary custody. Harriett was flabbergasted. I collapsed. I'd lost my sons. How could this be? I had never imagined this could happen.

It was very unusual for the father to get temporary custody. Later I heard that the judge had recently lost his two sons in a mountain climbing accident. Perhaps that made him more sympathetic to Harvey's claim. Maybe if I'd worn my uniform, if I'd had letters... but none of that would change the judge's ruling now. My attorney and I had done what we thought was necessary. Looking back wouldn't help.

I had a matter of days to move out. I did it when no one was home—I didn't want the kids to see me cry. I went through each room, took the things that were mine, and said goodbye. I also took the photograph albums—since Harvey had custody, I thought I should at least have the pictures.

I moved out and in to Frecia's (my PhD classmate) home in Seattle. I had visitation rights with the boys, which Harvey made sure I followed strictly. My week was arranged around these precious hours with my sons. My one room at Frecia's was a miserable place to entertain four anxious and wild children for the weekend. But we managed. I bought a mattress and sleeping bag for each boy and made sure the kitchen was stocked with their favorite treats.

After our first visit, I brought them back to Maple Valley. As we drove up, Harvey was on the porch, clocking me to the second to make sure I returned them at the specified time. I got the boys' bags out of the car as Harvey welcomed them. Then he turned to me and started to yell, "You dyke, faggot, queer!" I was speechless. I got in the car. Now he was laughing and calling out the names over and over. It was the first time but not the last. It became the boys' homecoming routine after being with me. Harvey would welcome them back, then he would scream, "Dyke, queer!" until the boys joined in. Looking back, I can see that the boys, having lost their mother, were trying to please the one parent (in their minds) they still had by mirroring his behavior. Each time I dropped them off, that farewell rang in my ears. I drove away crying, humiliated.

The collapse of my life, and now the anguish of these partings with my sons overwhelmed me. It was just as hard on the kids and it took them several days to be able to reconnect with me when we had time together. Their lives were being torn apart by separations; by hatred.

The judge's decision to give Harvey temporary custody was the shock of my life. I began to doubt myself as a mother. It wasn't something I could articulate. I still wanted my children. But now a fear haunted me. Was the portrait painted by Harvey and his attorney true? Could it be that I was not the better parent for my sons?

The court deemed that psychiatric evaluations were necessary before permanent custody could be awarded. A child psychologist was selected by the judge to interview each member of the family. He also was to observe how Harvey and I parented and, presumably, to recommend, or choose, the better parent.

I was terrified. This was an awful contest. Parents pitted against each other, the innocent children in the middle, and all of our futures at stake. I knew that more than anything I wanted to be with my sons. And I knew I would not survive if I stayed married to Harvey.

The day of my test as a good mother, I drove my boys to the psychiatrist's office, explaining to them that this was a meeting where we'd be asked some questions and they should say whatever they felt. I tried not to show my anxiety. But I'm sure they could tell how worried I was.

After stiff introductions, the psychiatrist asked us to play a game of "house" in his office. We were given a stack of cards that described family situations. We were each to draw a card and then play out the events while he watched. Of course, I knew that he would closely observe and interpret the way my sons and I interacted. And his first observation would be that we spoke only Norwegian together. I couldn't use English with the boys. It would be unnatural and confusing.

So we began. One of us drew a card and read out the instruction—in Norwegian, just as we would at home. The psychiatrist was not pleased; he didn't understand what we were saying. We began to play "house." The agony of knowing what was at stake was so overwhelming; I can't remember exactly what we did. I only know that we felt the game was stupid. I'd always encouraged the boys to be honest with me.

If they thought something was unfair or silly, they let me know. But now my unspoken message was entirely different. They sensed that this was important and they should deny their true feelings about it. And as we continued playing house in Norwegian, the psychiatrist became more frustrated. Though he could see how we interacted, he apparently felt excluded by our use of Norwegian and was unable to make the observations he needed. Finally he asked us to stop.

It was over. I just wanted to disappear. But then we were told we had to be interviewed separately. As each boy left the waiting room for his turn, I agonized for him.

The psychiatrist reported to the judge that after spending nine hours interviewing and observing all of us, he had determined that it was my decision to return to the academic and career world that brought this upheaval into our marriage. He noted that though I hoped to retain custody of my children, he felt I had "ambivalent feelings" about whether the boys would infringe on my own needs as I pursued my career. He described Harvey as managing the temporary custody well, though filled with anger and resentment toward me. Finally, the psychiatrist recommended that, because Harvey appeared to be slightly better able to provide for the immediate physical and emotional well-being of the boys, they remain in his custody. I was stunned and angry. But in light of this recommendation, the question now was: Should I fight for custody?

Not only did I not want to be in a relationship with Harvey, I didn't want to continue working twenty-four hours a day on the farm. And so I knew that I didn't want to go on living in Maple Valley and I suspect that was part of my "ambivalence" concerning my future plans that the psychiatrist observed. What could I say to the judge? I had no money. I had no home. I imagined a scene in the courtroom with the judge when I fought for custody:

The judge would say, "Where do you plan to live with your children?"

"Well, Judge, I thought I would start in the basement of a friend of mine."

"And how do you plan to take care of the younger children during work, classes, and Reserves?"

"Well, Judge, there's daycare. I'm sure I'll manage-I always have."

As I envisioned that conversation, I began to doubt I could convince the judge I should have custody. I had already tried to get my own credit card and had been denied one–it made me feel helpless. I had very little money.

With temporary custody, Harvey was taking the kids to daycare. He had joined the Mormon Church. This was after years of resisting his brother and sister's attempts to have us convert. Both Harvey and I were lifelong Lutherans. But as soon as we separated, Harvey became a member of the Mormon Church–he had always wanted a very traditional wife, and that is the view the Mormons promote. It also, I felt, made him look better. In the judge's eyes, he was being deserted by his wife and he was managing, joining a church and learning how to run the household. He hired a woman, Sally, to come in every day and take care of the kids while he was working.

The kids were in a stable environment, and what judge, once he had given temporary custody to the husband, would say to him: You've managed fine, but now it's your wife's turn to take over? I didn't think that was going to happen.

In addition, Harvey's depositions made so many inferences and such derogatory statements both about me and about my colleagues and friends that I realized how vicious this battle could become.

I shared these fears with Harriett. Her advice was firm. She said we could fight for custody, but she agreed that it would be an ugly struggle. Therefore, if I did go forward, I needed to be sure that the reason I made the boys go through a court battle was that I felt it was the best thing for them to be with me and not just to prove Harvey wrong.

I didn't want to lose my sons. But I had to be honest. Could I really give them the physical stability Harvey could? I'd moved many times as a child and had vowed not to subject my own children to that kind of upheaval. I talked with friends. A woman on the faculty at the university told me that her son lived with her ex-husband. She said it was very difficult for her but the right thing for her son despite societal expectations that children always stay with the mother. Other friends, John and Diana O'Laughlin, gave me the courage to fight social norms. Harvey's rage was directed at me, not at the boys. Once I was gone, their lives would be stable and secure with him.

I decided not to contest his custody. The home we'd built for them was where they belonged. And to fight seemed futile. I was beaten.

The divorce became final in December 1980. Harvey had custody and I had visitation rights and child-support payments. Our sessions with our attorneys to design the property settlement were marked by Harvey's rage. His abuse was directed also at Harriett Cody. Once he became so angry that she got up and left the room.

I'd lost more than my sons. I had no name, no credit, and no home. With the divorce, I decided to get my identity back and part of that was to reclaim my maiden name. It was, of course, hard to convince the kids that by changing my name I was not divorcing them, only their father. I was not Mrs. Hawken anymore and could not have that name. On December 12, 1980, I became Ms. Cammermeyer.

I had imagined that my father's response to my divorce would be difficult, but he was very understanding. When I called and told him, he wasn't shocked, as all our friends had been. "If you have to," he said, "you have to. It's not healthy to stay in the marriage just for the children."

My brothers were also supportive, though surprised. In our family it's not our style to ask one another's advice. I called only to tell them the news.

Harvey would not let me back in the house to get my share of the personal property agreed upon in the divorce decree. I had to have my attorney threaten court action. Finally he agreed to let me come over to get my possessions.

Our property settlement was one of those item-by-item lists —what was his and what was mine. Since I was not to enter the house to retrieve my family heirlooms, he packed up what he felt was mine and stacked it outside. Diana, our mutual friend, came with me to Maple Valley to pick up my things. Harvey allowed her to go inside the house and check for certain items. At times he became irate—once, he threw several pieces of my heirloom silver into the woods. These were pieces given to me by my great-uncle in Oslo when I visited Norway during my college years. Days later, the boys went out on their own to retrieve the silver and, with great excitement, secretly presented me with all the missing pieces.

My youngest son, four-year-old Tom, made me a house. One day, when I picked him up for visitation, he spirited it out of his room, past his father, and into the car. It is beautiful. A perfect house. Six inches square, built of wood with a sturdy roof to keep me dry, it even has my name written on the door (MOR-"mother" in Norwegian). It endured all the storms and sits prominently on my bookshelf today.

I was allowed one visitation in between the weekends. Since I lived thirty miles away, by the time I had driven all the way to Maple Valley to pick up the boys and all the way back again with them to my place, and we had had something to eat, our time would be up. So, instead, I bought each of the boys another bicycle (Harvey insisted they leave their bikes at home) and made a wooden rack for them on top of my car (I couldn't afford to buy a rack). I would pick the boys up and take them to dinner, and then we would go to one of the elementary or high schools, where they would ride their, bicycles in the schoolyard for the next two hours. I'd sit in the car or stand outside and admire them as they drove through the playground. Reluctantly, we'd load up and go to get a treat at a grocery store for the trip home. Then it would be time to drop them off and we'd go through the same horrible scene again: Harvey calling me disparaging names, laughing, taunting, and getting the kids to do the same. When I'd left them at the door of what had been my home, my tears would make it hard to see the road ahead. Each time, my heart felt as though it would break.

So, though the divorce was final, it wasn't over. Harvey never seemed less angry. The kids were sent as spies. Not only did he ridicule me, he made our friends and Aagot choose between seeing me or having a connection with the children through him. I felt worthless, and in this atmosphere I could make no progress at working through the boys' anger and pain.

All of a sudden Seattle seemed too small. Every place I turned there were memories of where we had been together as a family. Wherever I went, I wondered if I was going to run into Harvey. Every time I called the kids and he answered the phone, my entire defense system would break down. I felt as though I couldn't breathe, I was so stuck and entrenched, and he still had such power over me. I feared that our old friends viewed me the way he did: that I had sought the divorce, left the children without a fight, left a life of fullness and plenty for poverty and emptiness.

Because of the turmoil in my personal life, I'd taken a year's leave of absence from the doctoral program. Again, I was derailed from my doctorate. Again, I wondered if I was meant to go that route.

I began thinking that moving away from Seattle would help. I needed to rebuild my life. We all needed to heal. I began looking for other positions in the Veterans Administration medical system because I believe strongly in socialized medicine and wanted to stay with that agency. There are 172 VA medical facilities throughout the country, and I hoped there would be something available on the West Coast. I needed a position close enough to Seattle so that I could see the kids often and they could spend extended time with me during the summer.

I interviewed at medical facilities in Palo Alto, Menlo Park, and areas in Southern California. Finally a job in my area of neuroscience nursing opened up at the Veterans Administration Medical Center in San Francisco. They were looking for a master's-prepared clinical nurse specialist in neuro-oncology to coordinate care and research protocols, and provide general management of patients with brain tumors. Although I did not know neuro-oncology, I was experienced in neurology, and they agreed to hold the job for me for six months while I settled my personal affairs in Seattle.

My Army Reserves colleague Barbara was moving to San Francisco foe graduate school. We agreed to share expenses and buddy up for this move since neither of us had friends, family, or money to live comfortably alone in San Francisco.

It took months to tell the kids I was leaving. It put us all in another crisis. They were very upset. I tried to explain how difficult it was to leave them at the end of each visit and how this move would give us a better chance to grow and to heal. Of course, all they knew was I was leaving–again.

Just before my move down to California, I had the boys for a month in the summer of 1981. We went to Aagot's home on the Oregon coast for a wonderful and difficult time together. We built a tree house. In the city swimming pool, we played for hours. But this wasn't just fun. The boys wrestled with me–leaping on top of me, yelling in a wild flurry of arms, legs, and water. They needed to get mad at me, to gang up on me for having caused them to suffer so much. We'd leave laughing and exhausted to get ice cream, and then go crabbing at the ocean.

When our month was over, I drove them back up to Seattle and dropped them off in Maple Valley with Harvey. I promised again that I would call the permitted three times a week. And I would fly up every month for a weekend. They understood. Now they were stoic. We had become too skilled at saying goodbye.

With the memories of our month together, I began my trip down to California. Barbara drove her car and I drove a rental truck with our belongings. I wept the entire time. It was the end of life, as I knew it. I felt I was abandoning my children. But I knew that if I was ever to have a chance to get them back again, I had to find out who I was and make my own life.

I was thirty-nine and starting over.

CHAPTER 9

. . . .

On My Own

I stayed away from Castro Street. Not once during the four and a half years I lived in San Francisco did I go near that "gay Mecca." Would I be safe? Would "they" be out of control? Would I see two people of the same gender holding hands? Would I stare? (Which would be rude.) My expectations gave me the heebie-jeebies. Years later, I finally went there to give a speech during the 1992 election campaign. Haunted by those past thoughts, I tried to walk fast and inconspicuously. Still, a man jumped out and grabbed me. He hugged me as if we were old friends, not strangers on the street. As he gave me a kiss on my cheek, he cooed: "Hi, Angel. We love you!" My military demeanor dissolved. Laughing with him at the absurdity of it all, I said, "Thank goodness I finally got to Castro Street. "

. . . .

You don't become unmarried with the signing of the divorce decree. It's a long, slow process. It involves every part of your life, private and professional. And it's not just about becoming unattached. In fact, that's the least of it. Rather, it means fashioning a new identity even before you've understood your old one. Work takes on a different meaning. Your children are more important than ever—if that's possible—and more inaccessible than ever. Becoming unmarried means embracing contradictions. Looking back, I see that's what I did during my years in San Francisco.

Connecting with my children took precedence over every other aspect of my new life. I was determined to keep our bonds strong, to be there for them as much as possible under the circumstances, so my week revolved around the phone calls I was allowed to make to my sons. With every call I had to prove the hardest contradiction of all to them: I'm still here for you, even though I can't be there.

The divorce decree permitted me just three calls a week. If I called when one or more of the boys weren't there because they were at Scouts or 4-H, I didn't get to call back. If I called when they were in the middle of dinner, or Family Home Evening (a weekly event connected with their church), or some other activity, I would be intruding (I felt) and I'd get off quickly. It was a logistical challenge to make sure I talked with each boy during each call. I couldn't waste one opportunity.

No matter what I was doing, the best time to phone took precedence over everything else in my life. The boys were never allowed to call me. Harvey said it was too expensive. I told them to reverse the charges. Harvey prohibited them from using the phone. And so each of my calls was all the more precious.

Of course, getting them on the phone was only the first challenge. Because we spoke Norwegian to each other, we could have private conversations even around others. That was good, but other challenges remained. How do you let your child know you care, you're interested, on the phone? You ask a question: How's everything going?

The inevitable answer: Fine. Then, silence. How to engage them in conversation without seeming to pump them for information? On the phone, the most important signals from children, the nonverbal ones, don't come through. That makes it hard to know how they really are. And for children who are five, seven, eight, and twelve years old, a conversation is difficult to carry on without seeing someone's face or feeling her touch—particularly when this person is your mother, who isn't where you are.

In addition to the calls, I flew up every month for a weekend. I had left my van with Frecia, so I could pick up the kids myself for our two days together. Typically, I'd fly in after work on Friday evening. Taking a bus from Sea-Tac airport to downtown Seattle, I'd then transfer to another bus to get to my van in north Seattle, then turn around and drive thirty miles south to Maple Valley to get the kids. That Friday night, Saturday, and part of Sunday, we'd stay in a motel that had video games, a pool, and playrooms.

The first twenty-four hours or so were always very difficult. Even though they would run off to play and swim, return to the room for special snacks and meals or to pile on the bed with me and watch TV, their anger was never far from the surface. Whatever form it took wrestling matches, irritation at some disappointment, or outright comments—I knew they had to express it, and I had to prove to them that their anger wouldn't drive me away.

Sunday was sad. No matter what bike trips or games we embarked on, Sunday meant saying goodbye. By six that evening, we'd be heading up the long, tree-lined driveway. We'd go past the acres of manicured lawn, past the pond, past what had been our raspberry vineyard. I was no longer greeted by a heckler when I kissed the boys goodbye. Still, I would choke back tears because there was never enough time to get through the sense of loss or the reopening of old wounds.

I made these visits for a year. We struggled to get past the anger and the grief in our one and a half day visit. During the summer we had eight weeks, and at the holidays we had extended periods together. With more time we had fun, and that taught me what a difference an extra day made. I realized that despite their frequency, the short visits were harmful. At the very least, the boys needed three days with me: one day at the beginning to be mad, one day at the end to be sad, with one day in the middle to have fun.

So I went from a two-day trip each month to a three-day trip ever few months around a holiday or school break. This arrangement fit within my visitation rights and it worked.

But there was a problem. Parked on the street in front of Frecia's house, my van had been totaled by a hit-and-run driver. Since I needed a car in Seattle and enjoyed the long trip, I'd drive for fifteen hours up to Maple Valley and pick up the boys by four in the afternoon on Thursday. They could then get out all this pent-up anger on Friday; Saturday we'd have fun; and Sunday would be goodbye again.

They were growing into handsome, proud boys so fast. But I really was not a part of that. The calls, the visits were not a substitute for sharing their day-to-day lives. It was difficult to carry on normally.

During this dance of "I'm still here but I can't be there" with my children, I spent time looking inward. I recognized that I had used alcohol in my marriage as a way of not dealing with issues. I didn't want it ever to get in the way of my coming to terms with myself, so I quit drinking.

I was also experiencing what it was like to be a professional single woman. My new position at the Veterans Administration Medical Center in San Francisco marked my first full-time job since active duty twelve years earlier. I'd forgotten the joy that comes from a total commitment to work. Now I experienced it again as I created my own position on the neuro-oncology ward.

All of my patients were veterans. All of them had brain tumors. Although the patients did not know it when they entered the program, most people with brain tumors die. My job was to provide treatment after surgery, see them through moments of success and survival, and for most, work with them through the process of dying.

Before I was hired, patients with brain tumors had to fend for themselves through the hospital and VA bureaucracy, besides dealing with their life-threatening condition. My job was to act as their liaison with neurosurgeons and hospital staff. I also saw them through treatment, some of which was investigational and experimental, giving them an opportunity to be involved in the new technologies and the new possibilities for survival. I both coordinated their care and advocated for them at the weekly brain tumor conference, at which doctors analyzed and determined types of treatment. Neuro-oncology is a field in which advances are constantly being made, and I was fortunate to be able to work in conjunction with a team of brain tumor specialists at the University of California, San Francisco. When a course of action-radiation, chemotherapy-was outlined by the team, I met with the patient and his or her family to explain and discuss what was occurring and what options were available.

The combination of surgery, chemotherapy, and radiation would give the patient's a better chance of success–despite past statistics. I could never have done the work and talked to the patients about their treatment if I did not think there was a chance that it would help.

The greatest challenge for these patients is to keep believing in their survival. My role was to provide hope– or at least, to facilitate the opportunity for it. Part of my work was technical: coming up with the right mix of drugs and therapy, as well as the caring that would help and inspire the desire to survive. I also co-led a support group for patients who discussed feelings and strategies. There were no secrets; we had no private discussions that did not include their families. It was essential for everyone to be able to know the truth, to plan together, to share realistic goals.

Little could ultimately be done to reverse the course of most brain tumors. But I continued to feel that if I tried harder, worked harder, believed more, then more patients would survive. So I worked more. The smallest improvements inspired me. I became very attached to my patients, although I had to make sure that I kept a professional distance between us.

Once any patient became committed to a course of action whether new treatment or no treatment–I promised myself that that patient would not be abandoned by me. Death would be as peaceful and painless as was in my power. And always I made sure the family was included in all decisions.

For my patients, the tragedy was death; the blessing was that they went to sleep and died quietly. When I failed with a patient–that is, the patient died despite my efforts–I gave support to the family as they faced the loss of a loved one.

The courage and strength of the people I cared for kept me going as much as anything else. This work both tested and affirmed the philosophy of hope I had embraced in

Vietnam. Yet, always, even from the first months, I felt like an angel of death. Despite all our efforts, there was one truth: most of the people who became my patients were going to die.

I found a release from the tensions of that world by doing my military duty on weekends. As always, being in uniform and performing as a team member made me feel good and productive. Unlike my civilian work, one-on-one with patients, my position in the Army Reserves was administrative. It provided a much needed balance in my life.

In Washington State, I had been assistant chief nurse at the 50th General Army Reserves Hospital at Fort Lawton. Transferring to California, I was first assigned to the 347th General Hospital in Sunnyvale. I soon requested and received a transfer to a field hospital closer to where I was living in San Francisco.

I joined the Army Reserves 352nd Evacuation Hospital in Oakland and began some of my most rigorous and exciting work in the Reserves. An evacuation hospital performs a crucial role during mobilization. The staff's overall mission is to go anywhere, set up a hospital, care for patients, and evacuate them efficiently in response to the combat mission.

The 352nd was a MUST (Mobile Unit Surgical Transportable) hospital totally self-contained and movable. Because a field hospital must be established in a matter of hours where previously there has been bare ground, the wards were Quonset-type bubbles. Inflatable chambers that would be filled with air by portable generators created the roofs and walls. These expandable units had been used in Vietnam. They had one major problem: any shrapnel that penetrated a chamber would cause it to deflate and the ward would partially collapse. When this happened in the ward (as it did in Vietnam), it was quite frightening. You felt as if you were suffocating and did not know what was going on out-side the ward or if help was on the way.

The main job of the unit was to get everyone sufficiently trained so that if we were called to active duty we would be ready to provide medical services. Much of the fieldwork involved setting up parts of the hospital under difficult conditions. On drill weekends, we traveled on Friday night to a remote military reservation. There, we would erect a tent city as our own barracks, assemble the wards, and immediately receive mock patients and practice the types of activities we would be expected to perform in a war situation.

We trained in "light discipline," requiring blackout conditions even when convoys moved. Vehicles would travel with cat-eye lights—with coverings over the headlights so only a slit of light escaped to illuminate the way. Usually it was pitch-black when we were in such convoys, and we frequently had to have a foot guard walk in front of the vehicle both to act as a guide and to make sure that no one was asleep on the ground in our path. As healers, we played at war to train ourselves to be able to adequately care for combat casualties.

On other occasions, the hospital prepared for attack and practiced defensive actions: perimeter security and responding to hostility with perimeter guards firing duds to drive off the attackers. We also practiced "sound discipline," during which work had to be executed as silently as possible and phones were dismantled. The point was to learn how far noise carried and the risk sound created in a combat situation.

In addition to working in the evacuation hospital on training exercises, as a member of a nursing research team I was a consultant to the chief of professional services on special projects. We studied ways to reduce high-heat stress in soldiers during chemical warfare training. With new technology and weaponry, reservists and active duty soldiers alike were trained to perform their duties wearing special clothing to protect them from chemical warfare and radiation accidents. The four-piece suits restrict movement and vision. They also get extremely hot inside and cause claustrophobia in some people.

This fact led to a new area of study for me. My friend Barbara, also with the Army Reserves 352nd Evacuation Hospital, and I conducted an investigation into ways of reducing the physical and psychological stress of wearing this clothing. The results of our four-year research project were published in a series of papers in the journal *Military Medicine*. One of our papers was selected for presentation at the international meeting of NATO forces. We felt honored even to be considered, much less selected. Barbara presented our findings at the conference in England.

In 1985, as a lieutenant colonel, I was appointed Chief Nurse of the 352nd Hospital. The job was very challenging because in some ways I was an outsider, having been with the unit for only a few years, though I had diverse previous military experience. In this new position, I realized that one of the exciting aspects of being a leader is that you have the opportunity to teach people what you believe they need to know if the unit should be activated. My Vietnam experience also gave me a sense of urgency about making sure those under my command developed skills that would help them survive during mobilization or a real disaster.

The largest and most exciting exercise I worked on while in the Army Reserves was with the Air Force. We mobilized and transported the entire hospital with more than two hundred personnel, their supplies and equipment, from Oakland to the Yakima Firing Range in Washington State. There we set up a field hospital and began receiving "casualties." For this two-week simulated mobilization, the Air Force had a hundred Civil Air Patrol cadets act as patients. They were moulaged and trained to look and act the part of wounded. Each day, all one hundred "patients" were triaged through the hospital emergency room. The casualties were then transferred to the appropriate wards for treatment and care. The following day we prepared each patient for evacuation.

This was crucial training and entailed phenomenal organization and care by the staff and administrative personnel. Each detail of their training was tested. The wounded had to be fed, housed, cared for, and tracked by paperwork. During the night, in preparation for evacuation each of the casualties with the appropriate dressings, personal belongings, food, and blankets. The next morning, the evacuees were picked up by litter bearers, who carried them to waiting ambulances. Air Force personnel loaded these casualties onto aeromedical evacuation planes.

Evacuation–keeping the flow moving–is the most important aspect of providing medical care in a combat zone. If we have four hundred beds, then receive four hundred patients whom we stabilize but do not transport out to another facility, we cannot treat additional incoming casualties. A military hospital becomes totally nonfunctional if it is unable to evacuate patients.

One of the newer concerns during the 1980s was the expectation that in the event of war, the Red Cross symbols on the hospitals would no longer protect medical personnel from attack. Because of this change in military doctrine, health-care workers were not considered a special, protected group. Now we, too, had to be combat soldiers and learn how to shoot weapons. This change in policy came about, in part, when POWs were released from Vietnam and we discovered that the North Vietnamese and Viet Cong had not treated prisoners according to the terms of the Geneva Convention Agreement. Also during Vietnam, hospitals, medical evacuation helicopters with red crosses, all became targets of attacks.

With this situation as a backdrop, a number of training objectives changed. All of us were required to become proficient with firing weapons. This was more difficult in the reserve forces, because we were allowed only one weekend a year to practice and shoot for qualification with the rifle or pistol. Company-grade (Army or Air Force captains and below) and enlisted personnel were to be qualified with the M-16 rifle, and field-grade personnel (major or above) with .45 caliber pistols.

Since future warfare would likely mean that hospitals would need to be able to protect themselves and keep functioning under attack, I added a surprise segment into our two-week field exercise. With the help of the Air Force training team, and in total secrecy, we isolated and sealed one of the wards. When it got dark, we sneaked the Air Force training team inside. They renewed moulaged wounds for all the patients on the ward, applied new mock moulaged injuries to all the staff, and then trashed the ward so that the cots and bodies were upside down. When it looked as if the ward had suffered a total disaster, we staged a simulated attack. The perimeter guards fired into the air, staff and patients screamed in pain, and the electricity (generator was turned off) went off. Then we partially dislodged the tent walls and the ward collapsed on top of the wounded.

Within a few minutes the generator was turned back on. The rest of the hospital staff came running. They were shocked—truly shocked—at the devastation. As they surveyed the horror before them, they were stunned for a moment. Then they went into action. Finding a way to get to the patients in the collapsed ward, they discovered that the hospital commander and assistant chief nurse were wounded as well. It was extraordinary to see how each of the uninjured staff immediately went to work within his or her area of expertise. The acting supervisor took over directing personnel and assuring the movement of patients so that the new wounded could be treated. The medics began primary surveillance, making sure that the wounded were breathing and had no life-threatening bleeding. The doctors started providing treatment. The administrative people moved patients and accounted for each one. The supplies personnel began assuring that emergency equipment was available. The operating rooms immediately took care of the wounded.

Everyone felt they had indeed participated in a massive medical emergency. In our debriefing period afterward, everyone shared what a profound effect the exercise had had on him or her. Curiously, one of its most traumatic parts was seeing their friends, superiors, and comrades wounded and vulnerable. This increased their commitment to do everything possible to help. Those who were the mock wounded medical personnel felt vulnerable and frightened.

Even in training, the intensity of feeling helpless is profound. Although it may seem like a game, everyone involved takes the training seriously, for anyone of us may be asked or ordered to participate in a real crisis at any time. The point is to be prepared.

For all of us in the military, whether reserve or active-duty forces, there is something deeply troubling about the sense of uncertainty, of the unknown. When will we be called? What will we face? Will we be prepared? I attempted to give the staff the experience of encountering a sudden disaster, and through proper training, keeping one step ahead of each development that occurs. I would have proudly and willingly served with them in any situation.

I have since found out that many of the officers and enlisted personnel I worked with on that exercise were gays and lesbians. At the time, I was unaware they were: the fact didn't come up, it didn't interfere with the mission, and it didn't matter to me or to anyone else.

In December 1983, Harvey and the boys were called out of the matinee at a movie theater and told there was a fire at their house. When they got home, they found fire trucks at the property. The house had burned to the ground. Only the foundation and chimney remained. Investigators found two or three hot spots. They determined it was arson.

A friend called me with the news. I immediately phoned Harvey at his parents' to offer my condolences and ask if there was anything I could do. He became very angry and told me that I was a suspect and would be investigated. I was hurt that his response to this tragedy was to threaten and strike out at me.

No one was ever arrested for the fire, though it was believed that a few neighborhood hoodlums torched the house. There was speculation it was an act of revenge against Harvey. I don't know. The one certainty was the charred shell of a house that we had spent years building. The only early photographs of the children that still exist are the ones I took with me when I left.

I felt so bad for the boys. Their home was gone. Harvey took a leave of absence from the state patrol and moved with them to a small town in the foothills of the Cascades. He ran a little grocery store and gas station his mother had purchased, while Matt, then fifteen, managed the household and his younger brothers. They stayed there just nine months. Apparently, Harvey preferred being a trooper. In September 1984, he and the boys went back to Maple Valley. Harvey returned to the state patrol. He and Matt lived in a trailer on the land while the house was rebuilt with insurance money. The other three boys lived at their grandmother's.

During the year of rebuilding, Harvey married a woman named Jan, whom he'd met through the Mormon Church. I felt both relief that Harvey was moving on and jealousy that my sons had a "new mother" (although for that school year, while the house was under construction, David, Tom, and Andy lived with Leona, the grandmother). I treasured the fact that at least the boys and I had our private language, Norwegian, and we could talk about their feelings regardless of who was listening.

Jan moved into the trailer and helped complete the new house; then all the boys moved back to Maple Valley and under one roof. From the outside, the structure looked very much like the old house I had been a part of. I don't know what changes were made to the interior design—I've never been invited inside.

Communications with Harvey—whether about making arrangements for visitations or sharing expenses for the boys' travel—continued to be like wandering through a mined combat zone. Very little was predictable or safe, it seemed. Explosions occurred when I least expected them. He played some games with visitation times, and I always worried whether he was going to let me see the kids. But I said nothing adverse about Harvey in front of the boys. I told myself that he was angry with me and it didn't have anything to do with our sons. He loved them as much as I did, and so I tried to support him in all my interactions with the kids.

When Matt got his driver's license at sixteen, he had started a landscaping business that he pursued after school and on weekends. It began with odd jobs from neighbor and friends, and then became quite successful. Its profits, along with his money from selling 4-H cattle and picking raspberries, went into a savings account for college. David, eleven, and Andy, ten, were active in sports both at school and in church-sponsored events. All the boys, including Tom at eight years of age, joined the Boy Scouts.

I missed them all the time. Fortunately, I had work to focus on. My position at the Veterans Hospital brought many rewards. But the toll was heavy. By 1985, of the one hundred brain tumor patients I had treated, sixty-six had died. I was exhausted and began to feel that my efforts were futile. I did everything I could and still failed to save most of my patients.

My supervisors and colleagues thought my work in the hospital and as a clinical professor in the school of nursing was worthy of recognition. The Veterans Administration had just begun a new program to honor nurses. Our assistant chief nurse submitted my professional biography for consideration of the award.

There are more than thirty-four thousand VA nurses in the country. I felt greatly honored and humbled to receive the first award of Nurse of the Year from the VA in 1985. Along with the certificate, I received a letter of congratulations from President Ronald Reagan.

I was also named Bay Area Federal Employee of the Year for the Greater San Francisco Area, Woman of the Year by the Women's Veterans Association, and, in the military, I received the highest coveted Surgeon General's "A" Proficiency Designator. It was a full year of recognition for doing jobs I loved in both the civilian and military communities.

My dedication had paid off. These awards proved that I was an expert in my field. But being singled out was awkward. Did I really deserve the recognition? How could I know if I did? What had I done to be worthy of such recognition? I felt I had to prove myself even more now—and I had so little left to give.

Looking inward for strength, I found emptiness. Except for occasional bike rides or trips to bookstores with Barbara, I had no personal life to renew me. After four and a half years, I needed more than work.

My children were the most important part of my world, but I felt I was no longer a mother—in some ways it seemed I had deserted my family. The guilt and pain I experienced was not erased by military or professional accolades. I was stuck.

I needed a change. It was time to return to Seattle and be near the kids. During my Thanksgiving visit with them in 1985, I met with the chief nurse at the VA hospital in Seattle and asked her if she knew of any job openings for an old Army nurse. She didn't have a vacancy but made some calls and arranged for me to meet with the chief nurse at American Lake Medical Center in Tacoma.

I had planned to drive the kids down to Lincoln City for Christmas with Aagot. Since Tacoma was right on the way, I picked up the kids at Maple Valley and told them we were going on a brief detour. I explained I had a job interview. If I got the job, I would be moving back. There was a hush in the usually noisy car. Then the questions started in rapid succession, and we drove the next thirty miles to American Lake chattering about my possible return.

I left the boys in the car and went inside the hospital. The only job vacancy the chief nurse could offer me was as a staff nurse on night duty in the nursing home care unit. I didn't know what it entailed—and I didn't care. I told her I'd love it. She asked me to begin on January 19, 1986—less than two months away.

It was a sunny, beautiful winter day. Mist rose off the lake as I walked to the car of waiting, anxious kids. When I announced I had the job and would be moving back after Christmas, they went crazy. Andy, the "tough guy," who had been the most tight-lipped of all the boys, began to cry. In the five years since the divorce, he had never shown much emotion. Now tears. My first concern was he didn't want me to return. Then I realized this was a release from his years of acting the stoic. Now all five of us cried. I can't remember when there were more unabashed tears of relief and joy.

Deciding to return to live near my sons was a tremendous relief. Until then, I had not appreciated how lonely I was because my own brothers and I got together very infrequently. My brother Jan and his wife and kids were in Virginia, my brother Paal had married and lived with his wife and kids in Washington, D.C. My father lived with Paal. And Tom was in Park City, Utah, busy with his school. So even though my family of origin was on the east coast I really felt that Seattle was my home and even more so because it was where my sons lived

My colleagues in San Francisco were surprised when I told them I was leaving, but understood when I explained I needed to go back and pick up the pieces of my life—to be closer to my sons and try to finish my doctorate.

I moved back to Seattle to be a mother again. I knew being a successful mother would take more than finding a job and an apartment and being closer for our visits. It had been five years since I'd last lived in the same house with my sons. They had grown and changed from the little boys I'd known. They had been toughened by it all. And on top of the normal challenges of living in a family damaged by divorce, they had lost their home and possessions in a fire, had lived in temporary quarters while the new house was built, had been taken care of by a grandmother, and then had seen a stepmother enter their world. There was still much we would have to work through.

On a chilly January day in 1986, the kids helped me move into an apartment located halfway between Maple Valley and my new job in Tacoma. We spent the first weekend together fixing up the apartment, each boy contributing decorating ideas and ensuring the kitchen was stocked with their favorite foods.

After six months, I bought a three-bedroom bungalow within walking distance of their grandparents' house. Leona and Howard had been devastated when Harvey and I got divorced. Yet they hadn't intruded, and until I'd moved to San Francisco, I'd kept in phone contact with them. But after I left, I didn't feel it was my right to intrude on Harvey's relationship with them, so I hadn't called or written. Even when I moved into their neighborhood, I kept my distance. After about a month, Leona walked down to my house and reminded me that in her mind I was still her daughter-in-law. I was very pleased, and from then on we talked and saw each other regularly.

The new home was very comfortable. It was just five blocks from Leona's, so the boys could bicycle there or to Lake Washington. There were two bedrooms for the four boys. I bought trundle beds that pulled out into separate units. The camouflage bedspreads I put on the beds were such a big hit, I also got each boy a set of BDUs (battle-dress uniforms) or, as called by civilians, fatigues. Our house looked truly military—"camo" everywhere for the kids. I loved hearing their happy voices in my home.

Several years before, I had finally found a simple way to make sure the kids could call me if they wanted: I gave them each a telephone calling card. Then they were able to call me from a friend's house or a phone booth. When I moved back, they continued that practice. As soon as cellular phones became available, I got one and it made me even more available to them.

Now that I was living near my sons, and we were seeing one another on a regular basis, I struggled with my new role. After the divorce, I used our limited time together to show them love, not discipline. But now, should that change? What were my rights? How could I best be more of a parent? Did I have the right to correct their behavior? It took time to work out all these issues.

There was another change within me because I saw my children differently. When I lived with them all the time, they were my babies, my kids, and part of me. Now, however, they had a whole set of life experiences of their own. When their opinions were different from mine, I didn't see those differences as expressions of rebellion, but as valuable points of view that came from their own experiences.

In other words, I considered my sons people. I didn't own them. I didn't control them. I resumed my role as mother, but with the appreciation that these were human beings. I was still an every-other-weekend parent—like a generous godmother. I wasn't authoritarian. When they were with me, they didn't have to do anything. We took all our time for fun. I bought a small motorboat and we played in that. I had them for only two days at a time, and I told myself I could deal with almost any behavior for forty-eight hours. I reaped all the benefits of their free time, and when they went back to Maple Valley, they returned to the discipline and chores there.

There was one positive part from my years apart from the kids. Even tough, cynical Andy said, "Mor, you don't act like a parent. You treat us like people." It was the most flattering comment I could have gotten. I don't always agree with them, but I try to offer them the same respect I want from them. And I might never have achieved that respect if I had lived with them or near them all those years.

My promotion to colonel occurred in 1987, and I was presented with my new insignia in an official ceremony. Harvey's father, Howard, had always wanted to pin the eagles on my uniform (he had retired from the Army Reserves with the rank of lieutenant colonel). But he was ill and unable to attend. So Leona and I made a surprise visit to his nursing home where he pinned the eagles on my shoulders with the bearing of a fine officer. I was deeply moved and pleased he could share that moment with me.

Reestablishing my life in Seattle had gone smoothly so far. My job at American Lake was calm and steady. My children and I had developed a comfortable routine. I had another loose end to tie up—my doctoral degree. Dare I try to apply, would I be able to finish it? Was my life settled sufficiently to allow me to succeed where I'd failed before? What other crisis or disruption could possibly arise? I was single, secure at work and in the military. I saw nothing that could distract me now.

My leave of absence from the doctoral program had expired, and I had officially withdrawn in 1982. As a result, I had to competitively reapply and was accepted for the Ph.D. program in nursing at the University of Washington. I resumed my studies in the fall of 1987.

After my return to Washington, I continued as chief nurse of the 352nd Evacuation Hospital in Oakland, California, and commuted back each month for drill weekend. Naturally, my ability to be involved and to supervise was hampered by being far away. The assistant chief nurse went to the staff meetings before drill and

called me so we could discuss issues that required
decisions about nursing activities. I was not available to
interview potential new members or deal with the day-
to-day problems.   As a commuting chief nurse, I was
not being fair to the people I represented.   I needed to
relinquish the job, so I began looking for alternatives.
The Washington National Guard was seeking a state
Chief Nurse. I applied for the position.

The National Guard has a mission similar to that of
the Army Reserves, with one addition: it also responds to
state emergencies. Thus, the Guard functions as both the
state militia and a federal agency, as part of the military.
People who are in the National Guard have to be approved
by the Army and meet the Army's physical and mental
requirements.   The President can mobilize National
Guard units for emergencies, as happened during the
Persian Gulf crisis. But it also responds to the Governor's
request for help when there are local emergencies—floods,
fires, hurricanes, or nuclear accidents.

For many of us who have gone from the Reserves to
the Guard, there is a much different sense of commitment
because you are doing something besides preparing for
war—you are getting ready to take care of your own in a
crisis. The Guard provides more of a sense of serving your
own community that any other branch of the military.

My first interviews for the position of state Chief
Nurse were with the National Guard recruiter Major
Tom Doherty and the State Surgeon of the National
Guard, Colonel George Koss. They were energized about
the work ahead. Funds had just been allocated for a new
field hospital for Washington State. This would be a new
unit, completely equipped, that would have the ability to
assemble a hospital and receive patients anywhere in the
event of a crisis. Both Major Doherty and Colonel Koss
were enthusiastic. They particularly wanted to improve

the image of the nursing component of the new hospital. With my background in the Army nursing in Germany and Vietnam, as well as experience in the Army Reserved, I seemed like a perfect fit as Chief Nurse.

Colonel Koss and I hit it off particularly well. I was delighted when he offered me the position. I transferred from the Army Reserves to the Washington National Guard in February 1988, and began assisting in the planning, recruitment and development of the new field hospital. I worked about five days a month—one drill weekend plus additional meetings and conferences. Then, as in the Reserves, there was a two-week summer camp for war games.

By June 1988, things had fallen into place. At the university, I passed the rigorous progressional exams and knew I was going to make it through the doctoral program. I was a mother again, sharing the weekly travails and joys of my sons' lives. I loved my work in the military, and saw the possibility of becoming a candidate for the post of Chief Nurse of the entire National Guard within the next few years.

To celebrate all this richness, I planned a trip with my kids to Lincoln City for the Fourth of July holiday with Aagot. There we'd also meet new friends, go crabbing, play music and sing around the beach campfire, watch the fireworks over the Pacific Ocean. And there my life would change again, more than I'd ever imagine.

For there I would meet Diane.

CHAPTER 10

. . . .

Becoming Whole

Staring into the embers of the beach fire, I continue talking, adding another idea to the fabric of thoughts we've woven between us. Suddenly I realize it's daylight. We've talked all night just as though we were kids. I feel young and innocent again, like a teenager watching the sun come up after the senior prom, knowing a chapter of her life is over. But here the chapter is beginning. Just beginning. My first day of not trying to fit into anyone else's mold. My first day with Diane.

. . . .

Boundaries between people are crucial. Military officer, nurse, and teacher—each occupation requires a particular type of behavior and demeanor. I believe that achievement in these fields comes not just from skill and dedication, but also from respecting the boundaries of each role.

That means simple things: I'm not a friend to my patients or to soldiers under my command. I show respect for rank. Personal matters are not discussed or disclosed except with friends. Caring for others-my sons, patients, troops-requires a focus on others' needs and feelings, not my own.

These separations of roles are necessary. But what is also necessary is a place where they can all come together: a place where what I feel is permitted. For all the gifts in my life, I never had that place. I never knew it was even possible to have.

Until I met Diane.

We met through a former patient of mine in San Francisco. I had managed Jean's treatment for a brain tumor. Because I worked with patients' families, I met her partner, Phyllis, as well.

During those years, I had a few acquaintances like Phyllis and Jean—colleagues, patients, family members of patients—who I suspected, or knew, were gay. I had no prejudice or fear with them because I'd gotten to know them as individuals, not stereotypes. At some point, I would think, "Gee, I bet they're homosexual." But we never talked about it. It wasn't done. I respected their privacy. As a middle-aged woman, raised in the conservative 1950s, I didn't discuss intimate relationships, much less sex. (It wasn't a topic of conversation when I was married, either.) But during Jean's extended stays for radiation treatment in the hospital, I arranged a private room so Phyllis could visit her.

While I worked at the VA in San Francisco, Phyllis and Jean tried to develop a friendship with me, but I maintained a distance, due to our professional relationship. After moving to Seattle, when I was no longer Jean's primary-care provider, I saw them from time to time when they traveled through the Seattle area. I enjoyed their company. Jean was a writer and Phyllis an artist. Their interests and experiences were so different from anything I knew.

With them, as with all my friends, I was reserved. Though our time together was important to me, they usually initiated the contact. I still immersed myself in work and did not have a social life. But I was delighted when they offered to meet me and my sons in Lincoln City for the Fourth of July, 1988. I was driving down with Tom, Andy, and David for our traditional beach and fireworks holiday with Aagot.

Matt was on his two-year Mormon mission (a teaching assignment the church encouraged young men to take) in Norway and then the Midwest, so he did not join us in Lincoln City. I'd been ambivalent when he had discussed going on a mission. The church rule was that the young man has to pay for his own mission. That meant Matt would use all his savings.

He was engaged to his high-school sweetheart, Lynette, and they planned to marry as soon as he returned from the mission. My concern was that the two years away would put too great a strain on them financially and that it would not only delay but possibly prevent his going on to college. But Matt was adamant about going on the mission. The church was very important to him, and so, once he had decided to go, I supported him.

Meanwhile, Jean and Phyllis had invited three other friends from California to meet us in Lincoln City that Fourth of July weekend. Nancy and Virginia were coming from Northern California. They, too, had been together—as friends and then partners—for many years. Nancy worked in health care and was completing her degree in counseling, and Virginia was a social worker and artist. Then, from Southern California, another artist and university professor, Diane, was taking the plane to Portland and traveling by bus to Lincoln City. These five friends had a history that spanned decades. It made perfect sense that they were all meeting together, and I felt pleased I had the opportunity to join them.

At the time, however, I didn't realize that Phyllis and Jean had planned for Diane and me to meet. Though we rarely talked about my personal life, Phyllis and Jean were astute enough to realize I might be ready to meet someone, and they felt Diane and I would hit it off. In a way, it was like my younger days in Germany before I knew Harvey, when friends would set me up on dates with men. Of course, the difference here was we didn't talk about it. We didn't mention my being alone any more than we talked about Phyllis and Jean's being together as a couple. And we certainly never discussed their arranging for me to meet their single friend, Diane. I can see now that our silence made my knowing who I was harder still. (That's also why I'm so astounded when I hear people say that gays promote an agenda or recruit innocent straights. In that circle of women in their forties and fifties, we didn't even talk to each other about being gay!)

And because nothing was said, I had no unusual expectations for the trip.

The boys and I arrived at Aagot's in a flurry of hugs and hellos. Her place had become as familiar as our own homes, having served as the boys' and my vacation place during the time I lived in San Francisco. The other women were staying at a motel on the beach, just a block away.

After we settled in, Phyllis called to ask if I would drive her to the bus station to pick up her friend Diane. Phyllis didn't like to drive in the rain. I said I'd be happy to play chauffeur.

I picked up Phyllis at the motel, and then drove to the bus station. On the way, Phyllis gave me a quick update about Diane. She'd known Diane for more than thirty years. They shared their passion as artists. Diane had also taught art at a university for almost as long as their friendship. They saw each other only about once a year, but had a great time when they got together.

We pulled up to the station and Phyllis jumped out to find her friend while I waited in the car. When they returned, Diane and I met through the rearview mirror. We exchanged glances. But it was dark and raining, and as the chauffeur, I was quiet for the rest of the trip back to the motel. After dropping them off, I went to feed my tribe at Aagot's.

Later that evening, the boys, Aagot, and I joined the five women at their motel rooms overlooking the ocean. The kids, kept in by the rain, wanted to play a game of Pictionary. Everyone else, except Diane, agreed to participate.

As the women and young men began a raucous game, Diane stretched out on a couch with a book. Andy, Mr. Persistence, continued to badger her to join the game. She politely repeated, "No, thank you," several times and went back to her reading. Undeterred, Andy vehemently challenged her again. Finally, she said, "I don't play games. I'm just a dud." Without missing a beat, Andy calmly replied, "Well, come on, Dud, play." She laughed with great delight, put down her book, and joined us.

From that moment on, the boys called her Dud.

The next evening was the Fourth of July celebration on the beach. Aagot decided to stay at home. The rest of us staked out a good spot early. The boys built a large fire pit and, since the weather had been unseasonably cold and windy, put up a rain tarp. We left Jean's wheelchair at the sidewalk and carried her down to our beach camp.

The sun disappeared into the waves and the entire town congregated at the beach to watch the fireworks. There were campfires and laughing children as far as you could see. As we had done every year since they were very little, the boys and I made Some-mores over the fire—marshmallows, apple slices, and chocolate piled and melted on graham crackers. I had also brought my guitar. We sang folk songs together until the fireworks display began.

Near midnight, the fireworks over and conversation dying down, Jean said she needed to call it a night. I drove the adults back to their motel. However, I'd promised the boys I'd come back to the beach. There was going to be a very low tide at 3:00 a.m. and they wanted to stay and go crabbing. As I helped Jean to the room, I gave an open invitation to everyone to return with me. I expected Phyllis to jump at the chance, since Jean would have others available should she need anything. Instead, Phyllis encouraged Diane to join me. Diane and I had not spoken more than a few casual sentences to each other, and I suspected the poor woman only wanted to get some sleep. But Phyllis pushed Diane until she agreed to keep me company while I watched the boys. We drove back to the beach together.

By now the boys were crabbing with single-minded devotion. Diane and I got the fire going again. Here I was, sitting on a log across from a near stranger in the middle of the night. I felt rather awkward.

Then I did something contrary to my style. I began to talk, and while I spoke, I found Diane listening in the most extraordinary way. I talked more, and she asked a few questions, and listened with an intensity that illuminated everything. So I continued on about everything and anything. But most amazingly, I talked about me. Perhaps it was the fact that here was someone who lived thirteen hundred miles away, someone I thought I would never see again which make talking easier. In the dark, with a kind stranger, it was safe to share what I felt. It was, in fact, wonderful.

Not only was Diane a superb listener with inspiring questions and inexhaustible interest; she had great stamina. In what felt like no time at all, I looked up from the fire and noticed the sun was rising. I'd talked until dawn. We were alone together. The boys were asleep against the logs. The beach was deserted. We smiled at each other and chatted about how quickly the night had passed. Then we gathered up the boys and on the way back to home decided to cook everyone a waffle breakfast. Since it was 5:00 a.m., we detoured to an all-night grocery for supplies and bought enormous quantities of food. We left David and Andy sleeping in the car, and, with Tom, went to the motel room's kitchenette to cook and talk some more.

Delighted at our maternal fortitude, we spread out waffles, sausage, and fruit and waited for the hungry crowd to rush to the table. But nothing happened. After our amazing night of talking, Diane, who was fifty-two, and I, at forty-six, had energy beyond the range of the teenagers. I looked for the two boys in the car, but they weren't there. I found them at home at Aagot's: David was asleep in bed and Andy was snoring in the bathtub. I let them sleep and returned to the motel. Only Tom remained awake to make sure there was someone to feed. The poor, exhausted kid was almost asleep standing up. Seeing the mounds of food before him, he roused himself and ate just enough so Diane and I would feel it was worth the effort. We laughed at ourselves and did the dishes.

I felt like a kid. I'd had a wonderful nightlong marathon; our shopping and cooking spree had been crazy and fun. Now the time was over. I didn't want it to end. But I had to get the boys back to Maple Valley and myself back to work. So I said good morning and headed off to sleep a little before the five-hour drive home.

After a brief nap, I loaded up gear and kids to return to Seattle.

First we went down to the motel to say goodbye to everyone. They were amazed that I was actually packed and ready to go. "You were up all night," Phyllis teased, "and now you're off with less sleep than your kids."

"It's a trick I learned in Vietnam," I explained.

We all posed for photographs. A flurry of kids and adults mixing in every combination, arms around each other, laughing for the camera. Finally, I got each son back into the van and began pulling out of the driveway. Andy gave one last wave, then yelled, "See ya, Dud!"

On the trip home the boys slept. It was quiet the whole way. And I felt a happiness that was new. A few days later, I received a card from Diane. It was a quick note saying how much she had enjoyed the weekend. I sat down and wrote a reply, returning the compliment. Then I went back to my busy life. But the memories of that wonderful time together, sharing my life, feeling special, lingered.

A few weeks later, Jean and Phyllis wrote that they were planning a trip to Seattle in September. I wrote inviting them to stay with me. Just before I put the letter in the mail, I added a note on the back of the envelope. Trying to be nonchalant, I wrote that if Diane was in the area she would be welcome, too. Only later did I find out they had already planned that exact scenario.

Phyllis and Jean arrived for their visit over Labor Day weekend. Again we didn't discuss Diane beyond noting to each other how pleasant it would be to have her join us. All my friends knew me as a quiet, private person. But a few days later, when Diane arrived, I suddenly began to talk in a way they'd never seen. Diane was a kindred spirit–I felt a new freedom. We had a wonderful visit. Phyllis and Jean left after a few days. And for another week, Diane and I had time alone, as well as opportunities to be together with the kids again.

Andy, David, and Tom continued to be very comfortable with the Dud. Their teasing back and forth was, even from the first, good-natured. Though ever observant, the kids were not threatened by her relationship with me, and she was generous to them and accommodated their needs.

No one listens like Diane. No one I have ever known. Hers is a receptivity that's intelligent, compassionate, and amused. Her heart is light, her laughter warm and ready. It's laughter that is never mean or petty, but embraces, loves, values. The laughter of an artist and teacher who inquires into the mysteries of religion with the same intensity she gives to a succession of Scottie dogs.

I'd never known what it meant to be understood by one person. It is that simple. It is no different from what every other person in the world wants: to be special to one other person.

Meeting Diane and experiencing the rightness of being with her made me realize I am a lesbian. Finally being able to acknowledge that gave me the last, connecting piece to the puzzle of my identity.

It was a puzzle I'd tried and failed to solve since my adolescence. Not understanding—or not accepting—my difference, my sexual orientation, was like looking at myself through a faulty lens. If something didn't feel right, I couldn't find the reason because I couldn't see myself clearly. I attributed my social discomfort in school to various sources. I was shy because I was Norwegian, I didn't fit in because I was too tall, I didn't want to date because my clothes weren't fashionable—but none of those explanations was entirely right.

My on-and-off reclusiveness in college seemed to have no cause at all. I so wanted to fit in. I wanted to be accepted, to be like all the women in the movies I saw, like the heroines in the books I read, like the classmates I knew, like my mother, whom I loved. I tried to play the role of a woman they played: a woman who desires a man. But I really didn't.

But when I acknowledged I am a lesbian, I could look back and see clearly for the first time. All my life I had recoiled at being intimate with a man, but I believed that I could change those feelings with time. I enjoyed working with my male colleagues; I had affection for male friends like Doug and cared for Harvey. But when I dated and when I married, not only was I not attracted to my male partners, I felt physically violated whenever I was kissed or touched by them. Despite trying, wanting to be an accommodating wife, I withdrew physically whenever possible. Being sexual with a man felt like a violation. It wasn't Harvey's fault. It wasn't any man's fault. Some unchangeable part of me felt that sex with a man was an invasion and I resented it. Over fifteen years of marriage, those feelings only got stronger. At the age of forty-six, I finally had to face the fact that being heterosexual wasn't a choice I had.

Yet, when I left my marriage, all I knew about my identity was contained in a negative statement: Being in a relationship with a man is not what I want. When a friend wanted to fix me up with an eligible man, I said no. My friend assumed that as an older, divorced woman, I was going to stay single and unattached for the duration and was not looking for another relationship. I wasn't asked to explain my lack of interest in dating, so I didn't. But silently I tried to understand my disinterest in men. I read books and studied scientific reports. I learned that the medical profession does not consider homosexuality to be a mental illness, and many scientists believe it is genetically determined.

I didn't want to have a relationship with a man. I accepted that in the years after my divorce. But I didn't want to be with a woman, either. I feared being a member of a despised and stigmatized minority. And there was something more. Like the world around me, I was homophobic-fearful of those who are labeled gays and lesbians. In my ignorance, I had only negative images of them: they were taunted, beaten up, fired from jobs, rejected by friends and families. I didn't want to be part of that group.

My homophobia was also unconscious. Just recently, a former colleague told me that when we served together in Vietnam I mentioned that I thought some of the women on my high-school softball team had been lesbians and that I didn't approve. I was very surprised by his memory. First, because it's hard to acknowledge my own intolerance and prejudice, and second, because I have no memory at all of saying or feeling such a thing.

Only once from the time of my divorce until I met Diane did I let down my armor. In San Francisco, I began to care for a person. I avoided thinking this special feeling linked me to an ostracized minority by telling myself that this person "just happens to be a woman." That relationship never evolved but the memory of new kinds of feelings remained.

After that, as much as I might have liked to, I couldn't be as naive as I was in my youth. And I couldn't deny my suspicions that I might be homosexual. But my own homophobia continued to hold that self-knowledge in a kind of intellectual prison. I wondered if I was a homosexual, but I blocked out any feelings that might go with the concept. Also, I never said or thought the word "lesbian." "Lesbian" was too personal. It had ownership-and I wasn't ready for ownership. I could only use the term "homosexual"-it locked the feelings in a theoretical trap, keeping them impersonal, like the word itself.

Over the next couple of years, I focused on my military and professional work and my sons. But when I met Diane, I realized how lonely I'd been. I cared for her, and I realized that this caring was more than friendship. It was love. For the first time in my life I felt: I can talk to this person, we discuss things, we have feelings for each other, we express those feelings easily, and I don't try to keep my distance as I always had done with men. One of the things that most surprised me was that my feelings came not from attraction but from an emotional connectedness. For the first time, I experienced completely fulfilling love.

After one of the most remarkable weeks of my life, Diane went on to England for six weeks. Now we wrote letters. I learned more and felt closer through these letters than I thought possible.

By reaching out to another person all my separate selves came together. How amazing. All my parts—nurse, Ph.D. student, officer, mother, friend—were permitted here. This wonderful time—building a relationship with Diane—also seemed right—one of the most natural experiences of my life.

Yet we lived thirteen hundred miles apart. Neither of us wanted to give up our established, full life. Diane was a tenured, much-loved university professor and artist who regularly showed her paintings at galleries in California. I was not about to move away from my sons and my work. It was a big challenge. But I'd managed distances before. So, with great happiness, we decided we would commit to each other, and began our enduring partnership.

We're very different. In many ways, we're opposites. I'm a scientist and believe in calculated results. She's an artist, a free spirit. I'm from Norway and the snow and cold of the North, and she's from the Southwest and the heat of the desert. At the first indication of sun, I'm outside, stripped down, and basking in the heat; she's inside, cool, away from the harsh, too-familiar glare.

Diane's laughter is irrepressible. She adores poking fun at whatever and whomever is too serious. That includes me. Her wise counsel and concern, however, are always available to me—and to everyone else. As a teacher, a friend, a fellow artist, and now an ombudsman for my sons, she is giving of herself.

We visited each other about once every six weeks and went to art shows (a first for me), concerts, and flea markets, searching for great bargains or additions to Diane's Ugly Collection (a roomful of mementos so lacking in style or utility she finds them endearingly ugly). We kept our relationship private. When we went places together, I was introduced to her friends, but we did not discuss our commitment to each other. And I said nothing to my sons (although several years later they revealed they'd guessed).

In the late fall of that year, 1988, my brother Paal was moving with his family for a two-year tour of duty to Africa as a diplomat. Since my father lived with them in Washington, D.C., I'd offered to have him spend those two years in my home, and was making arrangements for that to happen by the spring of 1989.

Because he was coming to live with me, I felt I needed to tell my father about my sexual orientation. I knew I wanted Diane in my life, though I was not sure how our long-distance relationship would evolve. Though I was silent about my personal life at work and with my sons when they visited, I was not going to hide who I was for the two years my father would live with me. If my father knew I was gay, and then chose to move in, neither one of us would have to be dishonest.

So I wrote my father a letter. Remembering he came from a world in which homosexuals were considered mentally ill, I fashioned my explanation to him in words I hoped he could understand. I wrote: "I've come to accept I am a homosexual. I am perfectly happy. I don't feel I am sick and I do not need therapy. I just want you to know this before you come."

It was a difficult letter to write and to send. Before I put it in the mail, I called Paal and told him about it over the phone. He was understanding and offered to help me be clear with Father. So I added in the letter to my father that Paal was already aware of this fact, and if he needed to talk with him, instead of me, that was fine.

My letter arrived. Paal knew when he saw it in the mail. My father took the letter to his room and read it. Paal waited. Finally, Father came out of his room and said to Paal, "I have bad news. Your sister is homosexual. That's really very unfortunate.

"Paal said, "You're going to write her, aren't you?"

"No," Father said, "there's nothing to write."

"Of course there is," Paal gently insisted. "Don't you need to write and tell her how you're accepting all of this?"

My father thought about that for a moment. Then he went back to his room and wrote me a letter. His words were as much as he could bring himself to say at the time: "I'm sorry you had to say anything about this. I hope it doesn't hurt your career. I'll only come and live with you for two years."

Telling my father was the first time I broke my silence to someone whose response I dreaded. But the world didn't end. In fact, my letter opened up new possibilities between us. He didn't reject me. With his scientist's precision he simply reminded me he would stay only two years.

And he did. A man who had enjoyed a most sheltered and rule-bound life moved into our busy, unconventional household. In 1990, the second year of his stay, Diane took early retirement from the university, and alternated her time between my house in Seattle and her home and art studio in Southern California. She'd come up for several months at a time, then return to her primary residence. While she was here, she pampered my father a bit too much. She found him to be quite charming, which distressed me slightly (probably because he teased me as I was growing up and was still able to provoke me that way). She even laughed at his teasing-though I found it un-amusing. In short, we had a pretty traditional untraditional household.

Years later, at family and friend reunion party, he surprised me in the most wonderful way. He stood as if to make a toast and said, with the same certainty he would use to explain a neurological condition, that he found Diane and my home to be "perfectly normal". Diane's eyes twinkled. I was amazed. We were all silent, contemplating the extraordinary moment. Then I said in true Norwegian style, "Far, please pass the salt." I felt nothing more needed to be said by anyone-and Father seemed to agree.

However, that acceptance was in the unpredictable future. When I received the letter announcing his arrival, I was relieved and also somewhat amused. It was good he was coming to live with me, but the way he responded was just so typical. I had made this major disclosure, and he had moved past the emotional part to say, "I hope it doesn't hurt your career." When I read those words, I chuckled. What did my career have to do with it? This is private-it changes nothing about the way I do my job.

I was that innocent.

As 1989 began, I felt the excitement of new opportunities throughout my life. I would not have thought all these riches possible just three years before, when I moved back to Seattle from San Francisco. I had a true-life partner for the first time and that brought great joy. Soon I would complete my Ph.D.—finally Dr. Cammermeyer. And I was a mother again. Still, I wanted to achieve more in the military.

Since I joined the Army in 1961, I'd dreamed of becoming a General a National Chief Nurse. By the 1980s, there were three Chief Nurse positions in the military. The Chief Nurse of the Army Nurse Corps oversaw the work of the other two: the Chief Nurse of the Army Reserves and the Chief Nurse of the National Guard. The position of Chief Nurse in the Guard offered the best opportunity to make change, create policy, and bring about improved patient care for soldiers. Also, the role of medical units in the National Guard was becoming more important as states recognized the need for emergency treatment in natural disasters and local crises. As someone with active- and combat-duty experience, as well as a strong record in the Reserves, I felt I had a valuable perspective.

I loved my current position as state Chief Nurse, but it also encouraged me to plan for my next career opportunity. The Guard was more open to new people joining, contributing, and advancing in the ranks than the Army Reserves, and becoming national Chief Nurse seemed within my reach.

Of course, that position demanded impeccable credentials. My military record was without a blemish, and I was in the final stage of completing my professional education and earning my doctorate. I needed only to attend the War College (the military equivalent to doctoral work) to be competitive.

The course work at the War College involves classified information important in the nation's defense. Therefore, to attend, you must have a top-secret clearance. I had to upgrade my security clearance to top secret.

Thinking only of acquiring more training (and not considering my new relationship with Diane), I completed the paperwork requesting an upgraded security clearance. Then I had my fingerprints taken. The next step would be a routine interview with a Defense Investigative Service agent. That wouldn't be scheduled for a few months, so I went on with my life, not giving it another thought.

It was a busy time. Diane, who was up for a couple of months, and I began looking for a larger house in preparation for my father's coming to live with me. Every other weekend, David, Tom, and Andy would join us. Then at the Guard duty, one weekend and two additional days a month, I continued preparing for the new hospital. The rest of my time was spent balancing the demands of graduate school with my job at the VA hospital in American Lake.

I was no longer on night duty as a staff nurse. A year after I'd taken that position—content to have any work near my sons—I was offered a new position. The staff neurologist had a tremendous patient load and was anxious to find a way to consolidate care for his patients who were being treated for seizures. Because of his heavy schedule, he was able to see each patient only about once a year. Many of them still had difficulties and, out of fairness to them, needed to be seen more frequently. Since I had worked with people with epilepsy and seizures from 1975 to 1980, he asked me to develop and manage a new seizure clinic and oversee the primary care for these patients.

By now, the early months of 1989, the seizure clinic was entering its third year of operation. As a clinical nurse specialist, I had inherited 125 patients and had received new ones as they came for treatment.

Most patients who have seizures at a VA hospital have developed the disorder after they entered the military. That's because, theoretically, anyone with a history of seizures before enlistment is barred from the military.

The kinds of seizures we see are caused by a head injury, stroke, or brain infection that has left a scar on the brain. The scar can be as tiny as the head of a pin. Statistically, only 20 percent of people who suffer head injuries develop seizures. It's not something we can predict, but we can successfully treat an individual once the condition develops. The first seizure may not occur for up to two years (a period of time based on changes in neurons) after the initial head injury. If a person goes beyond that two-year period without incident, he or she will most likely not have any problems later.

Epilepsy and seizures are one and the same. However, the term "epilepsy" has unfortunate, and inappropriate, connotations. But even the less-loaded term "seizure" still carries a social stigma. So we have two main jobs in providing care at the clinic. One is to effectively analyze the patient's current condition, prescribe medication, and monitor progress, and the other is to help the patient deal with the social stigma he or she often meets out in the world.

Because some people in the general public are uneducated about seizures, they fear them or fear those who have had them. However, when seizures are controlled through proper treatment they have absolutely no effect on a person's abilities. Eighty percent of our patients who take their medication become totally seizure-free without any side effects. They are able to function and resume their lives.

Yet the social stigma remains. Our patients sometimes lose their jobs, or are not hired. Some irrational people even believe that seizure patients are possessed by the devil, and condemn them for it.

Interestingly though, nobody knows that a person is on seizure medications or is suspected of having seizures unless the individual discloses the condition. It is very similar to the stigma of being gay.

Because of this heightened tension of patients' fears not just for their health but also as to whether others will accept them, we've found there is a tremendous need for a supportive health-care environment. Caregivers must not only provide the right drug therapy; they must also deal with the social ramifications of this unfair stigma. I work hard to build trusting relationships with the patients, so they will know I'm not going to medicate them into zombies. I must make them believe our mutual goal is to make them seizure free without side effects.

Sometimes that also means helping them fight the system to avoid losing their benefits. With their seizures under control, their lives are less disrupted and the VA can discontinue their financial benefits even though the stigma attached to their condition prevents them from getting health insurance or a driver's license or a job. Once we provide the right medication to make them seizure-free, we still struggle with the bureaucracy and fight unfair policies. My job, then, also is to empower the disfranchised.

The seizure clinic operated on Fridays at American Lake. I was, course, always available, but during clinic visits it was my opportunity to meet individually with patients, deal with new concerns, follow up on their treatment plan. Since I was completing my doctorate,

I went to classes the other days of the week, as well as working at the hospital, and performing my duties as Chief Nurse at the National Guard.

It wasn't until April 1989 that I finally received a call from Agent Brent Troutman of the Defense Investigative Service to set up my interview to upgrade my security clearance. I explained how busy my schedule was. He assured me he would take only forty-five minutes of my time. I thought it would be least disruptive to arrange it for my lunch break on a day I had seizure clinic.

In addition to my work at the hospital, I was on the clinical faculty of the University of Washington School of Nursing. In that capacity, I acted as a mentor to students interested in neurology. At the time of the interview, a graduate student worked with me and knew enough about the patients and the hospital to conduct clinic in my brief absence. The student could call me during my session with the DIS agent, but I was still reluctant to be gone too long.

Going into the interview I felt another pressure. Right after work at six that same evening, I had an appointment to sign the contract for our new home. It had to be done that night because other offers, we were told, were coming in the following day, so I didn't want to be late for that meeting, either.

In retrospect, I knew subconsciously there might be questions that I would answer differently now that I had met Diane. But my belief that I had more to contribute to the military took precedence. By over-scheduling myself, I effectively blocked any fears, and as I sat down in my office with Agent Troutman, I only felt concern that I get out of the interview on time.

Of course, I have played that day over in my mind a thousand times. I see the close, bare walls of my dungeon-like office. I feel the press of the patients I should be seeing in clinic, even as I focus on the agent intently going through his notebook full of questions.

Then, about thirty minutes into the interview, he asked me something regarding homosexuality. I do not recall the precise question. However, I remember I requested clarification. He didn't elaborate, but just read the question again. There was a moment of silence in which I thought only, "Well, this is what I need to say." I was unfamiliar with the details of the military's policy on homosexuality. Almost every decade since World War I, the regulation had been changed to conform to prevailing social attitudes or the need for enlistment during times of mobilization, and I hadn't studied current policy. I'd never been involved in anyone's investigation for homosexuality. My job was to facilitate the professional development of medical personnel. The little information I had was that the mere statement that I am a lesbian would not be cause for separation. I also thought that each commander had discretion to retain a gay or lesbian servicemember if the individual's contribution exceeded the "perceived risk" of his or her sexual orientation. But none of that was true any longer. The regulation had been revised again in 1982, and the present, harsher policy excluded gay men and lesbians without exception. In the revised policy, a statement alone was grounds for separation. Additionally, commanders had no discretion and were obligated to initiate separation action regardless of the circumstances. Unaware of those changes, I believed only that homosexuality was frowned upon, just as adultery and going to off-post red-light districts was frowned upon. I really didn't know what I was getting into. Although, if I had, my response would have been the same: I said "I am a lesbian."

Suddenly, he was very interested and there was a change in the flow of questions. I thought he really wanted to understand more about homosexuality. He was so attentive and eager. As an educator, a mother, a nurse, I responded. He had a need to know—and I tried to fulfill it. I talked about what I had come to understand about myself.

I explained that homosexuality is not something a person chooses. It is an inherent part of an individual that has nothing to do with behavior. It is really an emotional bonding. For me, it is an understanding of my identity that finally made me whole.

He kept prodding for specifics about behavior, experiences, and relationships. I reiterated I was talking about who I am, and it really didn't have anything to do with anything else.

No matter how I defined the distinctions for him, how I explained, he wanted more. We were getting nowhere and I was feeling frustrated and wanted to be done. I was worried about my patients. The hours were passing. Periodically I'd call the clinic to check in.

Finally I told him, "I really need to get back to work."

"Before you go," he replied, "I need to have you sign a statement regarding what you have said."

"I'll get a statement to you in a few days," I promised.

"This report needs to be completed today," he insisted. "1 know what they want. I'll go type it for you. Then you can cross out whatever you don't agree with, and sign it."

Feeling the pressure of the late hour and the daylong interrogation, I agreed, anything was fine just to get it over with. I hurried back to the clinic as he went off to write my statement. An hour later, he returned with a statement for me to sign. Now it was five o'clock. We'd been at it since 11:00 a.m. In one hour, I was to sign papers to purchase the new house. All I wanted was to get out of there.

I read the statement he had written for me to sign. It had errors, innuendos, changed meanings, and statements out of sequence. Its tone was totally different from mine. I crossed out sentences. I added some others. I signed the document and felt guilty because at the bottom of the paper it said I had prepared this document, and obviously I hadn't. With reservations, relief, and dread, I handed it back to him and rushed off to my appointment.

As I drove to the realtor's and what was to have been a celebration of our new home, I realized my career was in jeopardy. Maybe it was over. Yet that was unthinkable. The military had been my life, it was where I belonged. It had taken care of me and in return I had given it my best. My rank, my position, and my years—they wouldn't take those away.

Or would they?

At least I had been honest.

Integrity was the basis of everything I stood for in my life and career. I was not a security risk. I'd told them I was gay; I'd proved no one could blackmail me. I remembered the times I'd seen other major military regulations changed. Hadn't I been able to challenge the military to correct the date of my rank change in Germany? Hadn't I succeeded in getting them to provide me, a married female officer, with the same housing allowance as my officer husband before the regulation had been officially changed? In Vietnam, hadn't our arguments to allow married officers to live together been accepted? And in a major revision of policy, hadn't the armed forces let go of their prejudice against women with children serving, so that I and thousands of other mothers could return to uniform in 1971? These experiences proved the military could also judge this situation on its merits—acknowledge me as an individual and realize I still had contributions to make to my country.

But there were many things I did not know then that I know now.

I didn't know about Regulation AR 135-175, nor that it had been revised in 1982. The Regulation states that a service member shall be removed from the military if "the member has stated that he/she is a homosexual or bisexual, unless there is a further finding that the member is not a homosexual or bisexual."

I am always asked why I didn't know about this policy at the time of my interview with Troutman since there is a whole bookcase containing personnel regulations. New ones are constantly being added and existing ones are often revised and sometimes removed. You cannot be aware of each one unless you are implementing the regulation or you are charged with violating it.

I didn't know—and the information wasn't in the media then—that from 1980 to 1990 more than fourteen hundred American men and women were discharged from the military each year, their self-confidence destroyed and careers ruined because they were thought to be, or found to be, gay or lesbian.

I did not realize that by saying to Agent Troutman, "I am a lesbian," I would lose my career in a country that espoused equality for all.

And I didn't know that by being forced to speak out, first privately, then publicly, I would find the most important mission of my life.

CHAPTER 11

· · · · · · · · · · · · · · · · ·

Investigation and Hearing

My attorney told me that if I chose to challenge the military I had to tell my sons I am a lesbian. I had, ironically, practiced a don't-ask, don't tell policy with them. Now I'd undo all that work. Nothing would silence my fears: They'll reject me. They'll be ashamed of me. They'll be frightened of me. They'll hate me. Finally, I couldn't delay any longer. In all the hours I'd spent imagining their responses, I never came close to suspecting what would actually happen. And I discovered, firsthand, "Don't ask, don't tell" doesn't work.

· · · · · · · · · · · · · · · · ·

The days following my interview with Agent Troutman were difficult. Diane was visiting, and we talked about what might happen now that I'd broken my silence. Her strength and good humor were a comfort. I felt that I should not be identified by my sexual orientation but rather by my contributions to the community in which I live. Yet I couldn't control what the Army did. How would my disclosure affect my opportunity to lead, to contribute, to serve? Would they judge me as an individual and make an exception for me? And if not, should I retire quietly and keep my rank and benefits in force, and my life private?

Diane and I could only speculate. I was the same, but if I challenged the military, how much hatred and fear would be directed at me? Speculations gave rise to fears.

I remembered the case of another Washington resident and how the regulation that banned gays from serving had targeted him. Perry Watkins was a fourteen-year, active-duty veteran of Vietnam and Korea. Early in his career, he had told the Army he was homosexual. He served three terms and each time reenlisted without any problem despite his prior statement concerning his sexual orientation. Then, without warning, his security clearance was revoked in 1982 and the military started discharge proceedings. His challenge to the regulation had inched its way through the courts and had just–in 1989–been upheld in the Court of Appeals. The judges ordered the Army to permit Sergeant Watkins to reenlist again. Now the Army was appealing that decision to the Supreme Court.

Sergeant Watkins's Court of Appeals victory was a good sign. His attorney was in the area, and I thought that the American Civil Liberties Union might be able to give me his name or assist me too. So, first, I called the ACLU in Seattle and briefed them on what had happened in my interview with the Defense Investigative Service agent. The attorney I spoke with said that ACLU would not be able to determine if they could be of help until the military took some action and announced they were going to discharge me. I thought that was an odd response, but this situation was new for me. Suddenly I was alone again.

Except for telling Diane, I maintained silence about my statement to Agent Troutman and continued my

National Guard work. I knew it would be up to the DIS to contact the appropriate commanders. I waited. Maybe nothing would happen. My performance in the Guard certainly had not changed; nor would it.

Daily life continued. My father arrived in May. The house I had signed a contract to buy on April 28 was to close in June. It was a bigger place than my current home in Renton, and could accommodate my father much better because there were no stairs for him to negotiate to enter the house. On the first level, along with the main living and eating area, were a bedroom and bath, all accessible for my seventy-eight-year-old father. Downstairs was three more bedrooms, another bath and a recreation room for the boys when they visited, It was a contemporary design—lots of windows and good light for Diane to paint when she came to stay. It had a view through the trees of Puget Sound and the Olympic Mountains. It fit my budget because it was in the flight path of the Seattle-Tacoma Airport.

Finances were tight because of child-support payments and graduate school tuition but everything about the house and location was perfect. The boys still lived in Maple Valley, a thirty-minute drive away. As they got their driver's licenses, I hoped they would come to my home more often, and I wanted extra space for them and their friends. This house would give us that.

In addition to moving, I was conducting research for my Ph.D. and working in the clinic. All those demands insulated me from constant anxiety about what the military was going to do. But it was never far away from my thoughts. Each day I waited for a letter, a phone call, or being called to a meeting.

It wasn't until the following November, seven months after my statement to Agent Troutman, that the military responded. It was during the monthly drill weekend. I was called to a meeting with the Washington National Guard Chief of Staff, Colonel Dines, and Colonel Koss, the man who had hired me as state Chief Nurse. Also there was Lieutenant Colonel Ryan, the legal adviser for the Guard. It was a formal and courteous session. They explained that the DIS had contacted the Department of the Army concerning my disclosure of my sexual orientation. There was an adverse report based on my own statement, and as a result, my security clearance was going to be withdrawn and my federal recognition was under consideration for withdrawal. Translated, that military language meant the Army was going to kick me out.

With those words, my world collapsed. The Army was actually thinking of discharging me? It made no sense. I could continue to serve and contribute with the same energy and success I had shown for the past twenty-four years. Nothing had changed. Why couldn't they see that? But like my fellow officers around the table, I kept my thoughts to myself. These men, my colleagues, were transmitting information from their superiors. I did not feel animosity toward them. And for their part, they treated me with respect. Like them, I showed no emotion. We were all good soldiers.

Colonel Dines went on to say that the National Guard had the option to withdraw my federal recognition and immediately discharge me from the Guard, or I could resign. But then, almost as though they had read my mind, they said that the National Guard would not take action. Since this whole affair had been started by the Army, they'd let the Army do it on its own. If it was not disruptive to my unit, they wanted me to remain serving as Chief Nurse until the Department of the Army undertook some formal action.

Colonel Dines stated that if I remained with the Guard, I would at least have a support system around me.

He had expected great things of me and was very sorry for having to act on this issue.

Colonel Dines outlined the next steps I could expect in the process. Once I was officially notified of my hearing date, I would have ninety days to respond to the impending separation action. He explained that the Army would institute all of these procedures.

That this action came from the Army was the hardest news yet. It was as though the most important part of my military career—my years of active duty–was being negated. The Army was saying that what I'd done in Vietnam did not matter. It was a devastating feeling. I was being notified, in effect, of the pending execution of my military life.

But until that termination, Colonel Koss said, the Guard wanted me to stay on. That message was clear. Even though everyone at the meeting knew my sexual orientation they wanted me to continue to serve. Perhaps that would be the result from the Army inquiry as well. Perhaps the Army would make an exception for me. But it was now clear to me that I needed legal counsel to get this result.

This prompted me into immediate action. The next day, Monday, November 6, 1989, I again called the ACLU in Seattle. Once more, I explained my situation to the complaint counselor. She was sympathetic and said a supervisor would get back to me. All day I waited, but no one from the ACLU returned my call.

Meanwhile, down in California, Diane worked the phones. She obtained the name of an attorney, Susan McGreivy, who had been at the Los Angeles ACLU in 1983 when they took on Captain Dusty Pruitt's case. I had not heard about Captain Pruitt or any other challenge to the military's antigay policy except for Perry Watkins's case.

My education was beginning. Captain Pruitt had been on active duty for eight years before transferring to the Army Reserves in order to attend divinity school in 1978. She became the pastor of the Metropolitan Community Church in Long Beach, California while still serving in the Reserves. In 1983 the *Los Angeles Times* published an interview with her in which she discussed her church's philosophy of valuing all people and mentioned that she is a lesbian. That exercise of her First Amendment right to free speech started an Army investigation that eventually led to her discharge. Her case was winding its way through the courts when I first met her.

When I didn't hear back from the Seattle ACLU, I called Susan McGreivy the next day. She said it sounded as if I had a strong case, but asked me to wait to hear from my local ACLU. If they were not able to help, I was to call her back.

During the next couple of days I still received no word from the ACLU. Finally a handwritten note arrives. It said they would not take my case because it was different from the Watkins situation, in which the Army had known of Perry Watkins' homosexuality from the beginning of his service and still had decided to discharge him.

Though the letter didn't say it in so many words, I took the ACLU's rejection as meaning they didn't think I had a chance. I was crushed. (Much later, after my case became known in legal circles, I received a written apology from the Seattle ACLU for their lack of response to my request for help. Apparently, a rookie volunteer lawyer had spoken with me on the phone. She had then misplaced my phone number and neglected to discuss my situation with other staff before rejecting my case.)

When I received the rejection note from the Seattle ACLU, I called Susan McGreivy again and left a message asking her to help. It was the second week in

November 1989. The Army could institute proceedings against me any day. The time pressure, increased by the unknown consequences, was enormous. When Susan returned my call, she explained she was also unable to take my case. She was now in private practice, I had no funds to pay her, and this case at such a distance was too expensive. But, she said, there were gay and lesbian groups who could help. She suggested I call Lambda.

Lambda. She said the name as though I knew what or who Lambda was. ACLU I knew. But Lambda? What in the world was that?

Suddenly I realized that I would be entering a new world if I chose to challenge the military. I wouldn't just be working through the Army-an institution I knew and had felt so successful and welcome in. This next step, *if I took it*, would mean going to a segment of society I knew little about: the gay and lesbian community.

I believed that a person's sexual orientation was no one else's business. After I met Diane, I told very few people about our relationship, and those only on a need-to-know basis. I told my father because he was going to move in with me. I hadn't told most of my friends. I said nothing to my sons, and still naively believed (or perhaps it was my own denial) they did not know. And I certainly had kept my private life out of my work in the military and the Veterans Hospital. Now I faced meeting, and possibly working with, people who made it a practice to say they were gay.

Except for a few friends—older professional women who were also "in the closet"—I didn't know very much about this world. My view of the gay community at the time was similar to the stereotype many heterosexuals have because that is the image I had seen in the media. It is a false image, focusing mainly on those who, through rage or despair, attack the majority culture by using outrageous or shocking tactics. While I may not always agree with the strategy of groups like ACT UP and Queer Nation, I would eventually appreciate that if they did not exist I would not be listened to now.

I would also learn, over the subsequent years, that the gay and lesbian community is as diverse as the heterosexual one. Most of its members are settled in their work and seek to be identified not by their sexual orientation but rather by their contribution to society. However, back 1989, I didn't know this. I worried I would meet, angry people who would not accept me because I came so late to understand about myself, or would disapprove of me because all I wanted was to stay in uniform and continue to serve my country.

With the word "Lambda" still hanging in the air, Susan must have interpreted my abrupt silence for the confusion it represented. She appreciated the decisions I faced. Before I did anything, she suggested, I must learn what my options were. She felt the best place to begin was with Lambda—which is a nonprofit legal defense and education organization. Founded in 1973, it was the first group in the country (and possibly the world) that had as its main mission fighting for lesbians and gay men in the courts.

Lambda had a distinguished history. One of its first clients was Copy Berg, when he was discharged from the Navy in 1976 after what can only be described as a witch-hunt into his private life. With the worst sorts of tactics, the naval investigators forced this exemplary graduate of the Naval Academy to admit he was gay, even though the military had no evidence of misconduct on duty. The D.C. Circuit Court upheld the military ban, but his challenge to his discharge was a courageous and important step in battling discrimination.

Over the years, Susan explained, Lambda had supported other military personnel who had risked their careers to challenge the military's institutionalized prejudice. The organization also provided gay men and lesbians with legal counsel in their fights against discrimination in custody battles, housing, and jobs. And in the earliest stages of the crisis, they began work in behalf of the desperate people with HIV and AIDS, fighting for their fair treatment.

Theirs was an impressive track record. Susan said I should use her name to get through the operator at the agency and speak with an attorney.

So I called them and did as told, stating I was "Susan McGreivy". My first contacts at Lambda were with David Barr and Sandy Lowe in the New York office. I reintroduced myself and explained my dilemma. They said they would review my situation and decide as soon as possible whether it was an appropriate case for them to take. It meant, of course, a great commitment of their resources—money and staff.

Since I was going to be in Southern California shortly after my call to Lambda, to visit Diane, they recommended I meet with the Military Law Task Force of the National Lawyers Guild. Run by Charles Bumer and Kathy Gilberd, the organization was based in San Diego. With a national membership of 150 attorneys, law students, and legal workers, the Task Force represents servicemembers with military law problems, ranging from challenges to the military's drug policies to complaints of racial and sexual discrimination.

I met with Kathy Gilberd a week later. What a relief. Her intelligent and thorough answers to all of my questions helped immensely. She told me not to discuss my situation with anyone or answer any questions, and to refer all inquiries to her office. It was good to have someone to tell me what to do.

Together Kathy and I reviewed all letters and documents relevant to my situation. She gave me examples of other cases and described how decisions in some had been reversed by the circuit courts. She stressed that past litigation over the military ban might not have a direct effect on my case, but educating myself would be useful in the long run.

She explained the sequence of events I should expect as the various agencies of the military processed, analyzed, and determined my future. She outlined how different organizations worked together. My decision concerning civil litigation could wait until later.

The first hurdle is the administrative military procedure. There would be more reports on me, on my background, and the hardest thing would be when the Army announces its decision to initiate discharge proceedings. I could then request a board of inquiry hearing or resign. The members of the board—the judges—would be a panel of my peers, most likely colonels in the National Guard. I'd be assigned a military attorney from the Army Judge Advocate General Corps (JAG) to defend me. She recommended that a civilian attorney represent me as well. She mentioned Lambda; her own group, the Military Law Task Force; and a volunteer attorney with the ACLU in Los Angeles, Mary Newcombe, as possible candidates.

At the board of inquiry hearing, my civilian and JAG attorneys would have an opportunity to present evidence. Then the board would make a recommendation to discharge me or to allow me to continue to serve. Kathy matter-of-factly stated that the board usually goes with the prevailing policy.

Then a second board would review these proceedings and send recommendations to the Secretary of the Army, who makes the final decision. Before discharge, the JAG and other jurists can request a restraining order and seek an injunction against acting on the recommendations until the case is heard in the military court. This is rarely granted. The results may then be submitted to the Board of Correction of Military Records.

Kathy assured me the Military Law Task Force would help with the administrative part of this process. If the Board of Correction favored me, then I would be reinstated into the military. If it did not, my only other recourse was to go public and into the civil federal court system. All the information and evidence we might want to use on appeal must be entered in the record during the military hearing. Once the case has left the Board of Correction and goes into civilian court, where we would seek to prove that the regulation itself was discriminatory and therefore illegal, new evidence cannot be added.

Kathy sent me away with stacks of regulations, documents of past cases, and articles to read. And even more to think about. As I got ready to go, I stopped for a moment. There was one question I hadn't yet asked. Here, with this expert who cared so passionately about overturning the military's ban, was my opportunity to get an answer to the most important question: did she believe there was a good chance the regulation could be changed?

"Not very likely," she said.

So, I wondered, was I fighting a losing battle? Here was my first glimpse into the moral dilemma I would encounter again and again: if there is no hope your action will right an injustice, do you still take that action? Kathy showed me case after case in which men and women had already risked everything—had not resigned quietly—to fight the injustice of the military ban. All had lost their battle with the government and in the courts. On the surface, my case seemed hopeless.

But a soldier does not retreat. And nursing had taught me the possibility of turning even the most adverse situation into something that has meaning and value. As I left her office, Kathy urged me to contact other veterans who had fought back.

"You should talk with them about the emotional and personal cost," she said. "It's significant. The U.S. military is a pretty big opponent."

Particularly, I thought, if you love it as much as I do.

On December 19, 1989, Sandy Lowe called me with the great news that Lambda would take my case. She mapped out the steps ahead. It was up to the military to make the next move in this tortuous game with my career. In the meantime, we would assemble a team of lawyers and resource people.

To that end, I accepted an invitation to a dinner meeting on January 2,1990, at Mary Newcombe's home in Los Angeles. She was one of the attorneys who had worked on Dusty Pruitt's challenge to the Army's policy through the ACLU. Diane and I would join Mary, Susan McGreivy, who had worked with the ACLU on the Dusty Pruitt case, and Dusty herself to discuss strategies and the costs—personal and professional—of the work ahead of us.

It was to be my first face-to-face meeting with Mary Newcombe. During our two phone conversations, I'd been impressed with her intelligence, expertise, and compassion. Everyone who worked with her praised her. In the coming years, Mary would play a crucial role in my life. More than any other person, she was to be my legal counselor and, in many ways, my guide into this new world of the gay and lesbian community.

I remember thinking, when Mary greeted us at her door, "What a kid." Here I was, quickly approaching the age of forty-eight, seeking help and direction from a woman in her early thirties. Although she seemed relatively young, it was clear she was extremely knowledgeable about military law and injustice. And she cared. That quality of concern shown by the people representing the law was as impressive as her intellect. She insisted that the client always be put ahead of the case. From our first meeting, I cherished her contribution to my case.

I also spoke with Dusty Pruitt about her long ordeal. She described the bizarre lengths to which the military investigators went after reading the Los Angeles Times interview in which she'd stated her sexual orientation. Agents parked a van outside her church and a car outside her apartment and watched her, day and night. She noticed new and curious clicks on her phone suggesting that she was not the only one listening to her callers. She remembered how she had finally gone out to the men in the van one night and invited them in for coffee. They were embarrassed, did not accept her offer, but drove off and never returned. Though she smiled while telling me this story, it was obvious this had all taken a toll on her life— being followed, being labeled, being negated. Even then, seven years later, the struggle continued. Today, her case is pending in the Federal District Court in Los Angeles after the Ninth Circuit Court of Appeals reinstated her case and ruled the government must demonstrate with facts that the antigay policy is rational and not based on prejudice. That 1992 ruling would set the standard for how all the cases will be judged, including mine. But in 1989, that success was still in the future.

So I asked her, "Knowing what you do now, would you choose to challenge the military again?"

"Yes, in a second." Her words came from a place of great peace and strength.

That evening was my first experience of this community, and with it came the realization that my endeavor was much larger than me alone. Thousands of men and women–recipients of medals, honors, and awards–were being investigated and kicked out of the military. Their crime? Integrity.

As we shared our stories that night, I was both honored to be a new member of this community and outraged at the actions of my government. I thought of the McCarthy era. As had happened then, patriotic people were now being treated like common criminals. I kept thinking over and over: This isn't American.

Then I caught myself. Sitting here in this room with me was what I believed America should be: people fighting fear with love, challenging prejudice with knowledge, opposing hatred with humor and compassion.

As we were leaving, Mary suggested I consider discussing the situation with my kids soon. Up until then I had only mentioned I might be leaving the National Guard because the military was time consuming and I had to begin my dissertation research in the summer. The boys had been surprised by comments like that– they knew my devotion to the military. But they were teenagers, busy with their own lives, and I didn't think they were curious about pursuing my hints any further.

Mary, however, felt it was best to talk openly with the boys before anything else occurred. I told her I would find the best time to have this most difficult conversation with each son. Mary also warned me, "There will be publicity around this when we lose with the military and take our challenge to the civil court. You'll have to decide what your tolerance is for it. Talking to the media is a way to change social consciousness on the civil rights issues, but it will take a toll on you. You get to decide how much you want to be involved."

I smiled and thanked her. But the implications of what she said were lost on me then. I could not even dream of the level of scrutiny and the time commitment the publicity would eventually take. At that time, I wondered why anyone would want to talk to me unless it was about neurology, soldiering, or mothering.

And yet I was beginning to appreciate that if we lost in the military hearing, our only other recourse, to prove the policy was discriminatory, was by going to the civil court system. If I were unsuccessful in the Army court, I would lose my military job and income, and be stripped of my rank. I would perhaps retain my pension but not my gray-area benefits—that is, medical, Post Exchange and transportation privileges. Getting those back, as well as addressing the larger issue of social justice, could, most likely, be done only in a civilian court.

I continued to perform my duties as Chief Nurse as though nothing had happened. Very few people knew of my statement to Agent Troutman and the DIS investigation. Of course, from my point of view, nothing had happened. During this waiting period, I was often lulled into a fantasy that my rank, record, and medals would shield me.

However, the fantasy did not last. In February 1990, ten months after my meeting with Agent Troutman, Colonel Koss was told by the Sixth Army to initiate a commander's investigation of me. After his report, the Army would begin official action.

How ironic that the man most supportive of me was now ordered to do this difficult job. However, it was standard practice. Yet it caused me to see that the military was not the perfect, wise, all-knowing big brother I had always set it up to be. I felt bad for Colonel Koss because he was in a delicate position. He assured me he did not want me to retire or leave; we had much important work to do. He promised he would make sure that he complied with all his obligations under the investigation. It had to be very thorough since he suspected the case would go to federal court.

By the spring of 1990, my team of attorneys was assembled. Mary Newcombe, still in private practice at the Los Angeles firm of Hedges & Caldwell, had been selected to open Lambda's new West Coast office. She would work on the case, but everyone agreed I also needed local lawyers. Harriett Cody, who had represented me in my divorce, introduced me to her office mate, Jana Mohr, a member of the Northwest Women's Law Center. This nonprofit organization was eager to help. They had a roster of consulting attorneys, and turned to Jeffrey Tilden and Michael Himes to work with me locally. They were both with the large Seattle law firm of Perkins Coie, and so brought with them major resources. Interestingly, Michael had also been a law clerk for the prosecution in Sergeant Perry Watkins's case. This added a perspective and depth to the team that would prove vital in the years to come.

I began to check my mailbox with greater anxiety, expecting that the certified letter from the Sixth Army would certainly come soon to announce my hearing. Every day, all spring, I waited for that letter. It didn't come. Perhaps, I hoped, there would be no hearing. I would stay in uniform. They would make an exception for me.

Meanwhile, I had to tell my sons about the challenge to the military. First, I talked with Andy. He happened to be the only one who came for dinner on a particular Wednesday-night visitation in February. At fifteen, he was a freshman in high school, very self-sufficient, and a member of his high school basketball team.

In talking with Andy, I'd decided, I'd focus on the fact that I had told the military during the security clearance interview that I am a lesbian and that the Army would have a hearing and I might lose my military career. That would affect him and his brothers because I would have less of an income and, though I would still be able to afford the necessities, they wouldn't get as many goodies.

He shrugged his shoulders and said it was no big deal to him. He said he and his brothers already knew I was a lesbian, but he had not heard it from me and appreciated my talking to him now. I was shocked that he knew but I tried not to show it. I wanted this to be about him, not my feelings.

He had just one question: "When did you decide to become a lesbian ?"

"It was not something I decided," I explained. "It's something I discovered about myself. I think I have probably always been and never understood it until recently. And how fortunate, because, otherwise I wouldn't have had you and your brothers."

Then he withdrew into himself again. He's very quiet and contemplative, for all his other forceful qualities. Though I was surprised he said he and his brothers had already known, in retrospect, I understood. Harvey had accused me of being gay when I first began to question our marriage in 1979. Of course, I can see now, it was naive of me—if not stupid—to think that Harvey's accusations would not affect the boys. They probably had been subconsciously coming to terms with my being a lesbian longer than I had. Though I left the marriage to find out who I was, the boys didn't know that. Now I was back in their lives; they enjoyed Diane when she visited (in fact, found her to be an ally), saw how "normal" my daily life was, so they were accepting. I told him that I had yet to talk with his brothers about this, and encouraged him to ask me anything else he wanted to know.

Next, I invited Matt over. He had recently completed his two-year Mormon mission, was engaged to be married, and living with his fiancée's parents in Monroe, Washington, thirty-five miles northeast of Seattle. When I told him my news, he just beamed at the thought of taking on the military. He, too, said he already knew about my sexual orientation. I wasn't surprising anyone.

"No," he explained, "it was just how you were. We aren't dumb, you know."

"No, you're not," I said, smiling. "But mothers are rather dumb."

Matt explained he had discussed all this with his fiancée', Lynette, years before, and she was fine with it. Lynette was a frequent guest. Even during the years Matt spent on his mission, she'd often come over to watch TV with me, cook, or just visit. I was moved to learn she had accepted who I was even before I had. Oh, naïve parents. Matt also assured me his brothers already knew. I told him I had only discussed this with Andy so far.

None of my "coming out" conversations were any easier. Each time it was difficult. Each time I was immerged with my son's acceptance.

I next talked with David, a junior in high school, and the oldest son living with Harvey. After dinner one evening, I rather abruptly said, "Please come here. I need to talk with you."

A little sheepishly, he walked out onto the deck and sat down next to me. I could tell he thought I was going to admonish him for something. So I immediately said, "It's about me, not about you."

He let out a great sigh of relief.

Then I said, "The military has begun a process to discharge me because I've told them I am gay."

He, too, said he already knew about me. His surprise was at the military. Why would they throw me out after all my years of service? He was angry at this injustice. I also brought up my divorce, sure that he would remember what that was like and would want to talk about the stress of it on him. He talked about the times when I'd drop them off after a visit and Harvey would line up him and his brothers and urge them to yell slurs at me. He said that every time I drove away he'd run to his room, throw himself on his bed, and cry.

For the first time, I explained why I hadn't contested their father's getting custody: how much pain I felt, how confused I was, how I had no sense of myself. I talked about not having any money and how I wanted them to have the security of their home in Maple Valley and felt that only their father could provide that because I could not tolerate to live there any longer. Together we had a good cry. Then he got up and gave me a big hug.

Tom, my youngest, was the last to be told. My baby. The quietest. He didn't ask questions. Perhaps I didn't give him enough time to do so. Again, his response was "So?" His reticence worried me, but I was not going to push him to talk or ask questions if he didn't want too.

After my round of disclosures—news that was not news—the important thing for each son was: How does mother's challenging the military affect me? Clearly, during the years after the divorce, each of my sons, had come to terms with my sexual orientation, so that now the focus was on the Army's investigation and my possible discharge. After our conversations, they realized that the financial consequences wouldn't change their lives significantly.

We still had a house. I was no different and would continue working in my civilian job. Of course, none of us understood the ramifications then. Regardless of what Mary told me of the possible publicity in the future, life at our home continued at its hectic, noisy pace: school, work, and basketball games.

That spring, Colonel Koss sent me as our state's representative to a conference of the National Guard in Arkansas. Colonel Shirley Jones was then Chief Nurse of the National Guard, and had earlier invited me to come to Washington, D.C., to work with her. I took her aside and told her about my pending administrative discharge due to my disclosure. She asked if she could do anything to help. I said that it was too early in the process. Throughout the rest of the weekend meeting, she was very warm, often checking to see if I was okay. This encouraged me greatly. I was still naive.

As Colonel Koss had anticipated, his commander's investigation was taking many months to complete. I oversaw the two-week summer exercises at the Yakima Firing Range and continued work developing the new hospital for the Washington National Guard. No word came from the Sixth Army—they were waiting for Colonel Koss's report. Fortunately, I was so immersed in my Ph.D. research that I had little time to think about what might happen to my military career. I had almost completed my course work.

I was developing research for my dissertation, which would be finished by June 1991. Its subject matter was the causes and treatments of cognitive deficits such as memory impairment—associated with sleep apnea, which is a periodic disruption of breathing during sleep. I had been working with patients at the VA Hospital on this disorder, designing their treatment programs and collecting data for my doctoral dissertation. It was absorbing all my extra time.

My father was in his second year of living with me. He was content to do his reading and writing of the family genealogy in his room, emerging for meals. In this regular routine, I felt we were settling old issues. Not by talking–that is not our way, but through the routine of living together–accepting each other.

He had always been a pack rat, never throwing away a magazine or a piece of paper. Every few months, I would tell him, "If you can't clean up your room, I will." So he would then go to Diane if she was visiting (or wait for her if she was in California) and say, "The colonel says I have to clean my room." They would both laugh at his little joke, and Diane would get out the vacuum cleaner for him (he was too unsteady to get it for himself) and set it up, and he would push the thing around his room.

Those little events, the ways we found to be playful with each other, were good. But I was troubled by the inevitable progression of his hydrocephalus. His mental capacities were slowly deteriorating. His gait was less controlled and he was more likely to lose his balance and fall. But he was proud and stubborn and would still take off for walks in the afternoon. He'd frequently fall or become so fatigued he couldn't get back. Many times, I'd come home and he'd be gone. I'd start looking and find him leaning against a mailbox or, a few times, lying in the gutter blocks from our house. Sometimes neighbors would discover him resting or fallen in their yards, and bring him home. I tried to convince him not to take his walks alone. He'd smile at me, and his eyes would have a kind of childish mischief, and he'd say, "Oh, no, it's fine. I always just lean against a mailbox until somebody comes and picks me up." Fortunately, he was never injured, despite the fact that he didn't respect the limitations of his condition. It alarmed me, particularly because I knew that there were no interventions or treatments to stop the steady progress of this neurological disorder.

In the midst of these personal challenges, the crisis in the Persian Gulf erupted. Our National Guard unit was still involved in recruiting and training personnel for our new hospital. It was not likely we would be called up for duty overseas since we were not equipped or adequately prepared. All of us, independently, considered whether to volunteer on our own. My core ethic as a nurse was to care for casualties. I felt my experience in Vietnam and with heat-stress research would be particularly helpful in the Middle East should a conflict break out. I wanted to go but felt torn. It was the first time Diane and I confronted my duty to serve when it involved physical risk. Though she really tried to let me decide without pressure, I felt her distress also.

As the buildup in the Middle East continued, I struggled with the dilemma of volunteering. I had obligations to my dissertation research, my kids, my father, and my case. However, I decided to volunteer regardless. That was why I had trained and served all these years—to contribute when and if I am needed. Everything else was secondary to that obligation. It was a difficult decision but the right one. I bypassed protocol and contacted Colonel Shirley Jones. I told her about my research on heat stress, sent her articles I'd written with Barbara, and said I was available to be mobilized if needed. She thanked me and said that my request would be considered.

Fall brought a stalemate in the Persian Gulf. Another waiting game. Flexing of muscles. Testing your adversary's nerve. Our unit was not activated, and it became clear to me that I was too high-ranking to be separated from my unit and sent over alone to join another, activated unit.

Besides, Colonel Koss was eager for me to stay and complete our task of recruiting and training personnel for the hospital to reach its full complement. The summer mobilization had further delayed the completion of his commander's investigation of me, which was to our mutual advantage. I had been able to continue working on the new hospital.

Yet it was like sitting on a powder keg with someone else running around with a flame. You don't know when it will ignite. My legal team was in a holding pattern, waiting for the military to make its next move. The country was preparing for war. I was working with my seizure patients and doing my dissertation research at the sleep clinic.

All the while, I was beginning to hear reports from the boys that their relationships with Harvey were becoming more strained. Harvey and his wife, Jan, had custody of David, Andy, and Tom (Matt, now twenty-two, was on his own). They also had two young children of their own. Though life in Maple Valley was occasionally described to me, I stayed out of any interactions there. I refrained from contradicting Harvey and rarely communicated with him, except for a phone call now and then to arrange times of visits and trips with the boys.

There were several reasons I stayed out of things there. The children needed both Harvey and me, so I felt it was important to support Harvey as much as possible for the boys' mental health. As a part-time parent, I didn't have all the facts and there was no easy way to back up my point of view without going to court. There were a few times when the boys related a punishment they'd received that I thought was unfair, and I became irate-but felt helpless. I'd ask them if they wanted me to intercede, and they always said I shouldn't. And, too, I only heard one side—I didn't want to compete with Harvey or allow the boys to play us against each other. The kids were going through the normal rebellions of teenagers.

Harvey had always been a firm taskmaster, and there was much to do to maintain the eight acres of landscaping and pastures around the house. The boys' lives were filled with farm chores, Mormon seminary at five-thirty every morning as well as school and their basketball practice and games. There were many rules in the house governing what they did and what they ate. Harvey's frugality was sometimes difficult for the boys. Because there is no bus service between Maple Valley and my home, I bought cars and insurance for each son as he reached driving age. David, the oldest boy still living with Harvey, was the first to get a car. In his last year of high school, a star of his high school basketball team and a likely candidate for a college sports scholarship, David had many demands on him. Initially, Harvey forbade David to have the car at Maple Valley, so I said it was fine to leave it at my house. Soon, however, Harvey allowed David to bring the car to Maple Valley and drive his brothers to seminary at five-thirty every morning. The minute he got full-time use of his car, David was free to come and go, and that changed the already tenuous dynamic with his father. Harvey and David had confrontations until David moved out of Maple Valley to his coach's house. A few days later, he came to my house. Then Harvey's campaign began. He called David's grandmother, his brothers, the church, the bishop, and the coach to force David to return to Maple Valley. Because the issue was David's relationship with his father, it wasn't appropriate for me to intrude. I didn't give him advice. He needed to work out his relationship with his father on his own. After a few weeks, David, a very sweet and respectful young man, moved back to Harvey and Jan's.

But that lasted only a while. David felt nothing had changed, and so he moved to my home permanently around Christmas of 1990.

As I had since the divorce, I paid Harvey monthly child support for Tom, Andy, and David. But now that David lived with me, I called and asked, "Do I still need to pay child support for him?"

Harvey said yes, I did.

Any interaction with Harvey still intimidated me. Just the thought of talking to him on the phone reminded me of what it had been like that last year during our divorce. I did anything to avoid confrontation. When he insisted I continue to pay him David's child support even though he lived with me, I did. I knew that the only way of contesting this issue would be to go back to court. There were just six months left before David graduated from high school. It just didn't seem to be worth the emotional stress. I was sad the boys saw their father's integrity tarnished in this way. I didn't realize at the time that a precedent had been set for the future, when Andy, then Tom, challenged Harvey, encountered difficulties, and moved to my home.

But, happily, David's schoolwork and basketball playing got back on track. He had a bedroom downstairs next to the recreation room. He was happy to have the space and the autonomy. My father's room was on the first level, far enough away so that no one felt crowded. We were all involved with our own lives, and the transition went smoothly. The house was full and busy.

Andy and Tom reported that things were better in Maple Valley, too. Now with David gone, Andy was the oldest and enjoyed that position in the household dynamic. The tension was lessened and everyone was happier.

Then, just after the holidays, my house got even fuller.

Earlier in 1990, Matt and Lynette had been married. Lynette was devoted to my son, strong, tenacious, and loving. Because Matt had used his savings to go on his Mormon mission, they needed to rebuild their bank account. We had a spare room, and they joined us for a ten-month stay, which gave them time to regroup financially.

My resident family was growing rapidly. Leona, Harvey's mother, seemed to be caught between her son and her grandsons. Howard had died the year before. Harvey indicated to her that if she came to visit my home she would be condoning David's departure from Maple Valley. She felt a split loyalty, but decided to continue to join us on special occasions. I was glad for the kids that their grandmother spent time with them, regardless of the problems they might have with their father or with me.

On May 15, 1991, two days before my defense of my dissertation, Andy, sixteen, moved into our growing household. His departure from Maple Valley was pure Andy.

The precipitating event occurred when Andy and Harvey were on their way out to school and work. It was another typical struggle over authority. This time Harvey let the air out of the tires of Andy's beloved Camaro. This was Harvey's way of grounding him. But this did not stop Andy. He went over to a buddy's house, called me with a request to move to our place. Again, my role was not to encourage him to move out, but to be supportive of his decision. If he as going to leave, I'd rather he came to my home than move in with friend. So I said that if he needed to move, I trusted his judgment. He said he'd be over in a couple of days, after he "did some stuff."

The "some stuff" was orchestrating the release of his car. He enlisted three friends and mapped out a strategy. He explained they had probably no more than ten minutes to drive up to the Camaro, pump up the tires, and get out of there before Harvey returned, because Jan would call Harvey at work as soon as she saw them fixing the car. They got the equipment, were all prepped and ready for the great escape.

The next day, Andy and his friends drove up to the Camaro and madly began repairing its tires. Jan looked out and called Harvey in his State Patrol car, just as expected. As his pals finished with the tires, Andy ran to the Camaro, jumped in, and drove off.

Andy then moved into our house. Of course, Harvey once again began his campaign to get Andy to return. He called the roster of outsiders to intervene on his behalf once again. Then he called me.

As I listened to Harvey's litany of what had happened with Andy (his facts were identical to Andy's except that his interpretation of them was that Andy required discipline), I was silent. I didn't feel the old threat. This was really not my problem.

Harvey ended by saying he wished that I would support him in this effort.

Then I amazed myself: I laughed. I just laughed. I couldn't help it. Here was someone who for ten years gave me nothing but grief, who bad-mouthed me, who made it difficult for me to see the kids except on strict visitation dates, and he was asking me to support him?

Finally, Harvey insisted I tell Andy just to keep his mouth shut, go home, and do his chores.

"Well," I said, relishing the power of staying calm in the face of Harvey's apparent frustration, "I'll relay the message."

When I got off the phone, I realized that my response to Harvey was different from what I'd felt five months before, when David moved out from Maple Valley. Though I still did not want to antagonize Harvey, he no longer intimidated me. What had changed? I think it was the result of a process that had begun in my interview with Agent Troutman, and continued as I worked with my lawyers to prepare our challenge to the military's antigay policy. My immediate superiors in the National Guard knew of my identity and accepted me as they always had. Most important, I knew who I was, finally. I didn't feel so at risk with Harvey. After all, what could he do-go to the military and tell them I'm gay? By accepting myself, I had disarmed his accusations about my sexual orientation. Even after I had come out to my sons, David and now Andy had chosen to live with me. And in just two days I would defend my doctoral dissertation (I'd scheduled it for May 17-Norwegian Independence Day), earn my Ph.D. and the title of Dr. Cammermeyer. I felt more empowered.

I went downstairs and repeated Harvey's orders to Andy. "Your father says that I should keep the car and you should go back out to Maple Valley and behave and do your chores."

"So," Andy waited, "what did you say?"

"I said I would relay the message."

"Well, you have."

We looked at each other.

"Andy," I said carefully, "maybe I really am contributing to all of this. What would happen if I said you must leave the car here and go back to Maple Valley?"

"Hmm." He thought for a second. "I'd move in with one of my friends."

"Then," I said, "I guess it's rather hopeless and silly for me to do that."

"Yeah"-he grinned-"it really is."

Later, realizing the situation was permanent; I again suggested to Harvey that I didn't think it fair that I pay child support for Andy and David when they were living with me. Harvey repeated he hadn't given permission for them to move, and so would not agree to any change in our financial arrangements.

To stop the payments, I'd have to go to court. I was afraid of the way the court would treat a "lesbian mother." In this respect, I found it hard to stand up for myself with Harvey. Paying double–supporting David and Andy, as well as sending Harvey money for them–to prove my worth fit an old pattern. And though I had made strides in my self-confidence over the last few years, it was still easier to stand up for myself in an institution– the military–than to confront an individual. I decided I preferred the financial hardship of paying Harvey the child-support payments over the cost of challenging him. So I complied.

There were a few additional bumps in the coming years as the kids negotiated their relationships with their father. Tom, fourteen, now became the big brother to Jan and Harvey's younger children. He said there was a new sense of calm at home because the constant battle between Harvey and Andy was over.

Meanwhile, I had received the special delivery letter from the Sixth Army that I had been dreading and expecting. It arrived on March 18, 1991. Colonel Koss's commander's investigation had been completed in January. It documented my achievements, promotions, and excellent evaluations. In the interviews I gave for the report, I refused to retract my statement about my sexual orientation, although I had been given several opportunities. The Army wrote that Agent Troutman's report provided sufficient evidence to withdraw my federal recognition. The letter officially offered me two options: I could immediately resign, or I could elect to have an administrative board hearing.

This was the signal my legal team needed to begin working. There were meetings and conference calls to discuss what evidence and witnesses to present at the hearing.

It now seemed real. There would be a hearing at a date to be set in the future, and then it would be public. I had a long discussion with Matt and Lynette about the case, the possible publicity, and the stress. Living with me during this time might be more than they wanted to take on. I urged them to consider their needs. I offered them the opportunity to distance themselves from me and this mess.

They were appalled that I should even mention such a possibility. Their support was unwavering. They had already talked with their bishop. He told them to continue to do what they were doing: to be there for their mother. Then they offered to come to my hearing if that would help.

What a roller coaster. Receiving the Army's letter announcing the military's intention of kicking me out made me feel like a disgrace. But then, talking with Matt and Lynette, receiving their support and understanding, made me wonder why I hadn't told them sooner. Why had it taken so long for me to accept my own identity? Looking down at the Army's letter in my hand gave me the answer: in America prejudice against gays and lesbians is not only permitted but practiced by the government.

I would have to learn to live with these contradictions. I had a respite from them for a while in June when David and I both graduated. He was magnificent in his ceremony–handsome, happy, loved. He wore a silly nose with his cap and gown. Always the clown. Our entire family—Diane, Andy, Tom, Matt and Lynette, my father—went and cheered him. We had a celebration to mark the end of high school and his new beginning in college on a basketball scholarship.

Then, a few days later, it was my turn. Even my father came to watch me receive my Ph.D. It was 1991. A little more than thirty years since I had hit my first obstacle to becoming a doctor. But finally I was Dr. Cammermeyer. Of course, I was proud. Also I had a new sense of myself, a confidence that proved invaluable as I faced my battle with the military. A battle that came much sooner than I had expected.

Near the end of June, I received another letter from the Army. After two and a half years of waiting, and just as the members of my legal team were preparing for summer vacations, the military notified us that my hearing would be held in two weeks. Two weeks?

I called Mary. "Why now? What's the big hurry all of a sudden?"

"We don't know, but my guess is this," Mary calmly explained. "For quite a while the Army was willing to defer it to the Guard. But suddenly they realized they'd been dragging it out for over two years. Here you've been an admitted lesbian to your commander and some colleagues, and it's had no impact on your unit whatsoever. In fact, they still love you. They still need you and want you. So, the Army realized they'd better enforce this policy, because allowing you to stay undermines it tremendously."

"What about your vacation?" I asked.

"The Canadian Rockies will wait."

Captain Margaret Bond, the JAG attorney I'd been assigned to represent me, now joined the civilian legal team. Margaret Bond was in private practice in Tacoma as well as a respected lawyer with the National Guard. She was a valuable addition to our team. She requested the hearing be postponed until August 12 so she could become familiar with the case. That request was denied.

I asked several state National Guard chief nurses for letters of support, and although they wanted to write them, they were discouraged from doing so by their superiors. It was suggested that whoever supported me officially would find his or her own career in jeopardy. I spoke with Colonel Shirley Jones, Chief Nurse of the entire National Guard, who had earlier expressed her concern for me. She would not write a letter of support for me. She would not "go against Department of Defense policy," and my evaluations would speak for themselves. But she wished me luck. It felt like a slap in the face.

The American Nurses Association came out in support of me personally, and joined with the American Association of Psychologists and the Association of Social Workers in favor of overturning the military's antigay policy. General Adams, Chief Nurse of the Army Nurse Corps, wrote a letter to the American Nurses Association criticizing them for their stand. She said that my discharge had nothing to do with my professional abilities, but was a matter of military policy. I found General Adams's response particularly ironic; she told the American Nurses Association to support the status quo and stay out of Department of Defense policy. If the status quo had always been accepted, women would still be relegated to second-class positions in the military. If the policy that limited women had not been challenged years earlier, she would not now have the rank of general and the ability to contribute at such a level in the once-all-male organization.

The stakes were getting high. There were others in uniform who made the choice to support me in writing and in testifying at my hearing. The risks they took for me and for this issue fill me with gratitude.

Immediately, the lawyers began to choreograph our strategy. We had little time to arrange witnesses, exhibits, and prepare testimony. I was amazed at the dedication and pace as we mobilized for the hearing. Overall, our argument would be that the policy was irrational and based on prejudice. To prove that, we would show how each of the rationales put forth by the Department of Defense for excluding gays and lesbians from service lacked justification. The regulation stated that gays and lesbians are incompatible with military service because we adversely affect the "ability of the Military Services to maintain discipline, good order and morale"; that we damage recruitment; that we lessen trust and confidence among officers; and, finally, that we pose security risks.

Of course, my own experience contradicted each of those assertions, and we intended to show that fact through my own testimony, as well as by calling on my superiors and those who had served in my unit to testify. Also, we would present evidence outlining how the government had commissioned a number of studies that, without exception, found no evidence to support its own rationales for the policy. As early as 1957, the Crittenden Report, prepared for the Secretary of the Navy, stated that the concept that gay people cannot acceptably serve in the military was "without visible supporting data" and that "there have been many known instances of individuals who have served honorably and well, despite being exclusively homosexual."

More recently, the 1988 Defense Personnel Security Research and Education Center (PERSEREC) report, commissioned by the Defense Department, had reaffirmed those findings. It concluded that the policy was based upon stereotypical and outdated notions about gay people, including the erroneous belief that gay people were more likely to breach national security. The study found no evidence to support the claim that gays and lesbians were bad security risks. Nor did it find facts to support the false view that gay people disrupted order, discipline, and morale. Finally, it determined that "having a same-gender or an opposite-gender orientation is unrelated to job performance in the same way as is being left- or right-handed," and it even proposed that the policy be scrapped.

Rather than revise the policy, the Pentagon had instead buried the PERSEREC report. A year later, however, it was leaked to Congressional Representatives on Capitol Hill, where it created a furor. Although the Pentagon insisted that the report was merely a draft, and issued a revised report curtailing the study's broad recommendations, the damage had been done.

Along with those and other reports, we intended to introduce a memorandum issued by Vice Admiral Joseph Donnell of the Atlantic Fleet that clearly revealed the underlying hostility of the male-dominated military toward competent servicewomen. In this memo to his commanding officers, Admiral Donnell urged them to be vigilant in hunting out and discharging lesbian officers whose investigations, he warned, were often "stymied" because they are "hardworking, career oriented, willing to put in long hours on the job and among the command's top professionals."

So, what was left as a basis for this expensive, disruptive, and controversial policy? If there was no evidence to show that gay and lesbian servicemembers refused orders, or didn't perform their duties, or resisted becoming "part of a team," why exclude them?

We intended to show that what remained–in the military's own arguments–to fuel the regulation's existence was, quite simply, the fear that heterosexuals would feel uncomfortable around gays and lesbians, might ostracize or harass them, or might resign from the military. In other words, the problem is not due to gays and lesbians, but to the expected prejudice of straight servicemembers.

Interestingly, these reasons for banning gay people were exactly the same rationales put forth to justify excluding African Americans from serving with whites. Both of these policies of exclusion were designed solely to cater to the fears or bigotry of others. However, we would argue that accommodating private prejudice does not serve a legitimate governmental or military purpose.

In addition to submitting this vast amount of evidence that undermined the rationales for the policy, we had a second purpose. We wanted to reach the hearts and minds of the members of the board and convince them to recommend that I be retained in the military. We devised a strategy that would require them to explore their own feelings about the policy, rather than simply rubberstamp my discharge. As Margaret Bond pointed out, because the Secretary of the Army retains some discretion in enforcing the Army's regulations, we decided to argue that the board should search its conscience as to whether discretion should be exercised here.

Since Margaret was an experienced military lawyer, who knew best how to speak to fellow officers, she was to be the lead counsel in the military hearing. She would present the legal arguments to the board. Captain Bond also conducted the questioning for my testimony and others about my career. Then Mary would follow with our expert witnesses: Dr. Laura Brown, who would explain what it means to be gay and how it is part of the normal spectrum of being human. Dr. Lawrence Korb, a former Assistant Secretary of Defense would testify on the implications of the antigay policy developed by the military. With this strategy, we hoped to engage the officers on the board and help them understand what it is like to face discharge and the termination simply for being honest.

After many more hours of preparation, the day of the hearing arrive–July 14, 1991. Ironically, it was the thirtieth anniversary of my swearing in to the military.

At home, the entire household readied for the ordeal. As I ironed my jacket and placed the insignias and medals in place I couldn't help feeling as if I were preparing for an execution. I knew I had a choice. I could still resign. But if I did, if I buckled under pressure, could I face myself again? I remembered the stories from my childhood of Norwegians resisting the Nazis, and my own question: Would I have their courage to stand and be counted? This was, perhaps, my test. There was no choice but to fight.

I got out my class A blouse and skirt—the green Army uniform to be worn on the most formal occasions. I'd bought it in the mid-1970s, with matching dress slacks. For the last few years, I had worn the pants with the jacket, but today I needed to wear the skirt. After pressing out all the wrinkles, I tried to put it on. It didn't fit I was too fat (I'd relieved the stress by eating and had gained weight). I was frantic. How could I go to what felt like a court-martial in an inappropriate uniform?

Lynette rushed in holding a doll-size girdle. "Put this on," she said, "and your skirt will fit."

I roared with laughter. I couldn't believe anything so petite could fit on my body. But I forced it on. My body fat shifted and, not only did the uniform fit, but the absurdity of the situation released some of my tension. In fact, I'm still enduring its comic absurdity: my most recent birthday gift (for my 50th) from Matt and Lynette was this very girdle, painted in camouflage green and black, mounted and framed with the title "I Support a Great American."

Now properly attired, I finally emerged from my room. Everyone was waiting. Matt, Lynette, David, and Andy looked wonderful. My father was ready to go to support me—though he seemed tired, old, and stressed. Diane was her quiet, supportive self. Tom did not join us—it was not a scheduled visitation and he still lived in Maple Valley.

Driving down the freeway toward Camp Murray, you'd never guess that it was the headquarters for the Washington National Guard. It looked like an old campus. The single-story brick and concrete buildings were vintage World War II. And hidden away in the trees was the only two-story structure on the post, where the adjutant general and his staff worked. It resembled a majestic, colonial-style building. Attached to this was a gray concrete addition that served as command headquarters during state emergencies. This portion of the complex, where the hearing was to take place, looked like a World War II bunker.

Inside, the walls were dingy and light barely came through the windows. People were busy doing their military jobs all around us. They appeared oblivious to the fact that during the next few days a board of inquiry would listen to testimony to determine whether or not I would be discharged. I felt like shouting, "Hey, you! How can you go on about your day-to-day business when what's happening here is so important?"

Obviously, I didn't say that out loud. The people working in the building didn't know or care. But looking around the office area, I knew there were "others like me" who were not going through a discharge hearing and would continue to serve honorably in the military regardless of what the board decided. Even the PERSEREC report said that investigations and discharges removed only a small percentage of the gay people who served.

Though my family and I had been haunted for two years by the possible public exposure of the hearing, it was private almost to the point of being secret. No one was allowed into the hearing room and no mention was made around the headquarters that the proceeding was taking place.

As we assembled in the room, the board members and the prosecutor, Captain Robin Davis, were formal. They made no eye contact with me. The administrative board consisted of four Army and National Guard colonels. The President of the Board was Colonel Patsy Thompson, former Chief Nurse of the National Guard. It was her former job I was seeking and that had prompted me to request the top-secret clearance. We had met several times before at military functions. Colonel Thompson came over and said how hard it was to have to sit in judgment on a colleague she respected. Clearly she didn't want to do this.

It was agreed that any family member who was not testifying could sit in on the proceedings. One of my attorneys, Michael Himes, talked with my kids and decided that Matt and Lynette would testify at the end of the hearing, so Andy and David could sit with me. While we were waiting, an obviously (to those of us who are) gay sergeant walked through on some business. Mary and I exchanged looks of ironic acknowledgment. I was about to be kicked out, whereas this sergeant continued doing her job adjacent to the hearing room without causing any breakdown in order or morale. The policy truly is absurd.

The preparations were taking a long time. We agreed it was better for my father to wait at home. He was too frail to endure a long session, and Diane needed to accompany him, so they reluctantly left.

Captain Margaret Bond began her opening statement for us. In a clear, strong voice she called me to the stand and asked me questions about my life. I outlined my careers in the armed forces and nursing. I noted how I was discharged from active duty in 1968 because it was against regulations for women with children to serve in the military, and how, when that policy was overturned in 1972, I joined the Army Reserves and had served without interruption since.

To establish my record, she asked me to describe my academic work, including my more than thirty published articles and book chapters on neuroscience nursing, plus awards and public-speaking appearances. This testimony was to show the board the importance of judging me by my contributions rather than excluding me for my sexual orientation.

I was then asked when I became aware of my sexual orientation, I admitted it was a hard question and described the difficulty of my divorce and the time afterward, as I searched to understand myself. Even now, I said, I could only explain it as an evolving process, so that when Agent Troutman asked the question about homosexuality, there was no other answer that I could give. I outlined the discrepancies between my own answers during that security clearance interview, and the statement the DIS agent wrote and asked me to sign. I said that the sentences I crossed out from the document before I signed it were then reinserted in the agent's own report, and there he alleged the statements to be mine. I explained that once I received a copy of his report, I objected, and that despite my written requests to the DIS to correct the record, they had not done so-in fact, they hadn't even responded to my last letter. This caused two board members, Colonel McAleer and Colonel Arrington, to interrupt. They felt it was unreasonable for the Sixth

Army to have pushed the scheduling of my hearing before the DIS had completed my file or responded to my requests on this crucial inconsistency. When we added that Agent Troutman did not sign his own statement, and, because the Sixth Army had given only two weeks' notice for the hearing, he was unavailable for cross-examination, Colonel McAleer got angry.

Colonel McAleer's concerns stopped the proceeding. My attorneys and the prosecutor went into conference. Michael Himes, brilliantly suggested, that instead of Troutman being summoned to testify and thereby postpone the hearing, that his contradictory statement should be dropped from the hearing evidence. The prosecutor agreed. My own words "I am a lesbian" would be the only "crime" considered at the hearing. The government reasoned that my statement alone was sufficient to win its side of the case. But this decision was actually very helpful to us. Its value would be most evident later by focusing my case in the federal court on the issue of whether a person can be denied the right to serve not because of anything the individual has done but simply because of who he or she is.

When the hearing resumed, I suggested that David and Andy leave. They had heard my testimony and had a good sense of what was going on. The remainder of the evidence would be more technical. Happy to be relieved of duty, they took off for home.

The hearing resumed with a variety of witnesses from my unit, as well as testimony from Colonel Koss, my commander, the State Surgeon. All were supportive of me. They stated they had known about my sexual orientation as the Army began to bring proceedings against me, and it never affected their view of me and my performance or the unit's morale.

Mary Newcombe then called our first expert witness, Dr. Laura Brown, who talked about sexual orientation and identity. Colonel Koss asked to stay and listen. He felt these issues would arise again, and he wanted to understand them better.

Mary presented Dr. Brown's credentials as an author of more than fifty publications, and a professor of psychology at the University of Washington who specializes in the psychology of women, human sexual development and sexual orientation. Dr. Brown provided insight on research about human sexual development and orientation. I was struck with how like a brief outline of my own life her description was.

"The first thing," Dr. Brown began, "is that we have a biological sex, If you have two X chromosomes, you end up with a body that most people consider female. If you have an X and a Y chromosome, you end up with a body that most people consider male.

"The next process happens between eighteen months and two years. That's the period during which a person develops what we call gender identity: I am a boy or I am a girl. Those of you who have had children will remember this period as one during which children show enormous interest in genitals—their own, other people's, yours—because they're very curious about this thing. It's a process of interaction between a person's internal experience and body, and external feedback from the social environment around them, that helps them come to label them-self. By about age three, most children can reliably answer the question: Which are you, a boy or a girl?

"Somewhere between the ages of two or three and about age five, sexual orientation develops. Sexual orientation is the predisposition to a sexual attraction to one or another or both genders. Now, this is not something that the child is aware of, because although children develop their sexual orientation at around this age, sexual interest and expression doesn't happen for most people until puberty. According to current scientific research, sexual orientation-whether heterosexual, homosexual, or bisexual-develops prior to age five.

"Then there's a long period which we call latency. This is between the age of about five and puberty. Children aren't particularly interested in, nor are there any progress in, the development of sexual identity or sense of sexual self.

"For most people, though not all, they begin to develop a sexual identity—that is, [they] begin to experience sexual feelings—at puberty or young adulthood. They begin to notice to whom and with whom those sexual feelings are directed. And they begin to develop words to call that sexual identity and what it means to them.

"Finally, again beginning usually in puberty and continuing throughout adult life, we have the development of sexual behavior choices. This is really the only aspect of this process where choice is involved, That is, a person can make choices about whether to behave sexually in committed or not-committed relationships. A person can choose not to act on sexual feelings during specific times or in specific settings. That process of choice in behavior is constant for us throughout our life span. Although we may believe when we're nineteen years old that we've made the decision for life, in fact what we find is that people continue that process of sexual behavior choices and development throughout adult life and into old age.

"We don't know precisely the factors that determine sexual orientation, there seem to be some combination of biological predisposition and perhaps some kinds of early environmental factors."

Mary then asked, "If you have a gay or a lesbian parent, what are the chances of you having a gay or lesbian child?"

"About the same as if you are a heterosexual parent," Dr. Brown stated. "Most gay men and lesbians were raised by heterosexually oriented people. Approximately ten percent of the population appears to have a minority sexual orientation of homosexuality." This description of events certainly fit my experience. All my sons are straight.

Mary's next question struck at the myth I heard as a child: that homosexuals are mentally ill. "Can you explain what makes a mentally healthy person in terms of their development of sexuality?"

"That's one of those questions psychologists are always asked about." Dr. Brown smiled. "I think there are several components. Broadly, the ability to work and to love. Specifically, the opportunity to act in congruence with yourself, with who you are, and with your values and ethics about how you should be in the world. Empirical studies have found fairly conclusively and consistently that there are very few, if any, psychological differences between gay and heterosexual men, and between lesbian and heterosexual women. The American Psychological Association in 1975 issued a statement that homosexuality is not per se a predictor of an individual's mental illness or mental health."

Dr. Brown then described how an important part of coming to understand one's own sexual identity is finding models in life that are like oneself. Of course, in our society, there are fewer role models—often, none— for gay and lesbian teenagers. That means the process of self-understanding takes longer. It is also more difficult because of the distress caused by "the fact that perhaps one belongs to a group that's not the dominant group, that may be stigmatized or punished. There may be attempts to deny one's identity and feelings, or to temporarily act as if one is not a member of the group." If one is homosexual, the search for one's "identity can last far into adulthood, unlike heterosexual identity development, which is strongly supported and mirrored and encouraged by the culture around us."

Dr. Brown said that my description of my long evolution to understand myself "is almost like reading a textbook case of sexual orientation identity development in women of her particular age cohort. "

If my life had been so textbook-clear, why was it so hard for me to understand? I found my answer in Dr. Brown's next response,

"Can one," Mary asked, "change one's sexual orientation?"

"No. Sexual orientation, as far as our research tells us, is not changeable. A person can behave heterosexually even though they have a homosexual sexual orientation, although because that behavior is incongruent with their orientation, it's likely to have negative mental health consequences. But sexual orientation is something that appears to be, from all scientific research available to us, an immutable phenomenon."

"What," Mary asked, "happens when one tries to change or suppress behavior that is consistent with the person's sexual orientation?"

"The person's self-esteem is affected," Dr. Brown replied. "Their ability to form intimate relationships is affected because they're trying to make themselves be intimate with a gender for whom there isn't a sexual orientation towards. They may feel badly about themselves,"

"Why then would one want to change one's sexual identity?"

"We live in a society in which there have been enormous numbers of punitive consequences for being a member of a sexual minority. People have been placed in jail, have lost custody of their children, lost jobs and homes, been victims of violence by individuals who are prejudiced and biased. So, people have attempted to escape these negative consequences by behaving as if they were members of the sexual majority.

"This is not an uncommon phenomenon for people who are members of stigmatized minority groups. In Hitler's Europe, it was not uncommon for members of the Jewish religion to attempt to pass as non-Jews because the consequences of being a member of that particular religious minority were, as we know, fatal."

Dr. Brown went on to describe false stereotypes often ascribed to gay men and lesbians-for example, that we make unwelcome overtures to heterosexuals and are not able to control our sexual urges, These biases are simply unfounded, she said.

She cited a study by Dr. Gregory Herek, published in the official Journal of the American Psychological Association, entitled "Gay People and Government Security Clearances."

"The research shows that, contrary to the stereotype, in all cases involving the breach of a government security clearance because of blackmail of the individual with the clearance, none of those cases, involved gay men or lesbians. In fact, there's some evidence, because of a lifelong experience of having to practice discretion and having to manage the way in which information is shared, that gay men or lesbians may be better capable of managing the demands, placed upon an individual with a government security clearance."

The members of the board asked for a copy of Dr. Herek's article to consult. They had listened attentively to Dr. Brown. We hoped her testimony would provide scientific analysis to replace their stereotypes or myths that the board members may have held about the issue; their openness and receptivity to our evidence encouraged me. Then the board adjourned for the afternoon.

The next and last day of the hearing began with the testimony of Major Duane Opp. Major Opp had worked with me for the last four years, and testified to the high level of morale and discipline in our unit.

Matt, and then Lynette, took the stand. They provided a picture of our family life. They described how I had told each family member of my sexual orientation a year and a half before, and that it never affected any of our relationships. In fact, Matt said, contrary to my disclosure causing damage, it had strengthened our bonds. Lynette began to cry when she talked about how much the military meant to me. "If the military is taken away from her—it's twenty-six years, it's like a baby. That's a long time with something."

And finally, we called our other expert witness, Dr Lawrence Korb, former Assistant Secretary of Defense for Manpower, Reserve Affairs, and Logistics during the Reagan administration. He holds a doctorate in international relations with a focus on national security policy and is the author of seven books. His view, shaped while at the Pentagon, is that the policy excluding homosexuals from the military should be changed, and that any problem that might arise would be temporary and overcome through leadership and education—two areas in which the military excels.

He talked at length about the PERSEREC report that recommended the ban be overturned. His testimony allowed us to enter the document's findings as evidence into the records. He also pointed to the success of the military mission in the Persian Gulf War as evidence that gay men and lesbians do not damage unit cohesion or morale.

"They used to tell me when I was in the Pentagon," he said, "ten percent of the force may be gay or lesbian. PERSEREC indicates that in their report also. Even at five percent that's 100,000 people on active duty, so they're already there. Since only roughly 1,400 are being discharged each year, there's another roughly 99,000 in there, and the last war demonstrated cohesion was never better."

Dr. Korb's testimony was impassioned and wide-ranging. He explained that the policy banning gays was formulated many years ago, when myths concerning homosexuals were more widely believed. But the policy, his study of the facts showed, is based on prejudicial attitudes rather than on empirical evidence. He equated it with fears about blacks and whites serving together. When President Harry S. Truman issued his executive order to integrate the armed forces in 1948, many within and without the Pentagon predicted wholesale disaster. Yet, Dr. Korb pointed out, once the military was given this directive to change, it became a model for the rest of society.

Dr. Korb's testimony was tremendously valuable. I felt we were presenting the most detailed case possible. But I kept reminding myself; this board cannot determine an Army policy wrong, they can only make sure the policy is properly enforced. However, I still believed, despite what everyone told me, the board might make an exception for me. Of course, my attorneys knew better, and were pleased that we were able to get so much evidence in the record that could be used in the civil court to prove the regulation itself has no rational basis.

Finally, it was time to give my final statement. I had spent a long time preparing what I would tell this jury of my military peers. I stood up and faced the board again. But my prepared statement left my mind and my heart spoke.

"Thirty years ago," I began, "when I joined the military, I had a dream of one day being in a position of becoming Chief Nurse of the Army Nurse Corps. And so as part of that process, I began both preparing educationally in the military and in my civilian world. I applied for top-secret clearance, and knew, I think, at a subconscious level that there might be some questions and it may be an awkward time because I had come to understand a little bit more about myself in terms of my sexual identity. And yet I felt so strongly that this was what I'm supposed to do with my life that I applied for the top-secret clearance, willing to take whatever chance came my way.

"And when the time came whether or not to disclose to the investigator, I told the truth. It seemed like that was the very premise of everything I stood for in my entire life and career. And because of previous experiences that I'd had in the military and changes that I had seen in the course of my own career, I believed in it as an organization that could deal with the individual and look in terms of the human component and contribution that someone could make to the service."

"In October of 1989 I was called to the chief of staff's office and told that my federal recognition was being considered for withdrawal. My world dropped out, and I was very—I don't know why I should have been surprised, but I was, and I felt—-very, hurt in some ways because by this time I had more than twenty-three years in the military and had served well, both here, on active duty in Vietnam, and in the Army Reserves and now in the National Guard, and felt abandoned and very alone. At the time I believed very strongly that I had something to contribute to the military. And for the past twenty-six months have continued to serve with every bit of the effort and energy I had beforehand."

"And when the time came now to decide whether or not to resign or retire, I felt that this was one of the decisions I had to make in my life. A crossroad. Do I back down or do I stand up for what I truly believe is my right as a human being, which is to be acknowledged as a human being. My professional career, my abilities, my contributions have nothing to do with my sexual orientation."

"Throughout my career and throughout the world there are times when change can be made only by someone stepping forth, being willing perhaps to expose themselves and their vulnerability so that others become aware of the fact that there are differences in the world. So that people will understand these differences are okay and don't affect our ability to be part of an organization or to make a contribution."

"And so, I choose to be here. To sit before you and my family, and be vulnerable in hopes that perhaps it can influence making a change and allowing us to serve as we have in the past and will continue to do in the future."

"I appreciate your presence, your attendance, your attentiveness, and I thank you very much."

The two days of testimony was over, and the board began its deliberations.

Waiting with my family for the board to reach its decision, I knew it had no choice, but maybe... I kept believing maybe it would make an exception for me.

There have been a few very difficult times in my life when I doubted I would survive and wondered if I was really living a nightmare. One was when the judge awarded temporary custody of our children to Harvey. The world disappeared around me; I nearly fainted. What was happening was unimaginable. And now, as I waited for the board to determine my fate, I fought off similar feelings.

After about an hour, we were told the decision had been reached, and we all reentered the hearing room. The board President, Colonel Patsy Thompson, got up.

"Would you stand, Margarethe," she said.

I rose and faced her, knowing that my uniform was flawless. And knowing that it made no difference.

Colonel Thompson then read the following statement on behalf of the board:

"I truly believe that you are one of the great Americans, Margarethe. And I've admired you for a long time and the work that you've done and all that you've done for the Army National Guard. When I was Chief Nurse, I said many times, I'm really glad that we have Margarethe Cammermeyer or Grethe Cammermeyer in the Guard. She's doing such an outstanding job. We're really fortunate that she came to us. And I really meant that. And I still do mean that."

"And we're really proud of you and all of your accomplishments; and I say that from the Army National Guard Nurse Corps perspective. And I think that one of the things that I read in your record pretty well sums it up. It really touched me. One young nurse summed it up when she said, 'It was a rare privilege to work under you during your tenure as Chief Nurse. I waited a long time in the trenches for your kind of nurse to come along. You were an inspiration for us all.' Another nurse wrote that you 'provided me with an excellent role model. She was one of the few members of the unit hierarchy who knew anything about being an officer. She has provided consistent positive guidance for those who cared enough to listen, Her ability to lead and inspire others was obvious, even to me, a person who did not know whether or not she was even going to stay in the military as a career.' But through your inspiration, that person did stay in and reached great heights, and those are just a few of the people that you've touched in your thirty years of military career."

"It's my sad duty to read what I'm going to read for you at this time, so I will proceed with that." Her voice caught. She stopped for a second.

"Colonel Cammermeyer has proved to be a great asset to both the active and reserve component, the medical profession as a whole. She has consistently provided superb leadership and has many outstanding accomplishments to her credit, both military and civilian. Notwithstanding, the board finds that Colonel Margarethe Cammermeyer is a homosexual as defined in AR 135-175 and as evidenced by her statement to DIS Agent Brent B. Troutman on 28 April 1989, and her admission under oath to this board that she is a lesbian, and statements made under oath to this board by five character witnesses. We recommend that Colonel Cammermeyer's federal recognition be withdrawn. In the event that subsequent action results in discharge from the USAR, an honorable discharge certificate should be awarded. We are aware that the DOD [Department of Defense] policy on homosexuality is currently under review. If the review results in change, these recommendations should be reexamined."

Colonel Thompson sat back down. And with that the board adjourned.

My military career was over.

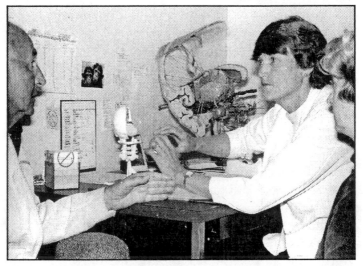

Discussing treatment options with brain
tumor patient, 1983 SFVAMC

1984 Thanking Martha Raye at military
Dining Out 352nd Evac, Oakland

MASH Hospital in background Colonel
Cammermeyer in MOPP gear

Diane the artist 1989

Matt wedding reception with Grethe
and his brothers 1990

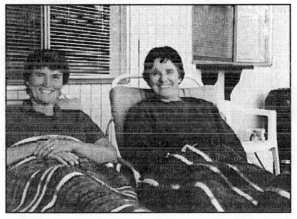

Diane and Grethe relaxing on porch 1991

PhD graduation 1991

First coming out event at Gay Pride, June 1992 Seattle

Presidential Inaugural Ball 1993, Washington DC

March on Washington, 1993 Tracy Thorn,
Grethe, Dusty Pruitt, Joe Steffan

Grethe and Diane in Norway 1991

CHAPTER 12

. . . .

Facing the World

The meal was over at the National Organization for Women luncheon. Politicians, journalists, activists were networking up a storm as I took some notes for a speech I was to give. A young woman came up and shyly asked if she could speak to me for a minute. Her father, she said, was a career Marine colonel. He had three children-herself and her two brothers. When he learned his children were gay, he disowned them. One brother died of AIDS without ever seeing or hearing from his father again. Now her other brother has AIDS. Overcome with the pain of this disclosure, she stopped talking for a moment. I put my hand on her arm. Then, she continued, her father saw me on TV. He called her and her brother and spoke with them for the first time in years. He said if I was a gay-rights activist, he was ready to be one now, too.

. . . .

The board of inquiry had recommended that my federal recognition be withdrawn and that I receive an honorable discharge under regulation AR 135-175. My attorneys had told me at the beginning that this would be the board's decision—but I hadn't believed it would happen. I was stunned. I had hoped that the board would make an exception for me. Now that they hadn't, I still felt the Army itself might overturn the board's recommendation and exempt me from the policy. If I was discharged, I would be stripped of my rank and privilege as though I had never served. I would also lose my monthly military salary, and we were not sure if I would lose my pension. As it turned out, I will receive a more limited pension, but have lost all gray-area benefits such as travel, life insurance, medical coverage, and use of military facilities.

As people got ready to leave the hearing room, I saw many with tears in their eyes. Several board members, particularly Colonel Thompson, came over to wish me luck in my uphill battle. I was grateful for their kindness and support. And I was amazed at the illogic of it.

Matt and Lynette offered to drive back with me, but I sent them on ahead. I needed to be alone. My sorrow was mixed with a curious relief that, at least, the hearing was over.

In the car, I called Diane, who had been at home with my father, waiting for the verdict. I told her what had happened and felt her presence. But I was glad to be by myself. I didn't want even her to see my tears—I was in uniform and still a soldier needing to be in control.

I arrived at the house. David came out to meet me. His big blue eyes were filled with concern. His was the last sympathy I could deal with. My facade of control dissolved. He held me in his arms as I wept. Fortunately, only he saw this tough old colonel lose military bearing.

Entering the house, I was surrounded with support, compassion, and outrage at the result. My first need, however, was to get out of my uniform. I changed immediately. I wanted to store it out of sight to symbolically reject my uniform as the military was rejecting me. But I couldn't. There would still be weekend drills and administrative work to do until my actual separation. And I dreamed of a reprieve.

Attorneys being attorneys, they were already thinking about taking the case to the Federal Court. We'd scheduled a dinner meeting for that evening to plan the next step. Even Dr. Korb was coming. Ironically, we had chosen a restaurant named *Winners* for our debriefing and strategy session. It didn't seem the appropriate place, but perhaps it signified their belief in the ultimate outcome. For the lawyers, this was the beginning of the next battle. For me it was the end of a twenty-six-year marriage.

The scene at the restaurant was lively. In a matter of hours, the focus was off me. Everything was out of my hands. The attorneys pitched ideas back and forth, as though I no longer existed. The legal battle was up to them.

Then the question arose: Would I remain silent? Till now, I'd shunned publicity. That was in keeping with my promise to the National Guard that while we proceeded through the investigation and hearing, this was a private struggle between me and the military. Now that I'd lost, if I remained quiet, it could all be swept under the carpet. No one would know, and nothing would change.

To continue to fight, the lawyers explained, our strategy had to change in a significant way. If I pursued this, I had to go public. We needed community and Congressional support, generated through letters, personal contact, and speaking out through every avenue possible. This battle could only be fought in the media. It meant my life would no longer be private.

Despite my earlier hope that I would be exempted from the policy, I had heard my lawyers' warnings that I would have to take my case to the Federal Court and go public. Consequently, Diane and I had talked about that possibility. We always came back to the same point: my service, like my life, was based on the values of integrity, honor, and duty. And values, to have any potency at all, carried with them moral obligations. Ethical tenets are made up of empty words if, at the moment of testing, one refuses to act.

Though we are both intensely private people, Diane and I had agreed that if the military discharged me I would take my case to the American people. Everyone at the dinner was pleased with my decision. They also knew it would carry a price—a price that I failed, at the time, to comprehend.

Mary said Randy Shilts of the *San Francisco Chronicle* wanted a chance to interview me and break the story. She felt that his commitment to exposing the institutionalized discrimination in the military would help bring national attention to my case and the regulation. Everyone believed this was the best way to proceed, and agreed to ask political and civil rights organizations to get involved. Our hope was to cause enough social outrage to encourage the Department of Defense to reevaluate its policy that separated patriotic Americans from the military not because of any misconduct but simply because of their identities.

Trying to resume my life after the hearing was difficult. For a time, I was in a daze. Worried that I might not feel focused enough to work, I had arranged a few days off from the hospital. I felt worthless—too distracted to provide quality care to my patients. The decision of the board was also an embarrassment and a failure-I didn't want to offend anyone by my presence. When I did return to work several days later, I was able to manage only a few hours; then I became too distracted and went home. It took several weeks before I became fully productive again at my job.

Fortunately, drill wasn't scheduled for several weeks. I didn't have to face the rest of the unit or deal with how they were reacting to my impending discharge.

Coping with these fears was an old struggle for me. To be formally rejected by the board confirmed my worst image of myself. My years in the military did not count. Nothing mattered—my awards, my professional and educational accomplishments. Being told I would be discharged, and my rank taken away, made me feel that even the lives I had saved in Vietnam were not important to the military. Each day I fought these waves of despair as I waited for a call from a reporter. Any reporter. Two weeks went by and nothing happened. I had put my career on the line and nothing was going to come of it other than losing my right to serve.

Finally, Randy Shilts called. I felt tremendous relief. During our phone interview, he was supportive and expressed dismay at the military's policy and tactics. He was in the middle of writing *Conduct Unbecoming*, and his grasp of the issues was impressive. When his article on my case was published at the end of August, I was out of the closet more than ever before. My role changed from that of a military officer to someone who publicly challenged the military policy of discrimination and sought to shift social consciousness.

That same month, August 1991, Mary had great news. The Ninth Circuit Court of Appeals had handed down its decision on Dusty Pruitt's case. She won reinstatement of her case, and a ruling that the government must demonstrate with facts that the regulation is rational and legitimate— that is to say, not based on prejudice. With those instructions, the Ninth Circuit remanded her case back to the district court. It marked a significant victory.

Soon after Randy's interview, *Time Magazine* published a story about gays in the military. When these national articles appeared, I gained a broader perspective on the social implications of my fight. Then there was the story about a highly visible Department of Defense spokesman who was gay. Defense Secretary Richard Cheney defended his aide by saying that one's personal life is no one else's business—job performance is what matters. The media heavily covered the controversy. People were beginning to take notice of the issue.

Consequently, I received a lot more requests for interviews on radio and television and from the print media. I began to appreciate the warnings I had received from my lawyers on how intrusive the media could be into my life. Though I thought I understood the cost, it wasn't until my story first appeared in a local paper that I experienced what profound impact publicity could have.

It happened the day my father left to return to his own home in Maryland, after living with me for two and a half years. Walking through the airport, we went by a newsstand. There on the front page of the *Tacoma News Tribune* was my story and my picture. I bought two papers. I gave one to my father as he boarded the plane and read the other as I went to work.

The article was excellent. Reading it, I blushed to myself. Then anxiety hit. Yes, I really wanted the military's treatment of gays and lesbians to be exposed and the regulation changed. However, when I was the focus of the story, I felt self-conscious and vulnerable.

I got to work at six-thirty in the morning. I looked at the newspaper box outside the hospital. There it was again. My face. A whole stack of papers with my story and my face. I froze.

I hadn't discussed any of this at work. I didn't believe many people knew. But now they would. And once they knew... My own homophobia went to work: no one would want anything to do with me. My patients would cancel their appointments. The hospital staff would be embarrassed and shun me. Colleagues would not work with me.

I had a fleeting impulse to put my quarter in the newspaper box and grab all the copies. But that would hardly undo the publicity. And it wouldn't be soldierly.

Instead, I slipped into the hospital via the back door. I stopped to check laboratory results from patients I had worked with the previous day. My intent was to sneak into my office unseen.

That's where this old Marine, a Vietnam vet I worked with found me. I'm sure he hadn't known.

Until this morning.

He came up. Close. In my face. I had to look at him.

"Do you know," he demanded, "what the most important thing is to an infantryman?"

I thought, His weapon. After all, that is what an infantryman uses to do his work. But he didn't wait for my reply.

"His buddy!" he said. I still held my breath.

"And you can be my buddy, and share my foxhole anytime."

Then he hugged me. And both of us old soldiers cried.

I'd been prepared for the hatred. I'd been prepared for the rejection. I hadn't been prepared for the love.

My intention was to be tough the whole day. That plan disintegrated then and there. But I did sneak up to my office to hide, contemplate, and work.

The world is so strange. Just when you think you have it all figured out—you don't. People came by my office who had never been there before, to offer kind words or an embrace. Many expressed their support for me in my fight against the regulation. To a person, they said the ban against gays and lesbians needed to be repealed. My patients, who are all veterans, wanted to make sure that despite losing my National Guard position and military career; I'd "still be their doc." I assured them I would.

Often their generous words included the thought that challenging the military took courage. To me it never felt like courage, but rather doing something you had to do. Although it was awkward—everybody knowing about my private life I could never hide again.

Later that month, Diane and I began our long-planned graduation trip to Norway. We left with great relief, thinking no one in Norway would know about my challenge to the military. But the world is a smaller place nowadays.

The news had even traveled inside the Arctic circle—to the town of Tromsø, where my cousin Mads Fredrick is a physician. I hadn't seen him since my last visit to Norway, twenty-six years earlier. When we arrived, I phoned him.

"Dette er din kusine fra Amerika, Grethe Cammermeyer (This is your cousin from America, Grethe Cammermeyer)," I said, worried he might not remember me.

He laughed warmly. "How is my fucking famous cousin?" he replied in English. "You have been my role model and I am so proud of you."

He had read about my suit against the military in the international edition of *Newsweek*. The entire family, including his parents, had discussed the case. Sexual orientation was not an issue to them. Why, they wondered, was it such a big deal in the United States? The family warmly welcomed Diane and me. What delighted them was my challenge to the government—the little guy standing up for what was right, particularly when this little guy's opponent was the strongest government on the planet.

Returning home after our marvelous trip, I was informed that the DIS was conducting a second investigation of me. Why? I had already been recommended for discharge. What more did they want? The lead investigator contacted me. He told me the Department of the Army had reopened the investigation. Later, when I again questioned the need for the second inquiry, the same investigator said the National Guard had requested it be reopened. Why couldn't the lead investigator keep his explanations straight? Who really was behind this second intrusion into my work and life? I never really found out.

As part of their second probe, the DIS interviewed my friends, colleagues, and acquaintances. I was told agents intimidated people by insisting appointments for interviews be set regardless of scheduling conflicts. Everyone assumed they had to comply with the investigators, but that was not the case. The DIS is not the police. It has no authority to force people to answer questions. I was offended that my associates and friends were being pursued.

Then the DIS set up another interview with me. Since I had experienced their interrogation techniques before, I felt I was an old hand and could manage alone–I wouldn't need an attorney for this. Mary did not share my opinion. I was confident of my skills, but Mary was not. Her tone and words of caution made me rethink my position. I recalled how odd it was that the second investigation was happening at all. There was the lead investigator's different answers to the question of who had ordered the second probe. Then Dusty Pruitt's and others' stories of harassment came to mind. Perhaps this was not the military I thought I knew. I massaged the knot in my neck.

"Well," I said to Mary, "if I didn't need an attorney, I guess I wouldn't have one."

"Good," she replied and immediately arranged for my JAG lawyer, Margaret Bond, to join me.

In October 1991, Margaret and I arrived together for my interview at the Defense Investigative Service offices in Tacoma. The two agents waiting for me said they were surprised to see I was accompanied by counsel. Julie Reddy and Schawn Schertzer had only three chairs in the windowless interrogation room. After an awkward moment, they brought in a fourth chair and we all sat down. At least the score was even: two on their side and two on mine.

I was again given privacy-act information—the military equivalent of reading me my rights—and they reminded me of the voluntary nature of my disclosures. They explained that Margaret could not speak for me, but I could consult with her. On the advice of my attorneys, I gave them a written statement outlining the details of my case and including testimony from the previous hearing.

Then they probed for details about my travels during the preceding twenty years. They included my recent trip to Norway as well as my tours of duty in Germany and Vietnam. They asked if I had met foreign agents. I had been contacted to present papers on heat stress, in Europe, and we discussed those occasions. It is amazing how intimidating "routine questioning" can feel.

Next, they focused on my previous DIS statement, going over and over each sentence. The repetition, the intensity, and their attitudes—it felt like harassment. In each case, I referred them to the hearing transcript, as well as the prepared statement I'd already given them. Agent Schertzer said he would read those but felt at a disadvantage; since he was not aware of the contents of the transcript or of the results of the board's action. I found that difficult to believe. He had my portfolio from the investigation, and I did not think he was being entirely candid. But I said nothing that questioned his integrity. I had agreed to this second interview. I did not want to jeopardize my security clearance, which was still pending, or my case. The Army had not yet acted on the board's recommendation that I be discharged, and, always the optimist, I thought I might still be allowed to stay in uniform.

As the interrogation continued, going over the same old questions and innuendos for no legitimate purpose, I became irritated. Though I felt pushed and manipulated, I worked hard to let none of it show. Then Agent Reddy asked if I could be pressured or blackmailed.

"No," I stated. Then, under my breath, I added, "Only by the government."

The agents heard it and rapidly made notes. I could have kicked myself.

Finally it ended. I had kept my temper and (almost) all my thoughts to myself. Afterward, Margaret said it had gone well. I still do not know the purpose of this second investigation. But one result was becoming clear: my view of my country and its military was changing from blind trust and obedience to suspicion.

The roller coaster of events continued. One day I was in a dungeon-like room being questioned about my loyalty and fitness for service, and the next I was an expected attendee at the National Guard's annual Militia Ball, held in the ballroom of a Tacoma hotel. Suffering from such mixed messages, I debated whether this year I should attend. Would I be accepted as before, or shunned? I decided to go regardless of the result. Now was not the time to hide.

During the VIPs' entrance, General Haugland, the new Chief of Staff, saw me and smiled. He seemed to nod in acknowledgment and approval of my presence. After dinner, I did not stay to socialize, though it had been my custom to do so in the past. Yet I went home pleased that I had attended, despite my trepidations. I had held my head up high. Because the people at the Militia Ball were primarily my own age, raised in the same culture I had grown up in, which rejected and stigmatized gays and lesbians, I half expected they would turn and walk away from me. But they did not, and because my homophobia persisted, I felt grateful to the 164th staff for their acceptance and support.

The DIS made no other requests and the Department of Defense took no further action. For months nothing happened, though everything loomed. To this day, I have not heard the final decision regarding my security clearance. But my legal team continued to press forward. Letters supporting my case from patients, colleagues, Vietnam veterans, as well as civic leaders I had never met, were sent to President George Bush, the Joint Chiefs of Staff, and Secretary of Defense Cheney. They argued for a reprieve or an exception—or a change in the policy itself.

Since no official word was announced, I continued to go to drill and to perform my duties as state Chief Nurse. For several years, I'd been working on a manual of standard operating procedures (SOP) for the new hospital, because there was no cohesive text to outline and standardize the tasks of all its areas. There was no manual on the National level, either. Writing the definitive document had been a task I wanted to accomplish if and when I became Chief Nurse of the National Guard. By January 1992, I was almost resigned to the inevitability that I would be discharged. So it now became a point of principle to complete this manual for the state National

Guard hospital I'd helped create. Major Opp had replaced me as Chief Nurse of the hospital (while I retained my duties as state Chief Nurse), and I wanted him to be able to take a completed document to the National Chief Nurse's Conference. Working against the deadline of my upcoming (though not yet announced) discharge, I would complete the SOP manual in six months, just in time to turn in the three-hundred-page book on my last day in uniform.

Then, in March 1992, my long ordeal with the Army went into its final stage. My records were flagged. In the military, individuals' records are flagged to indicate they are not meeting standards or have some adverse administrative action pending. You are then allowed to perform only minimal duties at your home base. Official travel, involvement in training exercises, and any favorable action (such as an award) are denied. I was therefore denied permission to attend the upcoming Chief Nurse's Conference or a continuing education seminar. That, in turn, meant I was unable to perform my duties as state Chief Nurse.

It had been two years and eleven months since I had stated my sexual orientation to the DIS agent. My record of service remained untarnished. As for destroying morale and damaging the mission, the only thing that impaired my unit's cohesion, effectiveness, and morale was my investigation and discharge.

By coincidence, the local TV stations contacted me to see if anything was happening with my case. Because my records were flagged, I told them I was not sure if I was going to be allowed to work as Chief Nurse much longer. The media interpreted this to mean I might not be allowed back on base. I tried to correct the misunderstanding, but the reports had already been broadcast.

On May 27, 1992, a reporter for the military newspaper at Fort Lewis contacted me. He had just heard from the National Guard Bureau that my discharge was imminent. I called the state headquarters and learned my records had arrived the evening before. The recommendations of the board of inquiry had been–as we had expected–approved. I was to be discharged. The Adjutant General for the Washington State National Guard, General Greg Barlow, wanted to meet with me the next day at Camp Murray.

My meeting with General Barlow lasted about thirty minutes. Despite his official demeanor and extraordinary military background, he was also a human being. We had a profoundly personal meeting, which I carry in my heart, rather than making it public. His sensitivity and caring meant a lot to me as he pronounced my ultimate sentence under military regulations: I would be discharged without shame, but with the dignity and respect of my rank and position. He wished me luck and success and escorted me to the door, outside which the press was waiting. I gave, and he returned, a final salute.

And so, two weeks later, on June 11, 1992, I was discharged. My dream of retiring with full military honors was not to be. Still, I decided to do something symbolic for the occasion, and arranged to have a last meeting with my staff for an official goodbye. At home, I ironed my uniform and precisely placed the medals and insignias. Each one brought a memory. I stood before the mirror and I looked at myself as a colonel for the last time.

Then I drove to Camp Murray and entered the post, returning salutes smartly to the gate guard and all who passed me on the grounds. Some stopped, gave me hugs, fought back tears, forced smiles.

I returned my keys and identification card, and turned in my completed, standard-operating-procedures manual. I said a brief goodbye to the staff. It was too hard to try to maintain composure and thank them for all they had done and had meant to me during the time I had served with them.

At 10:00 a.m., I met my team of attorneys in front of the memorial at Camp Murray. Camera crews from Primetime Live and The McNeil-Lehrer NewsHour, along with reporters from local papers and TV stations gathered before us.

I spoke of the meaning of my career and stated my resolve to fight discrimination in the military. We would file a suit against the Army that same day in civil court and argue that the ban was unconstitutional, must be overturned, and that I should be reinstated. Additionally, following the Ninth Circuit's ruling in Dusty Pruitt's case, we would also challenge the government to prove with facts on the record that the policy is "rationally related to a legitimate governmental purpose." If, as we would show, the antigay policy could not survive this rational-basis scrutiny, then the court would find it to be based on prejudice and therefore unconstitutional. My attorneys, Mary, Jeffrey, and Michael, took over, describing what the next legal steps would be. After all the questions were answered, the TV crews began packing up and I got ready to leave.

Then Mrs. and Mr. Ring pulled up in their truck. This personification of what we were to fight was sad and remarkable. Mrs. Ring yelled words of venom and hate. She raised her fists in a threat.

What false stereotypes, what broken path brought her to say such things? Though another civilian who worked at Camp Murray, the wife of a military person, came up to me, expressed support, and said that what I'd just experienced was not at all their feeling on the post, it was Mrs. Ring's words I remembered most.

Later, a reporter asked me why I had gone up to someone so clearly beyond listening. "She is the very person we need to reach," I said.

She hated me without even knowing me. So this is what prejudice feels like.

Weeks later, Mrs. Ring sent me a letter of apology. "I'm sorry I said I wish you had died in action," she wrote. "I didn't mean that. I let my emotions get the best of me. Please forgive me."

Her letter, of all the hundreds offering prayers and support, was the most memorable. It gave me hope that others could see us as people and not objects to fear. Perhaps I was not losing my career for nothing.

I shed my uniform and left my military world. Despite what everyone had said and what I knew, until my separation, until I was stripped of my rank, a part of me believed that my position as a colonel and chief nurse would give the military an excuse to make an exception for me.

But they didn't make an exception for me. And in that shock of it's happening to me, my perspective became larger. If they could do this to me, what were they doing to others who had less rank and visibility? The policy was unjust. My task should be to change it.

Yet, I still struggled with self-doubt. Out of uniform, without the identity I'd fashioned and loved, regardless of the letters and calls of support, I felt unprotected and displaced. I questioned whether I had the right to speak for anyone other than myself.

Less than a month later, at the end of June 1992, Diane and I were returning to Seattle from California. We were invited by State Representative Cal Anderson to attend the diversity concert of the Seattle Gay Men's Chorus at the Opera House.

Our plane arrived back in Seattle in the early evening, so we went directly to the performance. It was our first encounter with an event that had "gay" in the title, and neither of us knew exactly what to expect. As older ladies, we were a little nervous. Cal received us warmly, and asked us to wait backstage before taking our seats. He wanted me to say a few words to the audience.

The three thousand seats of the Opera House were full. It was the weekend of the Gay Pride Celebration, and also performing that night were the London and San Francisco Gay Men's Choruses. We waited in the wings until the crowd became quiet. I heard my introduction. A tremendous roar went up. I walked out on stage, into the lights.

I couldn't believe it. Everyone in the audience was standing, applauding, cheering. Flushed and embarrassed, I kept walking to the microphone. The ovation continued. It was the thrill of my life because this was Seattle. For a brief time, at least, I hoped people would listen to my message, and I could speak for those less visible.

The next day, Sunday, we were again being filmed by crews from Prime-Time Live and McNeil/Lehrer News Hour. The day started with an early radio talk show in Seattle; then our caravan headed to the Seattle Church of Religious Science, where Diane and I had been members for the last few years. This church has always been the place where I felt spiritually centered, and so, despite the TV cameras, it was good to be there with people who were our extended family.

Afterward, our group drove to the Gay Pride Day rally at Volunteer Park. I'd never attended this event before. It was a beautiful summer afternoon, and thousands of people were settling in around the open-air stage for the speeches and entertainment. The media crews had put a mike on me and were following Diane and me with their cameras as we wandered through the crowds, looking around, getting Cokes and hot dogs. I was swamped by well-wishers, amazed that so many recognized and supported me. I'd been asked to appear at the podium for a brief statement, and finally we made our way to the official area behind the stage. Looking up the hill, I saw folks of all ages crowded together as if at a vast community picnic.

I was introduced by Sergeant J. R. Stone, who greeted me with a proud salute, which I returned. The crowd's standing ovation was both empowering and humbling. I was moved and impressed by the diversity of my new community. When the crowd sat back down, I asked that others who had served in the military stand to be recognized. They did, and there were many. The audience cheered, and I saluted them.

We went from there to a local TV station, where I appeared on a Town Meeting program. It was a divisive setting. One of my patients from the VA came and expressed his support for me and for overturning the ban. But some in the audience adamantly embraced their stereotypical fear and hatred of gays and lesbians. As I fielded questions and statements from people who proudly repeated ignorant and malicious antigay phrases, I was struck by the fact that homophobia is one of the last socially acceptable prejudices in America.

Fortunately, though long overdue, the moral consensus of the country is that discriminating against African Americans is wrong. But in some people's minds it is still fair to deny gays their civil rights in employment, housing, and military service. That permission to hate those who are "different," I was beginning to see, is additionally fueled by the military's policy of discrimination. Yet shouldn't the American government's role be to protect its citizens from the prejudices of others?

Though I didn't imagine my schedule could be any fuller, the media attention had only begun. Requests for interviews came from every direction. Radio, TV, newspapers, magazines. News shows, talk shows, panels, debates. I used accrued compensatory and vacation time from work so was able to participate in these speaking engagements. At first, remembering my promise to my attorneys and myself, I accepted every offer-daytime TV, all-night talk radio, requiring red-eye flights to New York, California, Alaska, and points in between. I spoke at college campuses, town meetings, Rotary Clubs, Chambers of Commerce, high schools, and private gatherings. If someone would listen, my job was to talk.

Though I rarely encountered hostility, I never knew what to expect. I felt a guardedness, a vigilance similar to what I experienced in Vietnam and just afterward when I returned to the States. On college campuses, ROTC students often discreetly encountered me before I entered the lecture hall. They told me of their support and explained that their superiors had made it clear they were not to attend my speech. Those warnings, they added, were never put in writing. I told them I understood, and counseled them to wait for change to occur through the courts or Congress. When I read polls that showed a majority of enlisted personnel supported the military's ban, I doubted that the statistics were honest, untainted reflections.

As the country debated this issue, more facts were revealed about the cost of the anti-gay policy. In June 1992, the General Accounting Office report on the price of the governmental discrimination against gays and lesbians was released. People heard the numbers: fourteen hundred military personnel who wanted to serve their country and had been trained to perform specific jobs were eliminated each year. From 1980 to 1991, the cost of the anti-gay policy was $494 million to train people, who were then discharged. That number did not include the money the government spent on investigations. The GAO estimated that the cost of investigations for 1990 alone was more than $2.5 million.

The report also noted that "women in all services were discharged for homosexuality at a rate consistently ranging two to three times higher than their rate of representation." In the Marine Corps, the percentage of women discharged for being lesbians was almost six times their rate of representation in that branch of service, while overall, women, during the last decade, were separated at roughly three times the rate of men.

That supported the stories I was beginning to hear from women in uniform. Too often, I was told of a similar pattern: a female would rebuff a male service member's sexual propositions and soon would be investigated for being a lesbian. One service member told me how an investigation into her sexual orientation was stopped by her immediate male superior (using his commander's discretion). Then he raped her—he expected, she said, "payment" for protecting her. And she did not report his attack, because she was afraid that if she did he would reinstate the investigation against her. As women have attained more rights and opportunities in the military, the accusation of being a lesbian has become a weapon of sexual harassment. Continuing the ban is a perfect mechanism to perpetuate sexism either by keeping women out of the military or by controlling and abusing women who do serve.

As I became more visible in the media, I was often contacted by gay and lesbian servicemembers who were struggling to come to terms with a discriminatory institution that was also their only avenue for education and career advancement. I always counseled them to stay silent; otherwise their careers would be destroyed. I recommended to those who had already come out that they contact either the Military Law Task Force in San Diego or the Servicemembers Legal Defense Network in Washington, D.C., for possible assistance.

As I heard the stories of those hurt by the military policy, I realized another false image held about gays is that we all have good incomes and successful careers. That's not true. Just like society in general, only a portion of gay people have higher-than-average incomes and educational levels-and they are often the more vocal segment because they are better protected by their economic status. However, far more gays and lesbians find it difficult to obtain educational opportunities and jobs, and for some the military is the only way out of generations of poverty. But because of this policy that eliminates a minority group only to cater to the prejudices of others, the military careers of gays and lesbians are destroyed and their lives permanently damaged. This was the group I also needed to speak for.

As I became involved in these issues, I saw that all of the steps of my life were part of a necessary evolution. I was very fortunate to have experienced the heterosexual identity. Living the heterosexual life, I had had a husband, children, and an ideal home-and had received the mainstream culture's validation. I was recognized for professional competency. I knew what it felt like to be entitled to respect, dignity, and civil rights. That entitlement is invaluable, but it is often denied to members of a minority.

As I took my case to the public, my own expectations continued to be challenged. Steeled for rejection and hate, I kept receiving encouragement and support. At a televised town meeting in Seattle during the summer of 1992, I spoke with presidential candidate Bill Clinton. His promise to overturn the ban if elected, his view that everyone was important and had a contribution to make, inspired me to believe in him as an instrument for equal rights for us all.

His election signaled a positive change in the leadership and direction of this country. Many profound challenges faced America and the world. There was a continuing global recession, and our own economy needed inventive and vigorous attention. Violence was increasing alarmingly in our own neighborhoods and cities, while cynicism and resignation infected our national dialogue. The President and First Lady Hillary Rodham Clinton acknowledged these dilemmas as they assembled the new administration. The scope and magnitude of the issues facing our world called for the full participation of every human being. I believed that one of the first actions of the new administration would be to sign an executive order overturning the ban that prevented gay men and lesbians from serving their country. I dreamed of being in Washington, D.C., on that wonderful day.

Then, almost as good as my fantasy, Diane and I received an official invitation to one of the inaugural balls. If he's going to invite us to the big event, I thought, he's surely going to get rid of the ban, as he promised. With childlike excitement, we shopped for clothes, visited the hair stylist, and made arrangements to stay with my brother Jan and his wife, Kit, in their Virginia home.

Just before we stepped on the plane to Washington, I learned that more invitations had been sent than there were tickets, and we were not going to be able to attend the ball. Diane was tremendously disappointed; I felt a challenge.

A colonel—even an ex-colonel—is not so easily discouraged. We boarded the plane; confident this error would be corrected. Attending the inaugural ball was important, not for us individually, but for those we represented.

Washington, D.C., in January 1993 was charged with possibility, and for me, hope. With the help of the media, word was out that there was no room for us at the ball. Coming to our rescue, Seattle Mayor Norm Rice generously sent us tickets to join him in his box at the West Coast Inaugural Ball at the Kennedy Center.

But before that event, I had the sad honor of speaking at Navy Seaman Allen Schindler's memorial service, and I met his mother, Dorothy Hajdys. It was an experience I will never forget. Seaman Schindler, twenty-two, had been stationed on the amphibious assault ship Belleau Wood, notorious for the harassment of gays in its crew. He had complained of threats and abuse by fellow shipmates and was about to be discharged after telling his commander that he was gay. On October 27, 1992, Allen Schindler was beaten to death near the U.S. naval base at Sasebo, in southwestern Japan. His mother explained how the Navy had first told her he had died from injuries sustained in a fall, and how they had refused to send her his personal effects. It was not until her son's friends wrote to the military newspaper Pacific Stars and Stripes and disclosed that they believed he'd been killed because he was gay that the Navy acknowledged his death might have been a hate crime. Reporters for the paper itself investigated and began publishing facts that indicated a possible Navy cover-up. Mrs. Hajdys said that her son was so badly beaten that his eyes were pushed to the side of his skull and his body could be identified only from his tattoos. Eventually, a fellow shipmate, who had previously threatened Seaman Schindler, admitted that he, along with a fellow crewmember, had attacked and killed him without provocation, because they hated gay people. The serviceman pleaded guilty and received a life sentence. Mrs. Hajdys kept saying how much Allen had always loved the Navy. His murder showed the terrible price of a policy that condones hatred of those who are different. He is mourned by all of us.

The following afternoon, I attended a reception honoring the fund-raiser, gay activist, and former roommate of Bill Clinton, David Mixner. David was the force, which had raised $4,000,000 for the campaign of President-elect Clinton. Here reality interrupted my dream of overnight social justice.

In a corner of the hall, the Honorable Gerry Studds and I discussed the political challenge ahead. As an openly gay representative from Massachusetts, he, along with his staff, was aware of the new administration's negotiations with the Pentagon. He said there would be no Executive Order overturning the ban. Instead, a six-month moratorium on discharges would be announced while the policy was studied further.

As he explained the well-grounded rationale, I fought back tears. The votes just weren't there to support an Executive Order, he said. If President Clinton signed one, Congress would overrule it and submit a bill that would put into law a more discriminatory policy, and all our efforts would be lost.

Until then, I had not realized that Congress could overturn an Executive Order. It was the beginning of my political education.

On inauguration night, there were a dozen or more balls all over town-the city was one big party. We were invited to a number of events, and before we headed off to the Kennedy Center we went to the Triangle Ball at the National Press Club, the first gay and lesbian inaugural ball in history. It was an elegant celebration-former military personnel posted the colors (marched in with the flag), Joe Steffan, discharged Naval Academy midshipman, sang the National Anthem, comedienne Kate Clinton entertained, there were musicians and dancing, and the food was sumptuous. It was hard to leave.

Then, at ten o'clock, Diane and I grabbed a cab and went to the more official ball at the Kennedy Center. The contrast between the two events was fascinating. The vast hall felt empty and plain in comparison (granted, it was late and many had left). But we found Mayor Rice's box and had a delightful visit with his guests.

After the inaugural week of events, I departed from Washington, D.C., braced for the battle ahead. During the next months, there was a tremendous debate over the armed forces' policy of discrimination. The military hierarchy lobbied vigorously to keep the ban. That effort was countered by those of us committed to equal rights for all, who wanted Congress to permit service to be judged by performance, not prejudice.

Finally, Senator Sam Nunn's Senate Armed Services Committee held hearings. He did not want the anti-gay policy overturned, and so these were not genuine inquiries into the facts or the issues. Instead, they were designed only to justify the military's policy of discrimination. I watched in amazement the testimony of so-called experts who had no personal experience regarding gay people in the military. I listened to the top brass repeat fears and biases without being challenged. Prejudice was justified on the basis of "that's how we've always done it." The commander-in-chief was defied without consequences in what appeared to be insubordination. A parade of witnesses went before the Senate Armed Service committee, handpicked to support the existing ban and justify the prejudice. Continually, these witnesses spoke of how detrimental it was for gays and lesbians to serve-yet if there was truly a problem with our ability to serve, we would not be in the military. All of us would have already been removed. The repetition of such false stereotypes and unfounded fears made me sick.

Senator Nunn took his committee to military posts and naval bases, and interviewed servicemembers in front of TV cameras. A "top gun" pilot, Tracy Thorn, who had said he was gay and was currently challenging the attempt to discharge him, was heckled by more than a thousand spectators as he testified at Norfolk. The crowd's behavior was a disgrace. It reminded me of the comments of ROTC students I'd met on campuses around the country who said they were told they could not show support for me. And, later, I wasn't surprised to hear that some of the soldiers who had been interviewed by the committee revealed that though they wanted the ban overturned, their superiors had told them not to disagree with the existing policy. The military is superb at keeping order in its ranks when it wants to.

To counter misinformation, I visited more than fifty senators and representatives, one on one, trying to educate them and answer their concerns. These elected officials told me this was a politically explosive issue. Most would not take a position opposing the Pentagon without a strong signal from their own constituents. And the American people were receiving only biased views that were paraded as "expert" testimony in front of the Senate Armed Services Committee. I heard that Senator Nunn even prevented former Senator Barry Goldwater from testifying in favor of allowing gay people to serve.

Finally, in May 1993, four of us active-duty and former servicemembers who supported ending the ban were permitted to testify. I felt the events of the previous year had been preparation for this day. Curiously, our testimony was scheduled for late in the afternoon, after the media deadlines had passed and most reporters had gone. Still, walking into the Senate Hearing Room, a space so filled with history and power, I felt a profound responsibility to all who had been victims of this unjust policy and never had the opportunity to speak out in a public forum.

I appeared with Chief Petty Officer Steven Amidon, former Staff Sergeant Thomas Paniccia, and Sergeant Justin Elzie. Each of us described our experience in the military. Steven is straight. He testified that what disrupts unit cohesion and morale is the institutionalized prejudice that encourages heterosexuals to be fearful and bigoted toward gays. Tom, Justin, and I discussed the effect of the policy on our careers-we wanted the committee to hear about the personal side of this issue. We stressed that gay people will continue to serve well in the military, sacrifice, and die, if necessary, for our country.

When the hearings were over, we knew we had done all we could. Now it was up to people around the country to show their support for overturning the ban by writing their elected officials.

But the news was not so encouraging. After all the hearings, the panels of military experts advising the President, and Justice Department suggestions, the Clinton administration announced they would agree with a Pentagon "compromise," entitled "Don't ask, don't tell."

The Clinton compromise policy would end the practice of questioning recruits or those seeking security clearances about their sexual orientation. Investigations of unsubstantiated reports of homosexuality would be halted. But private disclosures of one's sexual orientation could still be investigated and servicemembers discharged.

So there remained, as before, the threat to our livelihood and careers. The symbolism of the government's saying you are unworthy to defend your country is powerful. It's just one step away from being told you're unworthy to vote, you're unworthy to be hired, you're unworthy to live where you want to live.

And yet I realized the magnitude of the task President Clinton faced. He didn't have the votes in Congress to take on the Pentagon policymakers and win. He had a broad political agenda—he was working to improve international trade, health care, and education, and reduce violence in our cities. He risked losing everything if he tried to buck the old-boy network of the government. And politics in a democracy is the responsibility of all of us—not just one person. The Pentagon, along with the right wing, said the policy should not change. Those of us with the opposite view weren't heard–in part, because we weren't loud enough. There was not the insistence in the gay and lesbian community that this discrimination must be ended, and we failed to enlist our co-workers and family members to lobby elected officials and the military.

However, a few gains were made with this compromise proposal. It showed a new realization that gays and lesbians really were in the military, and that their silent presence was not a problem and did not undermine the mission. This policy would enable incremental change, and it gave me hope that the ban would be overturned in the future. I had seen prejudicial policies regarding women in the military reversed in a similar fashion.

But then we received another, and this time a very surprising, defeat. The Senate and House Armed Services committees challenged the compromise policy Clinton had negotiated with the Joint Chiefs of Staff. They proposed and, over the next several months, Congress passed a law that excluded gays and lesbians from serving except in silence. The important difference was that instead of the discrimination coming from a Defense Department Directive, this was a law passed by Congress, and that made it only one of two congressionally controlled military personnel policies (the other is the role of women in combat). For the policy now to be changed, there will have to be a congressional hearing and a vote. The President no longer had an option to sign an executive order to overturn the ban.

This law excluding gay people from the armed forces punishes servicemembers more harshly than under the former regulation. Previously, if you said you were gay, you were usually dismissed administratively, with an honorable discharge. But under the new rules, a statement of identity alone could be officially used as an indication of misconduct that could lead to a court-martial and up to fifteen years in prison. This new law was a travesty.

It was now clearer than ever that we would have to fight both the old policy and the new law in the courts. Focus was turned on lawsuits similar to mine, brought by servicemembers like Keith Meinhold, Jose Zuniga, and Zoe Dunning. But this path, too, would prove to be difficult.

An early example of what we faced was the lawsuit brought by Sergeant Miriam Ben-Shalom. She was discharged after she had disclosed she is a lesbian. The policy at that time (before 1982) did not require separation based on self-disclosure. The courts found that the policy and her separation violated her rights to free speech and privacy. She was reinstated in the military, but when the U.S. Court of Appeals reversed the lower court's decision, she was discharged a second time, and the Supreme Court refused to hear her case. In that situation, the Court continued to endorse the government's stated, but unproven, argument that the antigay policy "serves legitimate state interests."

But there have also been fleeting victories. Joseph Steffan was one of the ten highest-ranking midshipmen in his class at the Naval Academy in Annapolis. Just six weeks before his graduation in 1987, he was questioned about a rumor that he was gay. He answered, "Yes, sir," and within a week was stripped of his rank, denied his degree, and told to resign or be discharged. He brought suit against the Navy and lost in the district court. But in November 1993 that decision was reversed by the Court of Appeals for the District of Columbia Circuit. The new ruling, in favor of Joe Steffan, stated the anti-gay regulation excludes "a particular class of individuals, identifiable only by their thoughts and desires, for no other reason than the military's fear and dislike of that group." The court directed the government to grant him his diploma, reinstate him to service, and commission him as an officer. The three-judge panel concluded by saying, "America's hallmark has been to judge people by what they do, and not by who they are." That decision is being appealed by the government, and may ultimately be decided by the Supreme Court. (Joe Steffan lost the appeal and was discharged from the academy. He decided not to pursue litigation).

Throughout 1993, a year of challenging the military, I was also looking forward to attending the dedication of the Vietnam Women's Memorial in November. The statue would be a tribute to the ten thousand women who served during that conflict.

My own views about Vietnam had changed in the last years. Recently, I'd read books that contradicted much of what I'd been told when I was on active duty in the 1960s. One in particular, *A Viet Cong Memoir*, by Truong Nhu Tang, the former minister of justice of

North Vietnam, allowed me to see the war from the other side's perspective. This scrutiny raised the possibility that our government was misinformed about the desires of the Vietnamese people. Truong Nhu Tang made a persuasive case that the South Vietnamese government we supported did not truly represent its people, and that the Vietnamese did not want Americans in their country. Though it was difficult, I began to realize that our leaders might have been misinformed or may have had a different agenda than the liberation of the South Vietnamese. That would mean that we, as a military, were misused. Additionally, I heard from other vets and read accounts of the "secret" wars the CIA ran in Cambodia—shocking stories of torture and murder. That, along with my own experience in challenging the Army weakened the trust I once had in our unchecked government and a military immune to scrutiny.

Regardless of the change in my views, the one thing Vietnam combat nurses don't talk about when we get together is whether or not America should have been in the war. We don't discuss it, because we can't. Too many lives were lost. We cannot regret or denigrate America's participation in the war, because to do so would take away from the sacrifice of those alongside whom we served.

That's why going to the Vietnam Women's Memorial dedication was important. It gave me a sense of closure and recognition. The monument itself is a sculpture of a nurse stroking the head of a fallen soldier while two other women search the sky for a med evac helicopter. The placement of the statue was also very significant-it stands near the granite wall of names. It's as though we nurses are still there, keeping an eye on our boys, the soldiers we weren't able to save.

I went to Washington, D.C., for the dedication of the memorial with four women veterans. Over the last couple years, we'd spent time together, working through our memories of Vietnam. We felt taking the trip would be an opportunity for us to mourn and heal. Even though I had lost the right to wear my uniform, I needed to do so on this occasion. I would not be denied the acknowledgment that I had served in Vietnam.

The day of the dedication was a powerful journey of memory and reconnection. Many GIs, wounded emotionally and physically, were there, looking for the nurses who had cared for them. The ceremony and speeches, as well as my time with other nurses, all helped me put Vietnam in the past. The guilt of not saving every patient, the pain and loss—that will not disappear. It was a gruesome time, and coming back was no better. But now I can finally say: we did what we could to heal and comfort, and I am proud of that.

In uniform, I was also recognized as one who was challenging the military's policy of discrimination. Several veterans in uniform came up, saluted, and encouraged me to continue speaking for those still serving who are muted by the policy of "Don't ask, don't tell."

Our first legal success in that challenge came in June 1994. Several months before, Mary Newcombe and Michael Himes of my legal team as well as the government had presented oral arguments in my suit before Judge Thomas Zilly in Federal District Court in Seattle. We asked that he rule the antigay policy unconstitutional and order my reinstatement. The government contended that the regulation should stand and that my separation was a legitimate action by the Army. The weeks of waiting for the court's ruling seemed to go on and on.

On June 1, the day we expected the decision to be announced, Mary and Michael called me. Michael started the conversation by saying, "Hello, Colonel. How you doing, Colonel?" He had not addressed me as Colonel since my discharge in 1992, but I was too anxious to appreciate his underlying message. Then both of them yelled at once, "You won!"

Besides the joy of victory, I felt a deep relief in the court's decision. I had devoted my life to defending America because I believed that it ultimately would not tolerate policies based on fear and hatred. Since my interview with the DIS agent in 1989, that belief has been sorely tested. But on this day my optimism was vindicated. At the hastily organized press conference in downtown Seattle a few hours after Mary and Michael's ebullient call, tears came to my eyes when I told the more than thirty reporters that for me the most important words in Judge Zilly's ruling were that the policy is unconstitutional.

In his fifty-one-page ruling, Judge Zilly said I had been discharged under a regulation "based solely on prejudice. Prejudice, whether founded on unsubstantiated fears, cultural myths, stereotypes or erroneous assumptions, cannot be the basis of a discriminatory classification." While acknowledging that the courts "must give appropriate deference to professional military judgment," he stated there "must never be a military exception to the Constitution," and he rejected every single rationale given by the government for the ban. Agreeing that my rights had been denied, he wrote: "a cardinal principle of equal protection law is that the federal government cannot discriminate against a class in order to give effect to the prejudice of others."

At the press conference, the reporters asked me if I intend to go back into uniform. Of course I would. That's what this fight is all about: returning to the military. I also will do it to send a message to young people who have said to me that they don't want to enlist because of what happened to me. Yes, it happened to me, and I'm going back in. We need a strong military. I challenged an unjust regulation not the institution itself-so that all Americans' service to their country will be judged on the basis of performance, not prejudice.

Throughout the day and evening, I received phone calls and more than one hundred telegrams from friends, colleagues, and strangers around the world. Even the Western Union operator congratulated me. That night I felt that the success of our mission—and there are many who share credit for it—was measured not only by the sweeping nature of the ruling, but by the broad and joyous support for our cause from people everywhere.

While the court's decision directly addresses only the old regulation under which I was separated, it does undermine the newer law of "Don't ask, Don't tell." In fact, the day after Judge Zilly's ruling, the Oregon National Guard announced that due to uncertainties and legal challenges to past and present policies regarding homosexuals, it was dropping its investigation of First Lieutenant Elli K. Work, an officer with fifteen years of service, who had told a legislative panel that she is a lesbian. However, these successes do not mean our work is over. Of course, we knew that the government would appeal. And it did.

The government also requested a stay of the judge's order, thereby blocking my return to uniform until appeals are heard. So our battle continues. Eventually, one of our cases—whether it's mine, Captain Pruitt's, Joe Steffan's, or another's—will make its way to the Supreme Court, and, as happened in the struggle for civil rights for African Americans in the 1950s, the constitutionality of the anti gay-policy will most likely be decided there.

Until that day, the domain of my life continues to grow larger. As Diane and I go into our next phase of work and family together, we are planning for her to move to Seattle permanently. And I find myself drawn to concerns of a much different and higher level than I ever would have dreamed possible.

Outside validation, once so crucial to me, is not so important now. Much of my new focus has come from being part of a spiritual community, the Seattle Church of Religious Science. It has taught me to look inside myself for spiritual strength and know that through our good works the world becomes a better place. As I reflect on these past years, I remember the joys and limitations of my military career.

Beginning in 1972, I had the best of both worlds—I was a civilian and a reservist, trained and available so that in the event of an emergency I would be ready to defend and protect my country. That's how I lived my life: being prepared, training myself and my unit for any contingency. The further we get from mobilization, the more important it becomes to maintain a state of readiness and discipline in reserve units.

I loved and believed in that daily commitment. Though denied the right to serve my country in the armed forces, I continue my work at the Veterans Hospital. My patients there encourage me to challenge the regulation. They only worry that I might lose this, my civilian job. Their fears are not completely unfounded. Without a civil rights bill that gives gay people the same protections against discrimination other Americans have, I could lose my position with the federal government because my sexual orientation is known. So our struggle continues.

My son Matt and his wife, Lynette, are now the proud parents of their first child, Makayli Kathlene. And I am learning to be a grandmother. In July 1993, David married a college classmate in a beautiful outdoor ceremony. They are busy completing their education and building their life together.

Andy graduated from high school and moved out of our home to attend school in Arizona. He now visits and talks on the phone, more the responsible young adult than the defiant kid. But always Andy.

And Tom, sixteen, who'd watched his older brothers move out of Harvey's Maple Valley house and into mine, called me one day in the summer of 1993. He wanted to come live at my home, too. I remembered the miniature house he made for me when he was four and I had no place of my own to live. I asked him if he was sure, he wanted to leave his father's.

He said, "Yeah."

He, too, had had a major confrontation and wanted peace. So he moved into David and Andy's old room. Tom would tell me he was waiting to be invited back to his father's house. He was disappointed when the invitation did not come. It took a long time for him to give up that expectation.

I again wrote Harvey to ask if the child-support payments I send him for Tom could be stopped and given to Tom directly. He wrote back that he maintains a house for Tom even if Tom does not use it and feels the existing arrangement is satisfactory. So I continue to send Harvey Tom's child-support payments, and Tom lives with me. He enjoys the benefits of being an "only" child in my house, is thriving in his classes, and was invited to join an all-state high-school basketball team. What matters is that all my children returned to my home. That is the greatest blessing of all.

My personal life remains full of love, laughter, trust, and respect. As Diane and I grow old together, we will always remember these extraordinary days when our very private world opened onto a universe of new opportunities, friends, and challenges.

I will continue to fight, now directing my energy to state and national civil rights bills to ensure that all Americans are protected by the Constitution. I want my sons and their children, my grandchildren, to live in an America that truly offers freedom and justice for all.

As I look back on my journey, I see many contradictions that have brought me here. I wanted only to avoid my father's specialty, neurology—and found myself, at every turn, drawn to it. I sought to be a healer—and did some of my most important work saying goodbye to young men on Stryker frames in Vietnam. I wanted only to be a good soldier—and had to shed my uniform in order to fight for justice.

I have learned there are many more important tasks on this beautiful earth than fearing one another. I believe the fine young men and women now serving with honor and discipline in our military are stronger than their superiors at the Pentagon say they are. They are not frightened so easily by stereotypes. What they cannot handle is the prejudice of their leaders going unchallenged.

My four words to Agent Troutman not only ended my silence; they inducted me into a new world: the gay and lesbian community. As complex as the heterosexual society I came from, my new community is made up of all kinds of people also. It is, in fact, wildly diverse: creative, indifferent, liberal, conservative, angry, tender, perennially immature, and wise beyond its years. Just like the world. Among its members are heroes and villains—just as in every community. And rarely is there a consensus on who is wearing the black or the white hat today.

We are your daughters, your sisters, your sons, your nurses, your mechanics, your athletes, your police, your politicians, your fathers, your doctors, your soldiers, your mothers. We live with you, care for you, help you, protect you, teach you, love you, and need you. All we ask is that you let us. We are no different. We want to serve, like you. Need love, like you. Feel pain, like you.

And we deserve justice, like you.

My family is getting larger.